JOURNAL FOR THE STUDY OF THE OLD TESTAMENT
SUPPLEMENT SERIES
157

JSOT Press
Sheffield

The Word *Hesed* in the Hebrew Bible

Gordon R. Clark

Journal for the Study of the Old Testament
Supplement Series 157

Copyright © 1993 Sheffield Academic Press

Published by JSOT Press
JSOT Press is an imprint of
Sheffield Academic Press Ltd
343 Fulwood Road
Sheffield S10 3BP
England

Typeset by Sheffield Academic Press
and
Printed on acid-free paper in Great Britain
by Biddles Ltd
Guildford

British Library Cataloguing in Publication Data

Clark, Gordon R.
    Word Hesed in the Hebrew Bible.—(JSOT
    Supplement Series, ISSN 0309-0787; No. 157)
    I. Title II. Series
    221

ISBN 1-85075-408-X

CONTENTS

PREFACE

The publication of this monograph marks the culmination of an interest spanning a quarter of a century. In 1967, I was a mature-aged student in a first-year Hebrew class at the University of Melbourne, and my attention was arrested by the lecturer's comment when we first encountered the word חֶסֶד. I acknowledge my gratitude to Revd Dudley Hallam who described it as 'a rich, old, covenant word'. His remark set a goal for me, and I offer as a tribute to his memory this account of some of the surpassing richness I have discovered in this word.

I am indebted also to other members of the Department of Middle Eastern Studies for their encouragement and help in various ways—to Professor Takamitsu Muraoka, to Dr Ziva Shavitsky, to Dr John Thompson for his careful guidance as he introduced me to the beauties and the intricacies of the Hebrew language, and to Dr A.E. Murtonen for his patient and competent supervision extending over eight years which led to the award, in 1990, of a PhD for the work which is now presented in revised form.

I express too my deep appreciation of the willingness with which Mary, my wife for 44 years, did all in her power to enable me to pursue the task. When we knew that her illness would prevent her from seeing me reach my goal, she encouraged me to press on and complete the work. To Ruby, my long-time friend and now my wife of two years, I say thank you for allowing me to spend so much time at the computer preparing the manuscript for publication.

Professor David Clines responded enthusiastically, encouraging me to undertake the task of revising the manuscript. I express my thanks to him and the staff of the Sheffield Academic Press, especially Dr Webb Mealy for his helpful advice and careful editorial oversight.

I also acknowledge with gratitude the grant from the Committee on Research and Graduate Studies of the University of Melbourne, which has assisted the publication of this monograph.

LIST OF FIGURES

Fold-out key to Figures 4.1–4.11

LIST OF TABLES

ABBREVIATIONS

AB	Anchor Bible
BASOR	*Bulletin of the American Schools of Oriental Research*
BHK	R. Kittel (ed.), *Biblia Hebraica*
BHS	*Biblia hebraica stuttgartensia*
Bib	*Biblica*
BJRL	*Bulletin of the John Rylands Library*
BT	*The Bible Translator*
BZAW	Beihefte zur *ZAW*
CBQ	*Catholic Biblical Quarterly*
CTL	T.A. Sebeok (ed.), *Current Trends in Linguistics*
DSS	Dead Sea Scrolls
GKC	*Gesenius' Hebrew Grammar*, ed. E. Kautzsch, trans. A.E. Cowley
HSM	Harvard Semitic Monographs
ICC	The International Critical Commentary
Int	*Interpretation*
JAOS	*Journal of the American Oriental Society*
JBL	*Journal of Biblical Literature*
JJS	*Journal of Jewish Studies*
JNES	*Journal of Near Eastern Studies*
JTS	*Journal of Theological Studies*
KB	L. Koehler and W. Baumgartner (eds.), *Lexicon in Veteris Testamenti libros*
NICOT	New International Commentary on the Old Testament
OrAnt	*Oriens antiquus*
OTL	Old Testament Library
OTS	*Oudtestamentische Studiën*
PMLA	*Publications of the American Modern Language Association*
SBT	Studies in Biblical Theology
Sem	*Semitics*
TDOT	G.J. Botterweck and H. Ringgren (eds.), *Theological Dictionary of the Old Testament*
TPS	*Transactions of the Philological Society*
TWNT	G. Kittel and G. Friedrich (eds.), *Theologisches Wörterbuch zum Neuen Testament*
VT	*Vetus Testamentum*
WBC	Word Biblical Commentary
ZAW	*Zeitschrift für die Alttestamentliche Wissenschaft*

GLOSSARY OF SPECIAL AND TECHNICAL TERMS

Additional lexemes: Lexical items that occur frequently in close proximity to elements of the *lexical field*. These 48 lexemes are listed in Table 2.2.

Agent: One of the parties involved in the activity specified by an element of the lexical field. The agent initiates this activity and directs it towards the other party. The nature of the field elements is such that the agent is almost invariably a person or a group of persons. These parties include God and humans, the latter being classified as a leader, a man or a woman. See also *Patient* below.

Collocation: A pair of *lexical items* that occur together in a reasonably restricted linguistic environment.

Corpus: The body of literature that forms the linguistic environment of the lexical field. For the present study, the corpus is the final form of the vocalized text as transmitted in the Codex Leningradensis as published in *BHS*.

Disinfected: A term used by Sawyer to describe *lexical items* that are never applied to the activity of anyone other than Yahweh, the God of Israel. See also *Restricted* below.

Distribution: The total set of linguistic contexts in which a lexical item can occur. In this study, the use of this term is confined to the persons and entities involved in the language event as agent or patient of an activity specified by an element of the lexical field.

Element: A member of the lexical field that consists of the derivatives of the six roots חסד, חנן, רחם, אהב, שׂנא and אמן. These roots were chosen because they occur frequently in interpersonal situations and because of their known relatedness in meaning. The 35 elements are listed in Table 2.1.

Lexeme: A unit of the vocabulary of a language, specifically the unit that is listed as a separate entry in the dictionary. The elements or members of the field are in fact lexemes, but in this study they are always referred to as elements or members and the term lexeme is reserved for the *additional lexemes* mentioned above, which were chosen because of their frequent occurrence in proximity to field elements.

Lexical field: A group of lexical items that have certain features in common. These features include their form (having the same ending or the same beginning), their sound, or their sense (being related in meaning). The lexical field investigated in this study is composed of lexical items whose meanings are related.

Lexical item: An alternative for *lexeme*; used in this study to include both *elements* and *additional lexemes*.

Paradigmatic: Language can be investigated along two axes, one of which is the *paradigmatic* axis. In any expression (e.g. a sentence), whether spoken or written, the lexical items are arranged in a definite order to form a chain. For one of these items, any member of a set of other items may be substituted and still produce a sensible statement, with possible adjustments to other items in the sentence; for example, for a noun, singular and plural forms may be interchanged, or for a verb past, present and future forms may be interchanged; a noun may be replaced by a pronoun or by an entirely unrelated noun; a verb may be replaced by an entirely unrelated verb. The pool of items from which the choice is made comprise a *paradigm* (compare the paradigm of verb-forms that may replace one another at a given point in an expression). An investigation along the *paradigmatic axis* is concerned with the relationships between the items from which a choice may be made to fill a given place in an expression. See also *Syntagmatic* below.

Patient: One of the parties involved in the activity specified by an element of the lexical field; more precisely, that party towards whom or for whose benefit (or detriment) the agent directs this activity. The patient includes the persons listed above under *Agent*, but is not restricted to persons; some patients are inanimate entities, which have been classified as non-personal. See Section 3A in Chapter 2.

PERDAT: The computer file in which is stored the data derived from the analysis of the elements when used in interpersonal situations. Obtained by deleting all non-personal entries from *WIDATA*, it consists of approximately 1100 records.

Restricted: A term to replace *disinfected* for elements used almost exclusively with either a divine or a human agent (or patient).

SRTKAP: The computer file in which is stored a rearrangement of the data in *PERDAT*, the columns headed CODE, KEYWORD, AGENT and PATIENT being sorted into alphabetical order in the sequence given.

SRTKAW: The computer file storing the data from *WIDATA* after it has been sorted into alphabetical order as in *SRTKAP*.

Synchronic: One of the two main temporal dimensions of linguistic investigation introduced by Saussure. The investigator attempts to freeze the language at a certain point in time and, disregarding any changes that may be occurring, to describe the existing state of the language. The present study examines the vocalised Masoretic text published in BHS and thus concentrates on the state of Biblical Hebrew as it existed early in the eleventh century AD.

Syntagmatic: A term introduced by Saussure to refer to the sequential characteristics of language. This is the second axis along which language, seen as a string of items in linear order, may be investigated. Each lexical item in a chain contracts syntagmatic relationships with the other items in the chain. A group of items that are closely linked together, such as a collocation, is called a *syntagm*. See *Paradigmatic* above.

WIDATA: The computer file containing the data derived from the analysis of every occurrence of each element of the lexical field. It consists of almost 1400 records.

Chapter 1

WHY IS ANOTHER STUDY OF חֶסֶד NECESSARY?

1. *Previous Studies of* חֶסֶד

Nelson Glueck's pioneering study of חֶסֶד, first published in 1927, is the sole authority cited under the entry for this word in the 1958 edition of the Koehler–Baumgartner Lexicon. Since Glueck's work many articles have been written to throw light upon the use and meaning of this 'rich, old, covenant word'. Several such works have been consulted during the course of this study, and acknowledgement is made here of the helpful insights that have been gained from them.[1] The focus of each author is, of course, primarily—and sometimes entirely—on the word חֶסֶד, and little attention is given either to other words that frequently occur with it or to words that may replace it in a phrase or clause.

This chapter sets out some of the important features noted in three major studies of חֶסֶד, all of which were presented as doctoral dissertations. They are:

1. Nelson Glueck's study, submitted to the University of Jena in 1926 and published in the following year (Section A);
2. Boone M. Bowen's unpublished dissertation, accepted in 1938 by Yale University (Section B); and
3. Katharine Doob Sakenfeld's revision of her 1970 Harvard dissertation which was published in 1978 (Section C).

After noting the relevant features of each study, the methods

---

1.   Authors of these publications are listed together at the beginning of the Bibliography. Other articles that appeared between 1933 and 1962 are discussed in Larue's summary of recent trends in the study of חֶסֶד which is prefaced to the English translation of Glueck's thesis (1967: 1-32). Others again, including more recent ones, are contained in Sakenfeld's bibliography (1978: 251-63) and also in Zobel (1986: 44 n. 1).

adopted by the authors are compared, with a view to delineating how yet another study of the root חסד may be approached.

A. *Nelson Glueck*

Glueck presents the meaning—as he discerns it—and usage in the Bible of the word חֶסֶד, but he does not discuss the method he used to analyse the passages in which it occurs, and he rarely provides reasons for the conclusions that he states. He devotes a separate chapter to each of the three categories to which he allocates the passages. The first chapter deals with people's conduct towards one another, and the second with people's conduct towards God. The third chapter treats God's conduct towards people, which Glueck also calls the theological meaning of חֶסֶד. Throughout his study, Glueck's main focus is on the mutually obligatory relationships in which חֶסֶד is the appropriate conduct, and he groups together, for discussion in the same section, those passages in which he finds a similar relationship between the parties. His use of the literary environment in which the word חֶסֶד occurs is often confined to a description of the situational context of the incident, and his discussion of this environment is usually directed towards a clarification of the obligatory relationship between the parties involved.

Glueck often suggests ways to convey the meaning of חֶסֶד in the various passages where it occurs; sometimes he lists these as possible translations. The first chapter deals with the secular meaning of חֶסֶד as human conduct, but it does not contain a list of translations as such. Glueck says that the essential components of חֶסֶד in the passages considered are mutuality and reciprocity, mutual assistance, service rendered in return for help given, and sincerity, friendliness, brotherliness, duty, loyalty and love. He adds that in the older sources חֶסֶד is never an arbitrary demonstration of grace, kindness, favour or love. In the second chapter, on the religious meaning of חֶסֶד as human conduct, he suggests that חֶסֶד, as mutual ethical and religious conduct, includes in its meaning loyalty, justice, righteousness and honesty; that it fulfils the demands of all these; and that the best translations are religiosity, piety, kindness or benevolence, and love of humankind. His third chapter deals with חֶסֶד as divine conduct, and as suitable translations he recommends loyalty, mutual aid and reciprocal love.

Other words that occur in conjunction with חֶסֶד are frequently mentioned, but Glueck does not often comment on the meanings of these words.

The essential features of Glueck's presentation may be summed up as follows:

When two parties enter into a relationship that involves them in mutual obligations towards each other, חֶסֶד describes the appropriate conduct of the parties.

The nature of חֶסֶד in such a relationship may be expressed by an adaptation of the ancient adage: One good turn demands another.

B. *Boone M. Bowen*

About a decade after Glueck's monograph appeared, Boone M. Bowen submitted the word חֶסֶד to a further examination that led him to challenge some of Glueck's conclusions. He was able to do this largely because he adopted a different methodology. He agrees with his predecessor's finding that the חֶסֶד of human beings is essentially a beneficent expression of a relationship that grows out of a tie or bond, but he criticizes Glueck's extremely brief treatment of חֶסֶד יהוה. Bowen arranges the חֶסֶד passages according to the literary strata in which they occur, devoting a chapter to each of seven general areas. Glueck and Bowen both separate their consideration of the human and the divine aspects of חֶסֶד, but Bowen departs from Glueck in that, before he considers חֶסֶד as a human quality, he first discusses it as a divine quality, thereby ensuring that he fills in the gaps that he has detected in this area of Glueck's study. Again, Bowen gives detailed attention to a greater number of the חֶסֶד passages than Glueck does, discussing 235 of the passages, many of them in considerable detail, whereas Glueck's discussion is restricted to 147 passages, although he lists a further 99 in footnotes. In some of these footnotes several references are given—all to passages in which Glueck finds support for the point he is making about the passage under discussion.

The term 'reciprocal' features prominently in Bowen's treatment of the meaning and translation of חֶסֶד; however, he frequently clarifies the nature of this reciprocity. In passages from the Hexateuch he finds (1938: 47) that 'loyal kindness' is the best translation. This is so both when חֶסֶד is a divine quality (pp. 26 [Exod. 20.6], 30 [Exod. 34.6-7], 33–34 [Deut. 7.12]) and also when it is a human quality. Bowen (p. 21; cf. p. 23 [Gen. 40.14]) says that when Abimelech requests חֶסֶד from Abraham in Gen. 21.23 he is asking for reciprocity: the חֶסֶד that he has extended to Abraham as a gracious host to a foreigner demands חֶסֶד in return. Abraham's 'loyal kindness' is partly an act of reciprocity, partly in fidelity to a solemn oath. This translation is not confined to the Hexateuch but it is recommended also in the prophetic literature (p. 139) as well as in some of the Psalms (p. 283).

Another translation suggested by Bowen is 'loving kindness'. This is particularly apt for the usage of חֶסֶד by some of the prophets, either for a social quality (1938: 124-25 [Hos. 4.1]) expressed in a person's relationship with others or for a 'social beneficence which is an expression of loyalty to a religious ideal' (p. 132 [Mic. 6.8]). In this latter passage, the phrase 'Godly loving kindness' is needed to make the thought complete; but this, as Bowen points out, is too long to use in practical translations.

A further contrast with Glueck's treatment is found in Bowen's frequent notice of advances in the content and application of the term. Thus, when summarizing the meaning of the word חֶסֶד and its areas of use in prophetic literature, he says (1938: 144-45) that חֶסֶד is 'a social quality incumbent upon the religious man', thus broadening the area of expression. It is an obligation that a person owes to everyone, not only to kinspeople, a guest in the home or a covenantee. A tremendous advance was made by Hosea when he showed that in Israel a person cannot know God if he or she fails to show חֶסֶד in general social relationships. In this same summary, Bowen (pp. 146-51) makes a detailed comparison of the meaning of the word as it is used in the prophetic literature and in the Deuteronomic material. He concludes by listing the new and distinctive emphases given in the prophetic literature. As a quality of God, חֶסֶד is

1. a mutual obligation between God and Israel, with Israel fulfilling its part of the obligation in social relationships;
2. the agent through which Yahweh will forgive and redeem the distressed penitent;
3. shown because Yahweh loves;
4. shown in all the earth—even toward Nineveh.

As a quality of a human being, חֶסֶד is

1. an obligation resting on every religious person;
2. not restricted by covenantal or family ties.

The main contributions Bowen's study makes to an understanding of חֶסֶד are:

1.   Using literary analysis of the text to establish a rough
     historical development enables him to note
       unique usages produced by different writers, and
       particular emphases related to specific periods.
2.   He pays greater attention to detail, which is especially
     valuable in relation to חֶסֶד יהוה.
3.   He recommends such translations as 'loyal kindness' and
     'loving kindness'.

C. *Katharine Doob Sakenfeld*

A further thirty-five years elapsed before a new enquiry into the
meaning of חֶסֶד was completed by Katharine Doob Sakenfeld; her
revised dissertation (1978) was published just over fifty years after
Glueck's monograph originally appeared. In this study Sakenfeld
follows the lead given by earlier investigators, but this is no slavish
following and she frequently presents fresh insights into the use and
meaning of the word. In her classification of the various passages
which contain the word חֶסֶד, she observes (1978: 14; cf. 1-2) the
traditional distinction between 'secular', 'religious' and 'theological'
usages, as did Glueck before her. The secular usage is concerned with
the practice of חֶסֶד between two human parties; in the theological
usage it is God who extends חֶסֶד to a human party. Sakenfeld (p. 2)
points out that Glueck, from his analysis of the religious usage, recognized that people's conduct toward each other and their relationship to
God are both inseparably a part of חֶסֶד, and she emphasizes (p. 152)
that in the case of religious usage the one who performs the חֶסֶד-act
has a responsibility—to God, not for another person.

Sakenfeld (1978: 3) acknowledges that Glueck's great contribution
was his observation that 'חֶסֶד is done within a relationship', but she
believes that he left the degree of the relationship too wide. She
objects (p. 53 n. 58) to Glueck's repeated use of the term 'חֶסֶד-
relationship' because it suggests that the term חֶסֶד could be applied to
any act appropriate to any human relationship of 'rights and duties'.
Again, in her discussion of Gen. 21.22-24, Sakenfeld says (p. 73) that
Glueck tends to generalize חֶסֶד, making it cover the performance of
any duty to another. She reiterates that 'חֶסֶד is regularly associated
with specific actions in special situations'. Claiming that only certain
types of action were called חֶסֶד, she proposes that a major thrust of her
work (p. 3) is to define the particular circumstances within a

relationship that render appropriate the use of the word חֶסֶד.

These 'situational parameters' (1978: 58) are set out in slightly different terms on three separate occasions. At the beginning of ch. 2 (p. 24), before discussing any of the texts, she states the four features that appeared, during the course of her research, to be normally present in situations when the word חֶסֶד was appropriate. These four characteristics are restated in her summary of Section A[1] of that chapter (p. 44). Her general Summary of Results (p. 234) lists the following principal features, which are common to all the secular examples in texts from the pre-exilic period; they 'provide the parameters for the use of the word' חֶסֶד.

1. חֶסֶד is always the provision for an essential need, never a special favour.
2. חֶסֶד is an action performed by the situationally superior party for the situationally inferior party.
3. The superior party, because of a more powerful status, is always free not to perform the act of חֶסֶד.
4. The potential actor has a recognized responsibility to act in חֶסֶד because of the relationship with the weaker party.
5. The superior party is normally the sole source available to render assistance to the party in need.

Sakenfeld pays very little attention to the reciprocity that features so largely in Glueck's study. She leaves the reader in no doubt that she rejects Glueck's idea of mutual reciprocity. The longest statement she makes on this point (1978: 53-54) is: 'Here as elsewhere the חֶסֶד action is onesided; it is not really mutual or reciprocal'.

Sakenfeld often conveys the content and meaning of the word, but she does not attempt to provide a single translation—or even a few— that can be used whenever חֶסֶד appears. Indeed, she claims (p. 233) that her study has given her a greater appreciation of the flexibility of the term. There is no adequate English equivalent, and it is both difficult and dangerous to select a single phrase to apply in all cases.

What is Sakenfeld's plan for her investigation? She builds up the analysis by an inductive study of texts, passage by passage (1978: 24)

---

1.   This section examines seven texts (Gen. 20.13; 2 Sam. 3.8; 16.17; Gen. 24.49; 47.29; 2 Sam. 2.5; Ruth 3.10) found in pre-exilic prose, in which the act of חֶסֶד is 'based implicitly in a personal relationship between the parties involved'.

and she describes (p. 14) the overall format of chs. 2–5 as 'a text-by-text analytical presentation of the biblical evidence'. In this she differs from both Glueck and Bowen; as she points out (p. 3), Glueck uses a topical arrangement of material drawn from various periods and sources, and Bowen arranges his texts to give a detailed analysis of each author's use of the word חֶסֶד. She also differs from her predecessors in that she gives a detailed discussion of only 96 of the חֶסֶד passages.[1] Sakenfeld does, however, briefly mention another 61 passages, most of which occur in Psalms, Proverbs and related literature. It sometimes appears that she treats the passages in a random order, but this is not so, for she states (p. 14; cf. p. 24) that she arranges the texts in each section in order to bring out the relationships between them and to enhance the development of the argument in that section.

On several occasions Sakenfeld notices words used alongside the word חֶסֶד. She comments on some of the verbs[2] that take חֶסֶד as object, as well as some of the nouns[3] with which חֶסֶד is frequently joined. In all these cases, Sakenfeld treats these other words as constants, that is, as words whose meaning is known (she regularly translates רַחֲמִים as 'mercy'), while she treats חֶסֶד as a variable and does not attempt to translate it. More importantly, she does not dwell on any influence these words may have on the meaning of חֶסֶד nor on the possible overlap in meaning between חֶסֶד and the other nouns.

What are the main contributions Sakenfeld makes to an understanding of חֶסֶד?

1. The type of relationship in which חֶסֶד is appropriate is not limited to a formal covenant relationship.
2. חֶסֶד is an action for a situationally inferior party by a situationally superior party who
   has a responsibility—moral, not legal—so to act,
   is, notwithstanding, free not to perform the act.
3. It is well-nigh impossible to find a single expression to convey the content, in all its usages, of this extremely flexible term.

---

1. Bowen discusses 235 and Glueck 147 passages; see Section B above.
2. For example, נשׂא in Est. 2 (1978: 160), נטה in Ezra 7.28; 9.9; cf. Gen. 39.21 (pp. 161-63), and משׁך in Jer. 31.3; cf. Ps. 36.11 (pp. 194-95).
3. Examples are אֱמֶת/אֱמוּנָה, מִשְׁפָּט and צֶדֶק/צְדָקָה in Jer. 9.23 (1978: 197-98) and also in Isa. 16.5; cf. Ps. 89 (pp. 205-206), and רחם/רַחֲמִים in Jer. 16.5 (p. 198), Isa. 54.7-10 (pp. 199-201) and in several other passages (pp. 206-209).

D. *Two Dictionary Articles*

Within the last 20 years, two theological dictionaries have appeared; they have been prepared by editors who have noted James Barr's criticisms of certain methods of handling linguistic evidence in theological discussions. Consequently the approach by Stoebe and Zobel in these articles differs considerably from that of the other works mentioned. In particular, each article considers larger groups of words that are related to the keyword either linguistically or semantically. The chief concern of these authors is not so much with suitable translations as with the content and meaning of חֶסֶד, which they attempt to outline as they consider various words that are used in close proximity with it. Margot (1974: 216) warmly recommends the detailed and comprehensive study in which Stoebe (1971) systematically analyses a wide variety of contexts where חֶסֶד occurs, considering history, literature, theology, syntax and semantics where he notes relations between חֶסֶד and other Hebrew terms belonging to the same area of meaning. Margot commends the sound linguistic method adopted by Stoebe (1971: cols. 600-21) in his discussion of the way in which words influence the meaning of חֶסֶד when they are used in close association with it, for example, the nouns אֱמֶת, אֱמוּנָה, בְּרִית, רַחֲמִים and חֵן, the verb עשׂה and various prepositions (cols. 601-607). Stoebe also considers the usage of the word in secular and religious contexts (between human parties, cols. 607-11; with God as subject, cols. 611-18).

Zobel (1986: 44-64) makes more than a passing reference to other words used in conjunction with חֶסֶד—such as the expression עשׂה חֶסֶד עִם in secular usage (pp. 46-48), and also in religious usage (p. 54), where he mentions other verbs. He notes the influence on the meaning of חֶסֶד of this and other expressions, especially 'nouns used in parallel with חֶסֶד or forming part of its semantic field' (p. 55). These nouns include אֱמֶת, רַחֲמִים, צְדָקָה, מִשְׁפָּט, יְשׁוּעָה and אֱמוּנָה (pp. 55-56). Among 'other syntactic structures' he includes verbs, adjectives, particles and prepositions that help to determine the content of חֶסֶד (pp. 56-57).

Both articles are based on sound linguistic methods. Indeed, in some respects Stoebe may be regarded as a forerunner of Barr, since the article shows close resemblances to the published summary (1952) of Stoebe's 1951 dissertation. He does not list any works on linguistics in his dissertation bibliography; but since he included only frequently-cited works, it is possible that Stoebe was well aware of developments in linguistics taking place at the time of his study. Yet neither this article nor Zobel's can be described as a study of a lexical field; but comments of both authors reveal interesting insights into the usage and meaning of חֶסֶד.

E. *Overview*

This section has drawn attention to some of the differences between the studies by Glueck, Bowen and Sakenfeld—differences of approach, difference in methods of classifying material, different insights into the meaning of the word, different conclusions drawn from the same material when it is viewed from another angle. But there are also important points of resemblance between these studies. In the first place, each is essentially a study of a *word*—the word חֶסֶד. Secondly, each is essentially a *contextual* study of a word: it investigates the word חֶסֶד in the various contexts in which it appears. While some—albeit very little—consideration is given to the influence that some of the words occurring in close proximity to חֶסֶד have upon its meaning, the possibility of substituting other words for חֶסֶד and the effect that any such substitution would have on the meaning of a given sentence is not considered at all. It is therefore possible to categorize each of the studies as a *one-dimensional* study of a word, and to assert that the studies were completed without reference to linguistic science. This must not be considered as a harsh judgment on those who were involved in the investigations, since developments in linguistics were occurring during the time-span covered by these three studies. However, it is necessary to highlight the weakness in the studies, namely their incompleteness from a linguistic point of view, and to note that this weakness is apparent in the work of many biblical scholars because of the prevailing tendency among such scholars either to ignore or to avoid the application of the principles of structural linguistics.

It is generally recognized that the syntagmatic and the paradigmatic relations between words are the two dimensions of linguistic analysis. Eugene Nida (1972: 84-87) considers that the unsatisfactory state of the lexicography of biblical languages is traceable largely to the reluctance of biblical scholars to grapple with the developments in structural semantics, and he asserts that 'critical studies of meaning must be based primarily upon the analysis of related meanings of different words, not upon the different meanings of single words'. He proceeds to illustrate how the different meanings of a given word are distinguished from one another in terms of that word's syntagmatic relations with other words occurring in the expression, that is, in the lexical chain. On the other hand, different words that have related meanings stand in a paradigmatic relationship with each other such that, in an expression containing one of the words, another word selected from the paradigm may be substituted, thus presenting the possibility of making a lexical choice. Here, then, are the two dimensions of linguistic analysis mentioned above—the axes of chain and of choice, of combination and selection, of syntagm and of paradigm. The three studies of חֶסֶד have concentrated on the syntagmatic axis and have ignored the paradigmatic axis; but, as Nida states, the paradigmatic axis is an important dimension that cannot be neglected in a semantic study.

In the next section, a brief account will be given of some of the developments in the science of linguistics—especially those that relate to the investigation of lexical fields. But first it is worth quoting the words of Larue from the closing sentences of his summary (Glueck 1967: 32):

> It is possible that the summarizing of some of the key studies of חֶסֶד may exercise a softening influence on Glueck's interpretation, and perhaps suggest that we are approaching a time when a new investigation of this important term and its relationship to words with which it is often associated including חֵן, אֱמֶת, בְּרִית, רַחֲמִים, אַהֲבָה, צַדִּיק and צְדָקָה, etc., will have to be made. Until the time when such research is undertaken Nelson Glueck's word study will continue its important role of providing the basic interpretation of חֶסֶד.

The authors of the articles noted in Section D above have made an initial approach to the type of study envisaged by Barr and Larue, but their valuable investigations can hardly be classified as studies of a lexical field centred on חֶסֶד.

2. *Lexical Field Studies*

In his review of Sakenfeld (1978), Yehoshua Gitay (1979: 584) points out that by concentrating on a single word and 'trying to draw relevant implications, there is a tendency to infuse more meaning than the word actually bears'. This, he says, could have been avoided by taking 'a methodological step which seems to be missing, i.e., a comprehensive analysis of the semantic field' of חֶסֶד. Since the present investigation is a field study, some consideration must now be given to the nature of such studies. While studies in comparative linguistics have been carried out, and are still being conducted, in the present century, many studies in linguistics are now moving in a different direction compared with those of the previous century, for the themes of such present-day research may be summed up in the keywords 'synchronic' and 'structural'. Tracing the historical development of a language over an extended period of time is a diachronic, as opposed to a synchronic, investigation; in the latter, an attempt is made to freeze the language at a certain point in time and, disregarding any changes that may be occurring, to describe the existing state of the language. From the structural point of view, a language is a network of interrelated units, and the meaning of the various parts can be specified only with reference to the whole. Structural semantics is, according to Crystal (1980: 335), 'an influential contemporary position, which is still in its early stages of analysing the sense relations that interconnect lexemes and sentences'. Hence, the researcher focuses attention on a single language, rather than a group of languages, and seeks to analyse that language as it existed—or exists—at a given point of time looking particularly at the network of relationships between the various elements which make up the language. Ferdinand de Saussure set this new direction in linguistic studies, especially in his lectures in general linguistics given at the University of Geneva between 1906 and 1911.[1] As Oehman (1953: 124-25) says,

> Semantics had almost passed over the fact that single words form organic groups with related meanings on the one side and related forms on the other. The synchronic consideration of language now opened new ways for the investigation of groups of words belonging conceptually together. Saussure had stressed anew that language is a *system* of signs. Actually it was only with this prerequisite that synchronistic investigation of the content of speech became possible.

This new direction in linguistics has been ignored in many lexical studies of biblical material. The position has not changed much since Barr (1961: 4, 6) surveyed the ways in which modern theological thinking had been assessing and using the linguistic material of the Bible. In the course of his survey he criticized certain methods of

---

1. These lectures were compiled posthumously from the notes of Saussure and of his pupils and were published in 1916.

handling linguistic evidence in theological discussion—and especially in some articles published in *TWNT*. Moule (1962: 26-27) in his review of Barr's work speaks of the author flashing 'a red light at the reckless driver who tries to take a short cut across a minefield' and warns that 'biblical theologians will ignore it at their peril'. Barr's work has more recently been described (Silva 1983: 18) as 'a trumpet blast against the monstrous regiment of shoddy linguistics', but much work needs to be done before Barr's hopes will be realized, namely to clear the way for a reassessment of biblical language and of the use that may be made of it in theology.

A. *The Nature of the Field*

The term *lexical field* is used in this study to refer to a field whose members are lexical items, that is, words.[1] However, the words that comprise the lexical field may be selected from various points of view. They may, for example, be derived from the same root, or have the same function in sentences, or be used in the same conceptual field. Examples of each type will be noted briefly.

As indicated by its title, the study by Riesener (1979) is essentially the study of a root in Biblical Hebrew. She is concerned mainly, but not entirely, with words derived from the root עבד. Riesener (pp. 75-76) defines her 'Wortfeld' as a group of overlapping words used to describe a certain area of life, and she arranges the members of the lexical field in three main divisions, which she names 'like concepts', 'correlative concepts' and 'antonyms or contrary concepts'.

Lyons (1963) investigates a group of nouns used frequently in some of Plato's dialogues. He classifies the elements of his field (pp. 142-46) either as nouns of occupation or as personal nouns of occupation; the former may be described as the names of skills, while the latter

---

1.   Erickson (1980: 91-137) devotes almost 50 pages to a careful discussion of semantic field theory. In his view (see pp. 129-31), a conceptual field is a theoretical construct, 'postulated in explanation of observed phenomena' and 'made up of concepts which are interrelated with one another by virtue of shared and contrasting "features"'. A 'lexical field is a set of terms [lexical items (words, phrases, etc.)—see his p. 73 n. 5] belonging together by virtue of their syntagmatic and paradigmatic relationships'. Following Lyons (1977), he calls these paradigmatic relationships sense-relations; and it is these sense-relations that are the members of his semantic field. While a semantic field consists of interrelated senses, a lexical field is 'the set of lexemes whose senses interrelate with one another to form a semantic field'.

are applied to persons who possess those skills. He also considers verbs of occupation, where they exist; but the nouns far outnumber the verbs and form the bulk of his investigation.

Matsuda, Burres and Erickson all take verbs as the members of their fields. Like Lyons, Burres and Erickson are both concerned with a field of cognition, but they differ from Lyons in that their fields are in New Testament Greek.

Matsuda's analysis (1976) of semantic relations between verbs denoting mental activities in Biblical Hebrew includes four verbs that also feature in the present study.

Burres (1970) studies 'the revelation field in the Pauline corpus', building up his field from two core verbs that are frequently translated by 'reveal'.

Erickson (1980) is 'a study of methods, with special reference to the Pauline lexical field of "cognition"'. Erickson states, on p. 10, that he attempts to carry out the methods of Burres and Lyons on the Pauline 'lexical field' of 'cognition'; consequently he also builds up his field from two core verbs, which are frequently translated by 'know'.

Each of the studies mentioned above can also be described as studies of words used in the same conceptual field—whether the words are derived (like Riesener's) from the same root, or whether (like those mentioned in the previous paragraph) they have the same function in the sentence. In his study of Hebrew words for 'salvation', Sawyer (1972: 35) lists eight lexemes that comprise the central core of his field; each lexeme is a verb but it is quite clear that these are not derived from the same root. Sawyer also includes other words derived from the core verbs, and several of these derivatives are not verbs.

There are several other studies of lexical fields in biblical Hebrew that can be included in this category. These are listed in the Bibliography.

B. *The Definition of the Field*

Opinions differ concerning the manner of determining the members of a field. It is generally accepted that a knowledge of the language is essential—whether the field be in one's native language or in a second language. What is open to question is the extent to which investigators may rely upon their knowledge of the object language to delineate the field. Such knowledge, it is argued, is intuitive and subjective, with the result that different researchers may—and probably will—produce fields that contain different lexical items for the same conceptual area.

Burres tried to reduce intuition to a minimum, and Erickson applied this method in another related area. Burres set out to establish and describe a lexical field using empirical means that were neither subjective nor intuitive. His study deals with words as they are actually used in sentences, and investigates the syntagmatic and paradigmatic relationships into which the words enter with other words in the same linguistic environment. Starting with two core transitive verbs, Burres (1970: 115) sets up environment classes of the form S–V–O, where S stands for the subject of the verb V, and O is the direct object of V. Using each verb in turn, he notes all the objects that they take, and allocates them to ten different classes. Four of these classes have an abstract noun as object, yet Burres nowhere discusses how he determines whether a noun is abstract, although he does mention (p. 163) that an abstract noun sometimes has the form of a neuter singular adjective. Using each combination of subject–object, he finds other verbs that belong to the same environment class and are consequently members of his semantic field. These two steps (from S–V to O, and from S–O to V) are repeated until no new verbs are produced, which means that all members of the semantic field have been found.

Erickson (1980: 183-96) applies this extrapolation method to the Pauline lexical field of cognition; he initially distinguishes 20 environment classes, but immediately discards 12 'non-crucial' ones. Four of the remaining classes are primarily determined by the presence of an abstract noun; these classes are identical with those that Burres had distinguished. Erickson recognizes a deficiency in Burres's treatment and discusses (pp. 190-93) what constitutes an abstract noun, deciding that this can only be determined by considering the referent of the noun—what the noun denotes. This, of course, depends upon one's knowledge of the language, and such decisions may be both subjective and intuitive. Since such a large portion of the fields of both Burres and Erickson depends upon a decision that is both intuitive and subjective, the method of extrapolation does not reduce intuition to the extent that Burres desires, and it can hardly be termed empirical. Erickson concludes (pp. 241-43) that the extrapolation procedure worked satisfactorily for Burres's field of revelation, but it was overproductive when he applied it in the same corpus to the notion of cognition.

This discussion has directed attention to the place that intuition may play in the formulation of a linguistic field. Burres and Erickson attempted to reduce intuition to a minimum, but their endeavours have not been as successful as they anticipated. What, then, is the place of intuition in a scientific discipline such as linguistics? In particular, to what extent may linguistic intuition be used when formulating a lexical field?

Some of the studies to which reference has been made above are of fields whose delineation depends upon the researcher's knowledge of the target language. Thus, Lyons (1963: 105-106, and n. 1 on p. 139; cf. also 1968: 433-34) claims that his knowledge of classical Greek provides him with an adequate cultural overlap that enables him not only to read the text but as he reads to write down the lexemes that belong to his field. Sawyer (1972: 34) makes a similar claim—'A knowledge of Hebrew implies that I can intuitively recognize words of related meaning'. It is his opinion that the 'criteria for building up this...field are in the last resort intuitive' (p. 33), but he is careful to emphasize that 'intuition is only a starting-point for semantic analysis, and no more'. Again, Silva (1980: 203 n. 1) refers to his 'lexicographical study of the semantic field of "mind" in the LXX...' In reply to a question regarding his method of delineating this field, he says,[1] 'My selection of terms was purely "intuitive", but I have to confess some doubts whether we're likely to come up with any method that will transcend intuition'. There is a place for intuition in such studies, but it must be kept in its rightful place.

The field investigated in the present study has been determined by intuition informed by a knowledge of the target language. It is not claimed that this field is complete in the sense that all the members of the field have been included so that they can be fitted together to cover the whole area. That the field studied is not claimed to be exhaustive is indicated by the use of the indefinite article in the subtitle. However, Even-Shoshan (1983: 386) provides some confirmation that it is a field centred on חֶסֶד. For, among the 16 words he lists as having meanings related to that of חֶסֶד, he includes four of the elements and also six of the additional lexemes that have been included in the field;[2] he also lists a few other items that have not been included, but only one of

---

1. Private communication, dated 30 September, 1983.
2. The terms 'element' and 'additional lexeme' are defined in Chapter 2, where the members of the field are listed. See also Glossary.

these occurs more than 20 times in the corpus. Similarly, the quotation from Larue at the end of Section 1E contains four elements included in this field as well as three additional lexemes.

C. *Methods of Investigating the Field*

Methods are here introduced that have helped to establish the guiding principles adopted in the succeeding chapters to study the various lexical items. Some of these methods have been suggested by Firth's notions of 'context of situation' and 'collocation'.

Firth's context of situation includes the linguistic environment (or 'verbal action') as well as features of the external (non-linguistic) world such as those appropriate to the participants; it is described by Robins (1971: 26) as a 'schematic framework by which the information relevant to the functioning, the meaning, of utterances can be stated'. A typical context of situation includes the following constituents:

1. the participants: persons, personalities and relevant features of these, including both the verbal and the nonverbal actions of the participants;
2. the relevant objects and nonverbal and non-personal events;
3. the effect of the verbal action.

These aspects are all relevant when one is investigating verbal actions while they are actually taking place; but when the corpus is a record of events which, having occurred in the past, involve participants who cannot be observed or consulted, it is not possible to determine with certainty such things as the nonverbal actions and events that accompanied the verbal actions and events. However, as many as possible of these features have been considered in the analysis of the relevant texts, described in Chapter 2.

In Chapter 3 attention is focused on the persons involved in each of the passages in order to discover differences in the usage of the various lexical items. For this part of the investigation the term 'distribution' has been adopted; this is normally used in linguistics to refer to the total set of linguistic contexts in which an item may occur, and according to one theory (see Ikegami 1967: 57) 'the meaning of any linguistic item is the sum total of linguistic contexts in which it may occur'. Ikegami notes the difficulties which arise from this view, but he does not dismiss the idea that there may be a relationship between distribution and meaning; he favours the position adopted by some linguists that, while meaning is not to be identified with distribution, clues to the meaning of lexical items may be obtained by considering the contexts in which they occur. He concludes (p. 61) that linguistic environments provide a very important tool for the analysis of meaning, and he recommends that this analysis should be carried out with the guiding assumptions that

1. The USE of a word is conditioned by the MEANING of the word.
2. The MEANING of a word... can be inferred from the way the word is USED in context.

The identity of the persons involved in each text can be determined by an examination of the linguistic context, even though it sometimes depends on a context that is wider than the immediate neighbourhood of members of the field. The term 'distribution' is applied to this one feature of the linguistic context—the persons who act as agent and patient[1] in each case. But the principles enunciated by Ikegami are still relevant, and differences in the personal distributions of the various lexical items highlight contrasts and similarities between the elements of the field.

'Collocation' is a term used, in the study of the vocabulary of a language, to refer to groups of words that occur together in the same lexical chain; a collocation may consist, for example, of a noun and a verb, or of a verb and an adverb, or of an adjective and a noun, or of a more extensive set of words. While the term may be applied to any group of words that co-occur, it usually entails their frequent co-occurrence in a given context; when one member of a collocation is given, the other member(s) may be predicted to a greater or lesser extent.

The present study deals with selected words that occur in a closed—and in a finite and therefore in a restricted—corpus. Hence it is possible to make the 'exhaustive collection of collocations' mentioned by Firth; this, however, has not been attempted because it is not intended to follow through Firth's remaining steps. Instead, collocations that appear to be significant—usually this significance arises from the fact that they occur reasonably frequently—have been selected for consideration. One important feature of post-Saussurean linguistics is its emphasis upon the two main aspects from which a

1. These terms are explained in Section 3A of Chapter 2 below. See also Glossary.

language may be viewed—the syntagmatic and the paradigmatic aspects or axes. The *syntagmatic axis* is concerned with the sequential characteristics of language, which depend upon the fact that in a specific (spoken or written) example the various linguistic units—whether they be letters or syllables or words or phrases, and so on—are arranged in order, one after another; from this aspect, language is seen as a chain of units linked together in a sequence. A compound unit, such as a phrase or some other group of words that are closely linked together, is called a *syntagm*. Collocations, being lexical items that occur close to each other in the chain, are determined by examining the text along the syntagmatic axis. Some collocations—such as חֶסֶד וֶאֱמֶת and עשׂה חֶסֶד עִם—are also syntagms, because they are closely linked together to form a compound unit. On the other hand, the *paradigmatic axis* relates to the aspect of choice that is a feature of language use: given a chain of units, there may be for each of the original units a set of similar units that can be substituted for it to produce another similar chain; for example, the second syntagm above may become עשׂה טוֹב עִם, by substituting a similar unit for the middle item in the chain. The list of units from which any one may be selected to fill a given position in a chain is called a *paradigm*.

In his earlier study, Lyons (1963: 59) claims that a solidly based theory of meaning can be established by defining 'the meaning of a given linguistic unit...to be the set of (paradigmatic) relations that the unit contracts with other units of the language'. These relations are discovered on the basis of pragmatic implications holding between sentences that contain the given units. Incompatibility, antonymy and hyponomy are 'the fundamental meaning-relations in any theory of semantic structure' (p. 70) and they are 'universal and essential meaning-relations' (p. 79). Context is relevant at all levels of semantic analysis (p. 80), and meaning-relations are established for particular contexts, not for the totality of language. In his later work he speaks of sense-relations instead of meaning-relations and describes the sense of a linguistic item by analysing the sense-relations (including incompatibility, etc.) that it contracts with other items in the vocabulary.

Sawyer's study also is guided by the method outlined by Lyons, and he looks for meaning-relations[1] between members of his semantic field

---

1.   Sawyer retains this term, taken from Lyons's early work, even though he makes frequent reference to Lyons 1968, where the term sense-relations is already being used.

for 'salvation' in the Hebrew Bible. He recognizes (Sawyer 1972: 74-75) that the parallelism of Hebrew poetry is a potential source for discovering these relations; but the precise nature of the meaning-relations, which admittedly exist in the structure of the poetry, does not depend on the structure itself. He draws attention (pp. 83-88) to examples of opposition, consequence and implication, but he does not incorporate such information in his final definitions (pp. 102-11) of the members of his field, where he lists points of distinction as well as features they have in common.

Semantic features have been used to obtain contrastive and differential relationships between members of different lexical fields. Matsuda (1976: 79) analyses 'the semantic relations that hold between seven Biblical Hebrew verbs which denote mental activities'. He does this by seeking the semantic features that distinguish the words from each other. A given verb and its subject and its object must have some semantic features in common (p. 82); and when dealing with the semantic component, the grammatical subject is 'the actor (or agent) ...of the "activity" in question', while the grammatical object is the goal of the activity. He first examines the subjects of each verb (pp. 83-84) and finds that 'all of the verbs in question can take as the subject the forms which designate "man" or "God", so that we can list as one of the semantic features common to these verbs the feature of "the actor being man or God"'. The tabulation (p. 99) in which Matsuda summarizes his findings does not include this common semantic feature. Among the seven features he tabulates are 'God as object', 'non-human object', 'desirable value of object' and 'favourable result to object'. Matsuda uses the symbols + (the feature is relevant) and – (the absence of the feature is relevant), while 'absence of mark indicates that the feature is irrelevant'.

The present study incorporates some of these distinctive features; in particular it takes note of the persons[1] involved in each situation where one of the elements of the lexical field occurs. Matsuda's categories have been increased by subdividing 'man' into 'leader', 'man' and 'woman'; together with 'God' and 'non-personal' (which corresponds to 'non-human' in Matsuda [p. 83]), they play an important role in highlighting distinctions between the field members. The last

---

1.   See Section 3A of Chapter 2 below.

category—'non-personal'—is utilized also in producing the file of material dealing with interpersonal situations, which is the subject of investigation in Chapters 3 to 10.

Chapter 2

THE LEXICAL FIELD

The purpose of this study is to examine the ways in which the various elements of the field are used, in an attempt to discover semantic relations between them. This chapter provides the essential details concerning the field: where it is found, how it was established, and the analysis to which it was subjected.

1. *The Corpus*

One of the important contributions that Saussure made to linguistics was his emphasis on the contrast between synchronic and diachronic methods of language-study. He made it clear that the two methods are fundamentally different and that they perform different tasks. Subsequently, it has been widely accepted that in semantic studies synchronic description has priority over diachronic description. One expression of this trend in semantics was the development of theories of the linguistic field, and it follows that the study of a lexical field is essentially—primarily but not exclusively—a synchronic investigation. This poses a problem when attempting to determine the members of a lexical field in a body of literature that has developed over a considerable period of time, and the Hebrew Bible has an extensive and extended literary history. The problem may be solved in various ways: for example, by confining the corpus to the known work(s) of a single author, or to works known to be contemporaneous, or to the text as it existed at a certain point in time. A decision must be made between these and other possible alternatives, a decision probably both individualistic and arbitrary, but one that will ensure precision in the study. But once the decision has been made, it is necessary to specify the literary corpus very carefully,[1] so that others who have access to the corpus will be able to verify the work that has been done.

For the present study, it has been found that the first two alternatives mentioned above do not produce sufficient material to investigate, and the third alternative has been adopted. The literary corpus being examined is the version of the vocalized Masoretic Text published in *Biblia Hebraica Stuttgartensia (BHS)*. The selection of this particular version does not imply that it is *the* text of the Hebrew Bible. Manuscripts discovered at Qumran have demonstrated clearly that several types of text were in circulation in the period immediately preceding the Christian era, and that some readings in these manuscripts were different from those in the traditional Masoretic Text.

Concentrating on the text as it existed early in the eleventh century CE[2] has disadvantages as well as advantages. It precludes any investigation of semantic development during the period of formation and transmission of the text. Again, because the text examined is remote from the original writer or speaker, the objective cannot be to determine the meaning of a passage or term when it was first written or spoken, nor to determine the meaning it conveyed to the original readers or hearers. This study aims to determine how the Masoretes understood the text before them.[3]

2. *The Members*

Studies of lexical fields have often been criticized because the elements in the field have been selected intuitively, with the researcher relying upon knowledge of the language itself rather than adopting a more objective method for determining the members of the field. Doubts were expressed above about the value of the method used by Burres and Erickson even when applied to the reasonably compact Pauline corpus. It was therefore decided that such an objective method would

1.   For examples of the specification of a corpus, reference may be made to Lyons 1963: 91-94; Sawyer 1972: 10-16; and Erickson 1980: 138-43. In each case, reasons for choosing the corpus are given.

2.   See Roberts 1969: 10-11.

3.   See Sawyer 1972: 10: 'in biblical research, semantic statements are not only about what a speaker meant, but also about what his hearers thought or believed he meant, and who the hearers in question are must be carefully defined'.

not be appropriate for establishing a lexical field in a corpus that is many times larger than theirs. Consequently, with Lyons (1963: 94-96) and Sawyer (1972: 33-34), decisions about what elements to include in the field have been based on intuition and a knowledge of the object language.

A. *The Roots*

Six Hebrew roots were selected—roots known to be frequently used in situations involving two persons or groups of persons. Most of these roots refer to attitudes adopted by one person towards another, or to attributes that are relevant to interpersonal relationships. The six roots are: חסד, חנן, רחם, אהב, שׂנא and אמן.

Five of these roots refer to interpersonal relationships that are basically favourable to the other person. שׂנא was included because it expresses an unfavourable attitude and provides a contrast, specifically with אהב, but none of the other four roots appears to have such a uniquely lexicalized contrast.

B. *The Elements*

Each lexeme derived from each of the roots was then considered as a possible element, or member, of the lexical field. It may be surmised that this step ignores Barr's trenchant criticism[1] of those who unduly emphasize the meaning of the root of a Hebrew word. This 'root fallacy', as he calls it, often occurs when interpreters are guided by etymological associations rather than by semantics based on the actual usage of words. However, Sawyer (1967) responds to one of Barr's articles that deals with derivatives of the root אמן and suggests that the root may be specially important in communicating information. He concludes that an etymological group of words does sometimes have a common semantic element; in particular, the root אמן contributes the idea of firmness to two of its derivatives. In any case, the current study is first and foremost an examination of the usage of words; it uses the meaning of roots solely to gather members of the lexical field.

To determine the derivatives, both the Koehler-Baumgartner Lexicon and the Lisowsky Concordance were consulted, and a subsequent check was made using the Even-Shoshan Concordance.[2] It was decided

1. See Barr 1961: 100-106, 159.
2. Neither of these concordances is based on the text of *BHS*, but careful checking as the study proceeded has shown that they provide a reliable guide to that text.

to exclude all personal names, all place names, and names of objects
(e.g., חֲסִידָה and רְחֵם), but to include the few occurrences of the second
root חסד. Following Lisowsky the nominal uses of the participles אוֹהֵב
and שׂוֹנֵא were listed separately, but their verbal uses were included
with the appropriate verb-form. There are differences in the treatment of אַהֲבָה, for Lisowsky lists nominal uses as well as those forms to
which ל is prefixed and which appear to be verbal uses of the feminine
infinitive of אהב. These latter have been included under the verb,
following K–B.

					חָסִיד	חָסָד	חסד	A
תַּחֲנוּן*	תְּחִנָּה	חִנָּם	חֲנִינָה	חַנּוּן	חֵן	חנן		B
			רַחֲמָנִי	רַחֲמִים	רָחוּם	רחם		C
		אוֹהֵב	אֲהָבִים	אֲהָבִים	אַהֲבָה	אהב		D
			שׂוֹנֵא	שָׂנִיא*	שִׂנְאָה	שׂנא		E
אָמוֹן	אֹמֶן	אֹמֶן	אָמֵן	אֱמוּנָה	אֱמֶת	אמן		F
אָמְנָם	אָמְנָם	אָמְנָה	אָמְנָה	אֱמוּן*				

Table 2.1. *Elements of the Lexical Field* (verb-forms are unpointed)

Table 2.1 lists the 35 elements of the lexical field, showing the code
letter assigned to each root. The three occurrences of lexemes that are
usually classified by lexicographers as derivatives of the second root
חסד were included. Two of these are nominal and the third is a verbal
use; only the latter appears in an interpersonal situation. Also included
are two instances where the lexeme חֶסֶד is very clearly implied
although it is not actually present in the text. The keyword lexeme has
been enclosed in brackets in the analysis of these two passages,
Gen. 21.23 and Ruth 1.8, which have an almost identical sentence
structure. These 'functional occurrences'[1] have not been included in
the statistics that are examined in Chapter 3. In Table 2.1 vowel points
have not been shown in the verb-forms.

Up to this point, the term 'lexeme' has been given its normal usage,
to refer to the words that are conventionally listed as separate entries
in dictionaries. However, since this term is later restricted to a more
specialized use,[2] the members of the lexical field are referred to either
as 'members' or, more frequently, as 'elements'.

---

1. For further discussion of this aspect, see the introductory paragraphs to
Chapter 3 below.

2. See Section 4 below. Note also the statement in Section 5 concerning the way
the various terms are used throughout this study. Refer also to the Glossary.

3. *The Analysis*

The total number of occurrences in *BHS* of the elements listed in Table 2.1 is quite considerable. Consequently it was decided early in the investigation to record the analysis in such a way that the information could be readily transferred to a computer file from which it could be retrieved either in the original order or in a rearranged order. The information obtained by subjecting each occurrence in the Hebrew Bible of each element to a detailed examination was first recorded on data sheets and then transferred to punched cards. Each card contained all the details for one occurrence of one element, and in order to facilitate the subsequent sorting process, it was essential to record similar items of information in the same columns of the cards. For example, the code letters for the roots were assigned to the first six columns; an abbreviated form of the reference to the biblical passage in which the element occurred was given in cols. 10 to 18; and cols. 20 to 28 gave a 'transliteration' of the keyword, using only the characters available on the computer line printer. There were almost 1400 cards—one for each occurrence of each element in the lexical field—each recording up to 11 items obtained by carefully analysing the context of the keyword, but only six of these items play a significant part in the subsequent discussion. When read into the computer, each card formed a single record in the file produced by the computer. While every effort was made to treat the text consistently during the examination, it was frequently necessary to make subjective decisions.

A. *Situational Context*

The six selected roots are frequently used in interpersonal situations where the function of the element is to 'name' an activity or an attitude that involves the two persons or parties. Such situations may be represented as 'A–R–P', where A, the AGENT, directs the activity towards P, the PATIENT, and R is an expression containing the element of the field. For example, R might be a form of the verb אהב, or it might contain a form of the verb עשה in the expression עשׂה חֶסֶד עִם.

The terms Agent and Patient are used because they are considered to be more appropriate than alternatives such as Subject and Object, which are applicable especially when R is a transitive verb. The following examples use different forms derived from the root אהב; there is no doubt in each case who is the agent—the person acting in the manner indicated by the keyword—and who is the patient—the person to whom (or to whose benefit) the action is directed; the names are determined from the immediate context.

'He loved him' (1 Sam. 20.17).

Agent = Jonathan, Patient = David. Here the agent is the grammatical subject, and the patient is the grammatical object of the verb.

'They were loved' (2 Sam. 1.23).

With the *niphal* participle, used here, the agent is not specified; indeed, this is a convenient form to use when the speaker either is not concerned to specify the agent or is concerned not to specify the agent.[1] However, in this case the basic thought may be expressed as 'Jonathan was loved by David', which by a simple transformation becomes 'David loved Jonathan', and fits the representation used above, with Agent = David, Patient = Jonathan. In the untransformed expression the grammatical subject is in fact the patient, not the agent.

'Your love for me' (2 Sam. 1. 26).

Here a noun, not a form of the verb, is used, so the grammatical terms subject and object are not applicable. However, reference to the context makes it clear that the thought can be expressed as 'Jonathan's love for David'; and once again Agent = Jonathan, Patient = David.

Of the parties involved in the situation, one is frequently *God*,[2] the other is frequently human; in the latter case the human parties are distinguished as a *woman*, a *man* or a *leader*—such as one of the patriarchs, a king or a prophet. The term leader is applied carefully; for instance, during the lifetime of Saul, David is not classified as a leader. But there are occasions when two leaders are present, as in Gen. 47.29, where Jacob the patriarch and his son Joseph the ruler (under Pharaoh) of Egypt (see Gen. 41.37-45) are both termed leaders.

It often happens that the patient is not a person but an inanimate entity. These are classified as 'non-personal' (*nper*). Again, elements of the field used in inter-personal contexts often do not fit into the

---

1.   See Lambdin 1973: 176.
2.   In this and the next two paragraphs the italicized terms appear under AGENT and/or PATIENT in cols. 30 to 48 of the computer file.

basic A–R–P representation. For these the categories 'adjective'—
when the element is used attributively or adjectivally—and 'adverb'—
when it is used as a modifier—have been introduced.

Sometimes it has been extremely difficult to decide whether the
person is divine or human. After examining the context very carefully
for clues, the classification 'unspecified' has been used in those cases
where it has not been possible to make a decision. This course has
been adopted to avoid introducing a skewedness into the statistics; but
at a later stage of the study, when the statistical trends became clearer,
the classification has been revised in several cases that had previously
been left undecided. This matter remains unresolved in such the
passages as Prov. 3.3 (agent) and 2 Chron. 32.32; 2 Chron. 35.26
(patient).

B. *Syntagm*

The immediate literary environment of the elements frequently contains a verb and a preposition that are closely associated with the
element. The coding in the columns headed SYNTAGM identifies
these; the first symbol refers to the verb, and the second symbol to the
preposition. In this portion of the analysis the particular interest is in
the verbs and prepositions used with חֶסֶד, and these were recorded
whenever they were used with any elements of the field; no attempt
was made to specify every verb and every preposition used with every
element. In fact, attention was confined to 19 verbs and 11 prepositions. The entry '11' indicates that the verb is a form of עשה and the
preposition is עִם.[1]

C. *The Computer File*

The previous sections have given some indication of the information
obtained for each passage in which any of the 35 field elements
appeared. This information was stored on magnetic tape in the
CYBER system housed in Computing Services at the University of
Melbourne. The records were first arranged in the precise order in
which the key lexeme occurs in the text of *BHS*, and consequently the
entries in the REFERENCE column show the names of the books and
the numbers of the chapters and verses in the correct sequence in
which they appear in the Hebrew Bible. Not only is this so, but also
when there is more than one field element occurring in the same verse

---

1. This and other syntagms are investigated in Chapters 7 to 9.

the order of occurrence is preserved. The letters A to F were assigned
to the first six columns under CODE; when a passage contained the
expression חֶסֶד וֶאֱמֶת which is treated in Chapter 10, this was indicated
by recording F and A against חֶסֶד and אֱמֶת respectively in the eighth
column. This file, with records arranged strictly in their biblical
order of occurrence, is called WIDATA.

With such a vast amount of information it is of great value to make
rearrangements so that it may be viewed, as it were, from different
perspectives. The software packages SORT MERGE and SORT5 were
available on the computer to perform these rearrangements. These
programs kept intact the information in each record, but rearranged
the records with entries in a single nominated column in alphabetical
order. This rearrangement could also be extended to a series of such
columns. One very useful rearrangement dealt with the four columns
headed CODE, KEYWORD, AGENT and PATIENT, and the sorting
process was completed very rapidly, taking no more than 15 seconds.
Files on which this sorted information was stored were named in such
a way that the name of the original file and the columns sorted could
be readily determined; the prefix SRT indicates an output from the
sort packages, and this is followed by three more letters, the first two
of which indicate the columns sorted while the last letter identifies the
original file. Some of the files are noted as the sources for statistics
presented in subsequent chapters. For example, the source for Table
3.1 is SRTKAW. Here, W is the initial letter of WIDATA, the file
sorted; and the letters KA refer to the columns sorted—K includes the
CODE and KEYWORD columns, and A includes the AGENT and
PATIENT columns. Inspection of this and other rearrangements of
the collected information reveals trends that indicate similarities and
differences in the usage of the elements.

Subsequently, a second file was prepared by deleting from WIDATA
all records that contained the entry NPER in either the AGENT or the
PATIENT column. This file consists of approximately 1100 records,
containing information about the use of field elements in interpersonal
situations. There are, however, approximately 30 instances in which
an element is used as an attribute of a person; these are also retained
in this file. Since it contains the basic information for the situations in
which the keyword applies to an attitude or a relationship between two
persons—that is, to the personal data which is the subject of this
study—the file has been named PERDAT.

Most of the information to be investigated is stored in these two files, WIDATA and PERDAT, and reference is made to them frequently in subsequent chapters. However, further information gathered at a later stage has not been included in the existing computer files. This later collection is outlined in the following section.

4. *Additional Lexemes*

As the previously described analysis was proceeding, other lexemes were frequently noticed in passages containing the field elements. Following discussions with Professor J.F.A. Sawyer, it was decided to record each occurrence, within a certain neighbourhood of any elements of the lexical field, of the lexemes shown in Table 2.2. As in Table 2.1, verb forms are indicated by leaving them unpointed. The lexemes יֹדע and דֵּעַת were included only when they referred specifically to knowing God, being used in expressions like דֵּעַת אֱלֹהִים.

			נמל			בָּחִיר	בחר
			דוד				בְּרִית
		דָּבַק	דבק		גְּאֻלָּה	גּוֹאֵל	נאל
			חבק		יטב	טוּב	טוב
			חשק	מִישׁוֹר	יָשָׁר	יָשָׁר	ישר
		נְשִׁיקָה*	נשק			מֵישָׁרִים	
			חוס			דֵּעַת	ידע
		חָמְלָה	חמל	מוֹשִׁיעַ	יְשׁוּעָה	יֵשַׁע	ישע
תַּזְנוּת	זְנוּנִים	זוֹנָה	זנה			תְּשׁוּעָה	
			נאף				נצל
					נִפְלָאוֹת	פֶּלֶא	פלא
				צְדָקָה	צַדִּיק	צֶדֶק	צדק
					מִשְׁפָּט	שׁוֹפֵט	שפט

Table 2.2. *Additional Lexemes Used in Collocation with Elements of the Lexical Field* (verb-forms are unpointed)

The lexemes appear in the same order in Table 2.2 as in the collocation profiles of Figures 4.1–4.11. The lexemes in the right-hand column of the table appear in the lower right-hand quadrant of the profiles, and the lexemes at the head of each group occupy positions from 3 o'clock to 6 o'clock in the key profile. Similarly, the head lexemes in the left-hand column occupy positions in the lower left-hand quadrant between 9 o'clock and 6 o'clock in this key profile.

Criteria for selecting the additional lexemes differed from those applied to the field members. The field elements are derived from six roots that occur frequently in interpersonal relationships and which are also known to have related meanings. The additional lexemes, however, are included simply because they occur reasonably frequently in proximity to field elements. While *every* occurrence of the elements in the field was investigated, these additional lexemes were considered only when they occurred in the vicinity of one (or more) of the field elements. The neighbourhood was originally taken as a chapter in *BHS*, except in the case of Psalm 119 where it was restricted to a stanza. Sheets were prepared containing the first three columns of WIDATA headed CODE, REFERENCE and KEYWORD, and, using Lisowsky's Concordance, the lexeme and the number of the verse in which it occurred was noted whenever any additional lexeme appeared in a chapter listed in the REFERENCE column. Subsequent inspection revealed that many of the words occur in much closer proximity to one another, so the lexemes occurring in the same verse (or, in some cases, within a few consecutive verses) were subjected to a more detailed examination. The extent of the neighbourhood was determined by the sense and content of the passage, not by setting a rigid number of lexical items either before or after each element. One of the larger neighbourhoods includes five consecutive verses, in Deut. 7.7-11, which forms a single unit of thought and is indeed marked as a *seder*—one of the 'paragraphs which correspond to the natural thought' into which the Hebrew text of the Bible was divided.[1] This passage contains five field elements—שׂנֵא, אוֹהֵב, אַהֲבָה, חֶסֶד (twice), and אמן—as well as four of the additional lexemes—בְּרִית, בָחַר, מִשְׁפָּט and חשׁק. These co-occurring lexemes are called COLLOCATIONS and have been subdivided into three categories, according to whether they occur in a parallel construction, or in a series (a group of two or more items, frequently joined by the conjunction ו but sometimes appearing asyndetically), or simply in contiguity. Among these collocations are found groups of lexical items that contain either elements of the lexical field, or members of the set of additional lexemes, or items taken from both of these word groups.

1.   Bruce 1963: 121.

5. *Overview*

This chapter has defined the lexical field, stating the corpus in which it is found, and the elements or members of the field have been listed in Table 2.1. It has also described the analysis of the passages in the Hebrew Bible where the elements occur, setting out the various terms and abbreviations used in the analysis. Several other lexical items occurring frequently in close proximity to the field elements, called 'additional lexemes', are listed in Table 2.2. Although the field elements are themselves lexemes, from here on the terms 'element', 'lexeme' and 'lexical item' are used in a specialized and restricted manner, so that 'element' always means a member of the lexical field, and 'lexeme' always means one of the additional lexemes. The term 'lexical item' always refers to 'elements and/or lexemes' and includes both elements of the field and additional lexemes.

The ensuing chapters discuss various aspects of the analysis to which the lexical items have been subjected, commencing in Chapter 3 with the distributions of the roots and of the elements included in the field. Chapters 4 to 9 will refer to the additional lexemes as well as to the field elements.

Chapter 3

DISTRIBUTION: AGENT–PATIENT

In structural linguistics, the term 'distribution' is normally applied to the set of linguistic contexts in which a unit, such as a lexeme, can occur. When a distributional analysis of a living language is being made, statements can be made only in terms of probabilities; the linguist investigates the wider and growing selection available, and attempts to draw up distribution rules for most of the lexemes. But in the case of a closed corpus in a dead language, the number of times each item occurs in a given context can be counted and these statistics can be used as the basis for deducing relationships between the meanings of the various items.

However, doubts have been raised about the value of statistics based on the actual occurrences of words in a given corpus. Concepts are frequently implied in a particular context without being expressly stated. Burres (1970: 103-105) tackles this problem by first distinguishing two different senses in which the word 'occurrence' is used. The literal presence of a word in a text is an 'ostensive occurrence', whereas a 'functional occurrence' includes the replacement of a noun by a pronoun, or the deletion (to avoid unnecessary repetition) of a noun or a verb which nevertheless still functions semantically in the construction. As an example, he cites the word 'boasting' which occurs ostensively once, but functionally five times, in Rom. 3.27. Statistics of the occurrences of lexical items in various books of the Bible are based on the ostensive level; and when linguists use the word 'occurrence' it is primarily in its ostensive sense. Burres proposes to rectify this defect by obtaining the functional occurrences of the words in which he is interested, and he claims that this can be accomplished by applying transformational analysis to the text in order to recover the simple basic strings from which the complex sentence has been built up.

Erickson (1980: 312) refers to Burres's plan to obtain a transformational analysis of the NT text and to adapt this analysis to a computer. He reports work commenced on Paul's letter to the Galatians, but that up to 1977 little progress had been made. No reasons are given for the apparent abortion of this project; but if too many obstacles hinder its application to a relatively small corpus like one of the Pauline epistles, those involved in the much larger corpus of the whole Hebrew Bible will certainly prove to be insurmountable.

Thistleton (1977: 97-98) has reservations about certain applications of transformational techniques. Nevertheless, he speaks approvingly of the use Burres makes of transformational analysis to obtain implicit occurrences that are functionally operative. He asserts that making linguistic elements explicit shows that the occurrence of actual concepts may not be reliably determined from statistics for word-occurrences.

There are problems involved both in the determination of distribution by counting the ostensive occurrences of words and also in using such distribution statistics to draw conclusions about relationships between the meanings of those words. However, three points should be noticed—

1. No satisfactory method has been devised for determining the functional rather than the ostensive occurrences.
2. There is a difference between a concept and a word, and statements about word-occurrences are different from statements about the occurrence of actual concepts.
3. It is possible—and useful—when dealing with a closed corpus to compare the actual—ostensive—occurrences of words, provided it is kept in mind that these comparisons cannot be used to produce quantified statements about meaning relations between the words involved.

The possibility of using distribution as a clue to meaning has already been noted. Since the present study is essentially a word (not a concept) study—more accurately, the study of several words in a lexical field—it is intended to apply the situational statistics, which relate to the actual occurrences of the words in the corpus, to obtain clues to relationships between the meanings of members of the field. Suppose there are three members of the field, such that one of them always occurs in a situation where both the participants are persons, and the second one only occurs in a situation where one of the 'participants' is a non-personal entity, while the third occurs sometimes in one, and sometimes in the other, situational environment. This is, at one level, a statement about the distribution of the words; but it carries with it implications about the relationships between the meanings of these words. However, it cannot be concluded that there is a semantic feature for which the value 1 can be assigned to the first word, the value 0 to the second word, and a value between 0 and 1 to the third word. Nevertheless, the relevance of this semantic feature to each word may be represented by assigning a plus sign (+) to the first word, a minus sign (–) to the second word, and a blank to the third word, as has been suggested by Matsuda.

The term distribution is applied here to the broader context which includes not only the linguistic environment but also the persons involved in the language event. Fuller consideration is given to the linguistic environment of the elements in later chapters, but the present chapter deals first with the roots that form the basis of the lexical field, and then with the members, or elements, of the field, concentrating on the persons involved as agent and patient. The additional lexemes introduced in the previous chapter are not considered here, for two reasons—first, only some, but not all, of the occurrences of these lexemes have been included in this study; secondly, the additional lexemes have not been subjected to the same analysis as the field elements.

1. *Distribution of Roots*

The statistics to which reference has been made above are set out in Tables 3.1 to 3.4 and they are also presented graphically in Figures 3.1 and 3.2. In these tables, which appear at appropriate points in the text, the categories of agent and patient have been reduced by combining Leader, Man, and Woman under the single classification Human, and by combining others under Varia. Tables 3.1 and 3.3 show the actual number of times the derivatives of each root occur in each combination of agent and patient. The statistics given in Table 3.1 for the original file, WIDATA, were obtained very quickly from SRTKAW; the source for those in Table 3.3 for the derived file was SRTKAP, produced by sorting the same four columns of PERDAT.

The total number of occurrences varies from one root to another, and also from one keyword element to another. Table 3.1 shows that the roots חנן and רחם occur almost the same number of times in a situation where God is agent and the patient is human. But the figures in the right-hand column of the table show that a חנן-derivative is likely to occur in any position 2.3 times more frequently than a רחם-derivative. In order to compare the roots, both the actual number of occurrences of each root in a given category and also its total number of occurrences must be taken into account: by expressing the actual number as a percentage of the total number of occurrences. These percentages are shown in Tables 3.2 and 3.4, which have been derived from Tables 3.1 and 3.3 respectively. Thus the figures recorded in any line of Table 3.2 are obtained from the corresponding line of Table 3.1 by expressing the figure in each column as a percentage of the total recorded in the right-hand column; e.g., in column 1 for חנן, 76 = 32.1% of 237. Hence, less than one-third of the חנן-derivatives occur in a God–human situation, whereas more than three-quarters of the רחם-derivatives are used in the same situation.

AGENT:	GOD				HUMAN					OTHER		TOTAL
Patient:	Hum	N-P	Uns	Tot	God	Hum	N-P	Uns	Tot	N-P	VA	
חסד	187			187	28	52		12	92	2	1	282
חנן	76			76	48	68	1		117	40	4	237
רחם	77			77	1	20		21			4	102
אהב	31	7		38	34	117	60		211	1		250
שנא	8	10		18	12	108	26		146			164
אמן	65	5	1	71	39	64	27	3	133	106	23	333
TOTAL	444	22	1	467	162	429	114	15	720	149	32	1368

Table 3.1. *Situational Distribution—Agent Patient: Number of Occurrences of Each Root in Each Category* (Source: SRTKAW)

AGENT:	GOD				HUMAN					OTHER		TOTAL
Patient:	Hum	N-P	Uns	Tot	God	Hum	N-P	Uns	Tot	N-P	VA	
חסד	66.3			66.3	9.9	18.4		4.3	32.6	0.7	0.4	282
חנן	32.1			32.1	20.3	28.7	0.4		49.4	16.9	1.7	237
רחם	75.5			75.5	1.0	19.6		20.6				102
אהב	12.4	2.8		15.2	14.6	46.8	24.0		84.4	0.4		250
שנא	4.9	6.1		11.0	7.3	65.9	15.9		89.0			164
אמן	19.5	1.5	0.3	21.3	11.7	19.2	8.1	0.9	39.9	31.8	6.9	333
TOTAL	32.5	1.6	0.1	34.1	11.8	31.4	8.3	1.1	52.6	10.9	2.3	1368

Table 3.2. *Situational Distribution—Agent Patient: Percentage of Occurrences of Each Category* (Source: Table 3.1)

The following discussion is based on the percentage figures given in Tables 3.2 and 3.4; it is these percentages which have been graphed in Figures 3.1 and 3.2 respectively.

A. *Agent–Patient Distribution of Roots: WIDATA*

Figure 3.1 presents graphically the statistics obtained from WIDATA and set out in Table 3.2. The graphs for each root have been separated into four sections. In the upper section, A, the agent is God, while in the next two sections, B and C, the agent is Human, and the lowest section, D, includes all the non-personal cases for which the agent is not specified as either God or Human. Sections A and C refer to a patient that is either Human (shown above the zero-line) or Non-personal (below the zero-line); and those portions which are hatched refer to the few cases that remain Unspecified. The patient in Section B is God. In terms of the columns of Table 3.2, the first three columns are graphed in the upper Section A; the graphs of the fifth column are in the next section, B; columns 6 to 8 are in Section C; and the data for the graphs in the bottom section, D, come from column 10. The data in the remaining three columns are not featured in the graphs.

The graphs of the three roots on the left of Figure 3.1 contrast with those on the right in some fairly obvious but nonetheless important ways, especially in Sections A and C. For convenience, the roots חסד, חנן and רחם are referred to as Class L (for left), and the remaining three roots—אהב, שׂנא and אמן—as Class R (for right). Then in Section A, when God is the agent:

1. The percentages of the Class L roots are much higher than those of the Class R roots;
2. A non-personal patient occurs only with the Class R roots, but never with the Class L roots.

In Section C, when the agent is Human:

1. The contribution of the roots אהב and שׂנא is much greater than that of the Class L roots as well as אמן;
2. A non-personal patient occurs very frequently with the Class R roots, never with חסד and רחם, and very rarely—in fact, only once—with חנן.

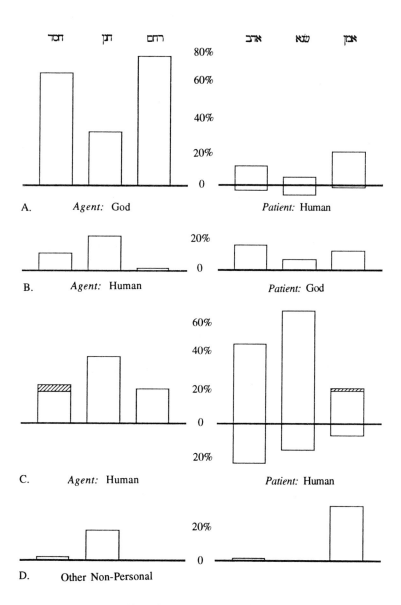

Figure 3.1. *Situational Distribution of Roots*

In Section D there is a relatively high incidence of non-personal cases, especially for the roots חנן (in Class L) and אמן (in Class R). This is traceable to the existence of derivative elements that are used either attributively or as modifiers. The small non-personal contribution under the root חסד applies to two instances of the second root of this form mentioned previously.

The controversy over the existence (or non-existence) of root-meanings in Hebrew has been mentioned earlier; it is not intended to assert that meaning and distribution are identical, but it is nevertheless true that the one is dependent upon the other. Therefore the contrasts just noted can throw light on the meaning relationships that exist between lexemes derived from the roots. Examination of the graphs in Figure 3.1 reveals that the scope of the agent–patient situations in which the Class R roots appear is much greater than that of the roots חסד and רחם. To adapt an expression of J.R. Firth (cf. 1951: 196), it is part of the meaning of derivatives of the roots אהב, שׂנא and אמן that they are used in a wider range of situations than the derivatives of חסד and of רחם and possibly also of חנן.

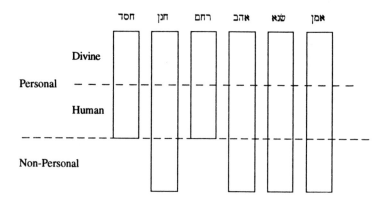

Figure 3.2. *Distribution of Roots in Agent–Patient Categories*

The diagrammatic representation in Figure 3.2 summarizes the fore-going discussion of the distribution of the roots. The tripartite 'universe of discourse' embracing the agents and patients is first divided into Personal and Non-Personal, and the former category is then subdivided into Divine and Human. No attempt has been made in the diagram to quantify the results.

Attention has been drawn to the extent to which the various roots are used in situations that involve a non-personal entity, but now the focus turns to situations in which both participants are persons.

AGENT:	GOD			HUMAN				OTHER	TOTAL
Patient:	Hum	Uns	Tot	God	Hum	Uns	Tot		
חסד	187		187	28	52	12	92	1	280
חנן	76		76	48	68		116	4	196
רחם	77		77	1	20		21	4	102
אהב	31		31	34	117		151		182
שׂנא	8		8	12	108		120		128
אמן	65	1	66	39	64	3	106	23	195
TOTAL	444	1	445	162	429	15	606	32	1083

Table 3.3. *Personal Distribution—Roots: Number of Occurrences of Each Root in Each Category* (Source: SRTKAP)

AGENT:	GOD			HUMAN				OTHER	TOTAL
Patient:	Hum	Uns	Tot	God	Hum	Uns	Tot		
חסד	66.8		66.8	10.0	18.6	4.3	32.8	0.4	280
חנן	38.8		38.8	24.5	34.7		59.2	2.0	196
רחם	75.5		75.5	1.0	19.6		20.6	3.9	102
אהב	17.0		17.0	18.7	64.3		84.0		182
שׂנא	6.3		6.3	9.4	84.4		94.7		128
אמן	33.3	0.5	33.8	20.0	32.8	1.5	54.4	11.8	195
TOTAL	41.0	0.1	41.1	15.0	39.6	1.4	56.0	3.0	1083

Table 3.4. *Personal Distribution—Roots: Percentage of Occurrences of Each Root in Each Category* (Source: Table 3.3)

B. *Personal Distribution of Roots: PERDAT*

The statistics relating to interpersonal situations, in which both agent and patient are persons, have been drawn from the PERDAT file, and are set out in Tables 3.3 and 3.4;[1] they are graphed in Figure 3.3. All records containing a Non-Personal entry have been deleted from the WIDATA file, and such entries occur predominantly under the roots חנן, אהב, שׂנא and אמן (as may be confirmed by referring to Figure 3.1); hence the entries in Tables 3.2 and 3.4 for these four roots differ considerably. The reductions in the totals produce an increase in the percentages and a consequent lengthening of the columns in the graphs of Figure 3.3 as compared with the corresponding columns of Figure

---

1. The percentages shown in Table 3.4 have been derived from Table 3.3 in the manner already described in Section 1 above.

3.1. The small hatched portions in Sections A and C of Figure 3.3 indicate the percentages of cases in the appropriate category which still remain unspecified.

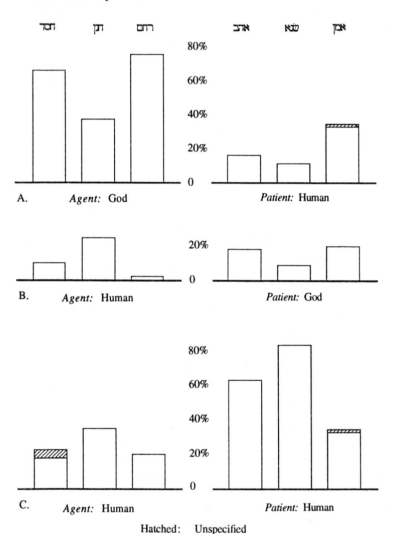

Figure 3.3. *Personal Distribution of Roots*

The notation introduced in the previous section is used here also, so that Class L refers to the roots חסד, חנן and רחם whose graphs are on the left, and Class R refers to those roots whose graphs are on the right, viz. אהב, שנא and אמן. Some of the previous observations still apply; these are incorporated here and they are expanded as more detailed consideration is given to the contrasts between Class L and Class R.

In Section A, when God is the agent and the patient is Human:

1. the percentages of the Class L roots are still much higher than those of the roots in Class R; but the greater increase in the אמן percentages brings the אמן graph into much closer equality with the חנן graph;
2. the total number of cases in Class L (340) is more than 3 times the total in Class R (104).

In Section C, when both the agent and the patient are Human:

1. the contribution of the roots אהב and שנא is once more much greater than that of the Class L roots; and again the greater increase in the אמן percentages brings its contribution almost up to equality with that of חנן;
2. the total number of cases in Class R (289) is more than double the total in Class L (140).

In Section B, where the agent is Human and the patient is God:

1. there is no longer the wide discrepancy between the percentage contributions shown in the two classes; in particular the distributions of חנן, אהב and אמן are very similar to each other;
2. the total number of cases is also very evenly distributed between the two classes—84 in Class L and 77 in Class R.

The distributions of the Class L roots contrast with those of the Class R roots in both Sections A and C of Figure 3.3. This contrast becomes even greater when comparison is made between the distributions of the Class L roots in Section A and those of the Class R roots in Section C, as well as between the distributions of the Class R roots in Section A and those of the Class L roots in Section C. As noted, the distributions of the roots חנן and אמן resemble each other both in Section A and also in Section C; also, the contribution of חנן to each of these sections is slightly greater than the contribution of אמן to the same section. This is also true when the distributions of these roots in the opposite sections are considered—for example, the distribution of the root אמן in Section A is almost equal to that of חנן in Section C. Hence concentration can be focused on the remaining four roots. This reveals that the distribution of

1. חסד in Section A is almost identical with that of אהב in Section C;
2. רחם in Section A is slightly less than that of שׂנא in Section C;
3. אהב in Section A is almost identical with that of חסד in Section C, and also of רחם in Section C.

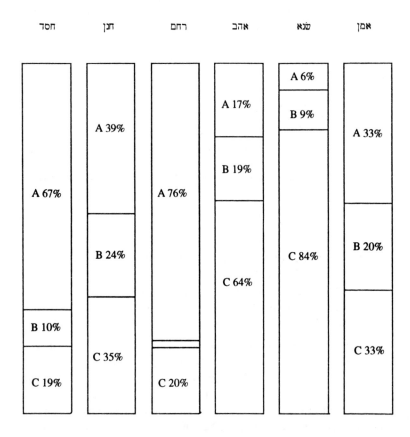

Figure 3.4. *Distribution of Roots—Sections A, B, C*

Figure 3.4 presents—approximately to scale—the distribution of each root as shown in the three sections of Figure 3.3. There is not sufficient space to record on the diagram the contribution of רחם to Section B; the figure is 1%. The percentages shown for the roots do not in all cases add up to 100 because the figures given in the columns of Table 3.4 headed UNSpecified and OTHer have not been included here—or, for that matter, in Figure 3.3. These columns account for almost 14% of the occurrences of אמן, but less than 5% of the occurrences of each of the other roots.

Figure 3.4 shows that considerably more than half the occurrences of four of the roots are concentrated in one of the sections—חסד and רחם in Section A, אהב and שׂנא in Section C. The other two roots—חנן and אמן—are more evenly distributed between the three sections, but each of these roots contributes considerably less to Section B than to Section A or Section C.

The following is a summary of salient features in the distribution of the roots, based on figures given in Table 3.2 above.

The roots חסד and רחם resemble each other in that

1. they alone of the six roots are not used in non-personal situations;
2. they are used most frequently in situations where God is the agent and the patient is human (66% and 76% respectively).

The roots אהב and שׂנא also resemble each other, and contrast with חסד and רחם, for

1. they are often used in situations involving a non-personal entity (27% and 22% respectively);
2. they are used most frequently in situations where both agent and patient are human (47% and 66% of WIDATA, respectively; and these increase to 64% and 84% of PERDAT).

While the roots חנן and אמן both provide a high proportion of non-personal usage (חנן, 17%; אמן, 41%), they are spread more evenly than the other roots between the three sections into which the personal situations have been subdivided. The contribution of both these roots to situations in which there is a human agent and God is the patient is appreciably less than their contributions to the other two categories.

The analysis has shown, as Matsuda found, that the nature of the agent and patient involved—whether they be non-personal, human or divine—affords a means of distinguishing between the roots. From this point of view, it is clear that the distributions of the roots חסד and רחם are very similar to each other, and they also contrast with the distributions of the remaining four roots.

The value of investigating the distribution of the roots is that it provides an overall picture of the usage of the roots in various contexts of situation. However, there are at least three and at most twelve elements derived from one or another of these roots; and in a lexical study concentration must be on the usage of the lexical items rather than the roots. It may be that some of the elements are used entirely in a single category, while others may be more uniformly distributed across the range of categories. For this reason the statement in the preceding sections has been brief. From this point on, the investigation is concerned not with the roots as such but with the field elements derived from these roots. The root חסד is no longer the focus of the study, for the examination will now be centred on one derivative of this root: the element חֶסֶד. Any reference to its other derivatives—חָסִיד and the verb חסד—will arise simply because they are related in the text in some way with חֶסֶד.

2. *Distribution of Elements*

Statistics resulting from a more detailed examination of the material are given later in Tables 3.8 and 3.9. There, the three categories that have hitherto been considered under the combined heading Human are separated into Leader, Man and Woman; reference is made to these statistics in Subsection B c below. In addition, the roots are subdivided into their constituent derivatives, which are elements of the field. Discussion of the distribution of the field elements takes into account two aspects of each element: it is first of all a lexical item in its own right; it is in the second place a derivative of one of the roots, and as such it plays a part in determining the nature of the distribution of the root—which has been already discussed in the previous section. The percentages introduced above, based on the total number of occurrences of the root, are necessary for making comparisons between the distributions of the roots, and they are also adequate for this purpose. But to consider both aspects of each element two percentages are needed—one based on the total number of occurrences of the element, in order to compare one element with another, and the other based on the total number of occurrences of the root, in order to compare the contributions made by each element to the distribution of the root. The variations between the distribution patterns of the roots are also evident in the case of the elements. Moreover, appreciable variations exist not only between the elements derived from different roots but also between elements derived from the same root. Because an element and the root from which it is derived do not always fit the same distribution pattern, the classes L and R are no longer appropriate to the discussion of the distributions of the elements.

A. *Non-Personal Situations*
All the roots except חסד and רחם are used extensively in non-personal situations. Table 3.5 lists the elements that occur in these situations, giving the number of times each is involved with a non-personal entity and the total number of occurrences of the element. The third column under Occurrence gives the percentage of the element's total occurrences appearing in non-personal situations; for example, the 7 non-personal occurrences of חֵן are 10.3% of its total (68) occurrences. This information is next related to that given previously for the roots, by showing the total number of occurrences of the root and also the percentage contribution made by the element to the non-personal usage of the root; for example, חֵן appears 7 times in a non-personal situation, which is 3.0% of the 237 occurrences of the root חנן to which חֵן is related. This table includes only elements used at least five times in non-personal situations; it excludes several elements used occasionally in such situations.

Three elements, חִנָּם, אָמְנָם and אֻמְנָם, occur only in a non-personal context; and another, אָמֵן, is used almost exclusively in such situations. Besides these, four more elements, אֱמֶת, אֹמֶן, אהב and שׂנא, have a relatively high non-personal usage, in terms both of the actual number of occurrences of the element and also of the percentage contribution of the element to the root. The elements listed in Table 3.5 account for almost all of the non-personal cases given in the non-personal (N-P) columns of Table 3.1. For the root חנן, 39 of the 41 have been included in Table 3.5; for אהב, 63 out of 68; for שׂנא, 34 out of 36, and for אמן, 135 out of 138. רחם is never used in a situation that involves a non-personal entity, and the two cases listed for חסד arise from a different root.

	ELEMENT Occurrence			ROOT	
	N-P	Tot	% N-P	Tot	% N-P
חֵן	7	68	10.3	237	3.0
חָנַם	32	32	100.0	237	13.5
אהב	55	169	32.5	250	22.0
אוֹהֵב	8	36	22.2	250	4.2
שׂנא	34	105	32.4	164	20.7
אָמֵן	23	25	92.0	333	6.9
אֱמֶת	57	127	44.9	333	17.1
אֱמוּנָה	5	53	9.4	333	1.5
אמן	37	97	38.1	333	11.1
אָמְנָם	8	8	100.0	333	2.4
אָמְנָם	5	5	100.0	333	1.5

Table 3.5. *Elements Often Occurring in Non-Personal Situations*
(Source: SRTKAW)

B. *Personal Distribution of Elements*

The detailed statistics for the personal distribution of the elements have been obtained from a rearrangement of the PERDAT file, and they are displayed in Tables 3.8 and 3.9 below. Table 3.8 gives the number of times each element occurs in each of the possible Agent–Patient groupings, and also indicates the number of cases in which the patient remains unspecified (in the columns headed U; the significance of the other abbreviations used for Patient will be obvious from the terms used, in full, for Agent). Figures in Table 3.9 are the appropriate percentages for the elements, based on the total number of occurrences of the element (in the extreme right-hand column headed TOTAL). For example, the first column of Table 3.8 indicates that חֶסֶד occurs 16 times when God is agent and a leader is patient. The right hand column shows that חֶסֶד occurs 245 times altogether. Now 16 is 6.5% of 245; and this is the figure recorded alongside חֶסֶד in the first column of Table 3.9. While Table 3.8 contains the details for *all* elements in the lexical field, Table 3.9 omits the elements that do not occur very frequently in the corpus, and gives the percentages for only those elements which occur more than 10 times in PERDAT. The graphs of Figures 3.5, 3.6 and 3.7 are based on these percentages, which have been amended by reclassifying the unspecified cases for חֶסֶד but not for the other elements.

Element	SECTION A God–Human		SECTION B Human–God		SECTION C Human–Human	
	Elem	Root	Elem	Root	Elem	Root
חָסִיד	6.2	0.7	87.5	10.0	6.2	0.7
חֶסֶד	74.7	65.4			24.9	21.8
חַנּוּן	92.3	6.1			7.7	0.5
חֵן	29.5	9.2			67.2	20.9
חנן	55.7	22.4	16.5	6.6	26.6	10.7
תְּחִנָּה	4.0	0.5	80.0	10.2	16.0	2.0
תַּחֲנוּן*			88.2	7.7	11.8	1.0
רַחֲמִים	74.4	28.4			25.6	9.8
רחוּם	92.3	11.8			7.7	1.0
רחם	73.5	35.3	2.0	1.0	16.3	7.8
אַהֲבָה	23.1	4.9	5.1	1.1	71.8	15.4
אהב	19.3	12.1	14.9	9.3	65.8	41.2
אוֹהֵב			53.6	8.2	46.4	7.1
שִׂנְאָה	11.8	1.6			88.2	11.7
שׂנא	8.5	4.7	9.9	5.5	81.7	45.3
שׂוֹנֵא			12.8	4.9	87.2	26.6
אֱמֶת	47.1	16.9	8.6	4.1	30.0	10.8
אֱמוּנָה	50.0	12.3	6.3	1.5	35.4	8.7
אמן	15.0	4.6	43.3	13.3	30.0	9.2

Table 3.6. *Distribution of Elements—Section A, B, C: Percentage of Occurrences in Each Section* (Source: ELEM—Table 3.9; ROOT—Table 3.8)

a. *Distribution—Sections A, B and C*
The percentages in the columns headed ELEM in Table 3.6 have been extracted from some of the columns headed TOT in Table 3.9—Column 5 for Section A (God–Human), Column 9 for Section B (Human–God) and Column 29 for Section C (Human–Human). The number of columns, and their headings, are the same in both Table 3.8 and Table 3.9. The percentages in the columns headed ROOT in Table 3.6 have been calculated from the entries in Table 3.8 by expressing the number of occurrences of the element as a percentage of the total number of occurrences of the root to which it is related. As an illustration, Table 3.8 shows that the element חֶסֶד occurs 183 times in Section A, and the root חסד occurs 280 times altogether. Now, 183 is 65.4% of 280; and this is the figure given for the element חֶסֶד in the column of Table 3.6 headed ROOT under Section A. Comparison of the figures in Figure 3.4 with those in the columns headed ROOT in Table 3.6 indicates that for some roots one or other of its elements predominate in the different sections, while for other roots the

different elements make more even contributions to the sections; this information can also be obtained directly from Table 3.6 by noting the figures given for each element related to the same root.

As an example, consider the roots חסד and רחם, whose distributions are very similar to each other and at the same time in marked contrast with those of the other four roots. The distribution figures for the elements חֶסֶד, רַחֲמִים and רחם are:

1. uniformly high and very nearly equal in Section A—74.7, 74.4 and 73.5 respectively;
2. very low in Section B—0, 0 and 2.0 respectively;
3. fairly low but still of comparable magnitude in Section C— 24.9, 25.6 and 16.3 respectively.

Not only the roots but also the elements, especially חֶסֶד and רַחֲמִים, have very similar distributions in Sections A and C. But when the elements are considered in relation to their roots, it is found that חֶסֶד predominates in Sections A and C (65.4 and 21.8 respectively), while חָסִיד alone contributes to Section B.

On the other hand, the amounts that רַחֲמִים and רחם contribute to the root are more nearly equal than those for חֶסֶד and חָסִיד; the percentages for רַחֲמִים and רחם are 28.4 and 35.3 in Section A and 9.8 and 7.8 in Section C. It is interesting that the combined contributions of רַחֲמִים and רחם amount to 63.7 in Section A and 17.6 in Section C—figures that are almost equal to those given above for חֶסֶד; but it is doubtful whether this fact is significant.

A distribution feature distinguishing חֶסֶד on the one hand from רַחֲמִים and רחם on the other is that חֶסֶד accounts for almost the entire contribution of its root in both Section A and Section C, whereas רַחֲמִים and רחם both contribute more evenly in these two sections. From the point of view of the personal distribution features considered so far, there is a greater divergence between those of חֶסֶד and חָסִיד than for those of רַחֲמִים and רחם. More specifically, for these four elements—

1. חֶסֶד predominates over חָסִיד in God–Human and in Human–Human situations;
2. חָסִיד, but not חֶסֶד, contributes in Human–God situations;
3. רחם contributes slightly more than רַחֲמִים in God–Human situations;

4. רַחֲמִים contributes slightly more than רחם in Human–Human situations; and

5. רַחֲמִים and רחם are virtually absent from Human–God situations.

Furthermore, חֶסֶד is distinguished from all other elements by the magnitude of its contribution to that of its root in God–Human situations. The figure recorded for חֶסֶד, 65.4, is much larger than any other percentages in the columns headed ROOT in Table 3.6; the nearest approach is 45.3, recorded for שׂנא, followed closely by 41.2 for אהב, both in Human–Human situations. These figures measure the part played by the element in the total contribution of its root to a given type of situation. The significance of these facts becomes clearer if we consider שׂנא. More than 80% of all the occurrences of the root שׂנא are in situations involving two human persons or parties; and, of this 80%, the element שׂנא supplies 45.3%. The distribution of the element שׂנא, therefore, is such that it is responsible, in Section C, for 45.3% of all the occurrences of the root שׂנא; in other words, the element directs less than half of the root's occurrences to situations that involve two human parties. The only element that directs more than half the occurrences of its root into any one section is חֶסֶד: its usage is such that it causes almost two-thirds of the occurrences of the root חסד to be concentrated in Section A, in situations where God as agent directs חֶסֶד towards a human patient. Hence it is a unique feature of the usage of the element חֶסֶד that it concentrates in one section—where God is agent and the patient is human—a great majority of the occurrences of the root חסד.

There is, therefore, a great disparity between the elements חֶסֶד and חָסִיד which are both related to the same root, and this disparity is, in the lexical field, unique for these elements. Table 3.6 confirms that there is more uniformity in the distributions of elements related to each of the other roots than there is in the distributions of the elements חֶסֶד and חָסִיד.

The concentration of the occurrences of the various elements in one or other of the sections in Table 3.6 reveals contrasts and comparisons between the derivatives of חסד, רחם, אהב and שׂנא; but little has been said about the derivatives of חנן and אמן which contrast with the other four roots in making more even contributions to the three sections of the table; their smallest contribution goes in both cases to Section B.

Some of the elements derived from these roots follow this pattern—
אֱמֶת, חֵן, חָנוּן and אֱמוּנָה all contribute less to Section B than to the
other sections. Table 3.4 indicates that 24.5% of the occurrences of
the root חנן are in Section B where the agent is human and the patient
is God. The percentages given for the derivatives of חנן in the column
headed ROOT in Section B of Table 3.6 add up to 24.5. Hence these
three derivatives—the verb חנן as well as תְּחִנָּה and *תַּחֲנוּן—are the only
ones that are used in a Human–God situation. The percentages in the
ELEM column of Section B show that both תְּחִנָּה and *תַּחֲנוּן are used
most frequently in such situations. Both elements also occur
occasionally in situations where both parties are human (Section C),
but only תְּחִנָּה is used when God is the agent. Thus the distribution
pattern of each of these two elements is divergent from that of the
root; but the pattern of the verb חנן is similar to that of the root.
However, a form of הִתְחַנֵּן always occurs in passages where חנן is used
with God as the patient. The other חנן stems never have God as patient,
although הִתְחַנֵּן is occasionally used also when both parties are human.
The nature of the patient provides a means of distinguishing between
the derivatives of the root חנן and it also distinguishes one of the
modified stems of the verb חנן from the others. Sawyer (1972: 96)
introduces the term 'disinfected' for members of his salvation field,
like הוֹשִׁיעַ, which are freed of secular reference. His earlier statements
(p. 81) clarify the signification of this term, for הוֹשִׁיעַ is always and
only applied to the activity of Yahweh, the God of Israel. In other
words, an element is said to be 'disinfected' if its agent is always, and
only, God. The more general term 'restricted' will be used when the
person involved as agent or patient is either divine or human, so that
תְּחִנָּה, *תַּחֲנוּן and תִּתְחַנֵּן are all restricted to a greater or lesser degree
with respect to God as patient, but the other חנן stems are not
restricted.

Since the elements אֱמֶת and אֱמוּנָה both contribute less to Section B
than to the other sections, their distribution pattern resembles that of
the root אמן shown in Figure 3.4. But Table 3.6 reveals that the verb
אמן contributes more to Section B than to the other sections, and hence
its pattern diverges from that of the root. The Hithpael of אמן is not
found in the biblical corpus, and so it cannot account for this divergence. The frequently used stems are the Niphal and the Hiphil, and
they together account for all the cases shown in Table 3.8 where God
is one of the parties. The Niphal is evenly distributed between the two

alternatives—when God is agent, 8 times, and 6 times when God is patient. The Hiphil, however, is used 20 times with God as patient but only once with God as agent. Thus the Hiphil, but not the Niphal, is restricted with respect to God as patient.

b. *Distribution—Agent or Patient Specified*

The preceding section has examined the distribution of the elements when both agent and patient are specified. Rearranging the statistics from Table 3.9, by bringing together all the cases in which the agent is human (in both Sections B and C) as well as those in which the patient is human (in Sections A and C), shows which elements are used exclusively with, or are restricted from use with, a specific class of Agent or Patient. Table 3.7 sets out in adjacent columns the distribution figures (as percentages of the total number of occurrences of the element) for the Agent classified as either God or Human; the figures for the Patient are also in adjacent columns.

Element	AGENT		PATIENT	
	God	Human	God	Human
חָסִיד	6.2	94.7	87.5	9.3
חֶסֶד	74.7	24.9		95.1
חַנּוּן	92.3	7.7		100.0
חֵן	29.5	67.2		95.1
חנן	55.7	43.1	16.5	82.3
תְּחִנָּה	4.0	96.0	80.0	20.0
תַּחֲנוּן*		100.0	88.2	11.8
רַחֲמִים	74.4	25.6		100.0
רחום	92.3	7.7		100.0
רחם	73.5	18.3	2.0	89.8
אַהֲבָה	23.1	76.9	5.1	94.9
אהב	19.3	80.7	14.9	85.1
אוֹהֵב		100.0	53.6	46.4
שִׂנְאָה	11.8	88.2		100.0
שֹׂנֵא	8.5	91.6	9.9	90.2
שׂוֹנֵא		100.0	12.8	87.2
אֱמֶת	47.1	38.6	8.6	77.1
אֱמוּנָה	50.0	41.7	6.3	85.4
אמן	15.0	73.3	43.3	45.0

Table 3.7. *Distribution Of Elements—Agent, Patient: Percentage of Occurrences for Categories Shown* (Source: Table 3.9)

Table 3.7 reveals that none of the elements is used in the corpus exclusively with God as either agent or patient. The elements that approach this exclusive use most closely are חַנּוּן and רַחוּם when God is agent, and *תַּחֲנוּן* when God is patient. The elements *אוֹהֵב, תַּחֲנוּן* and שׂוֹנֵא are never used with God as agent, but always with a human agent. Likewise, חַנּוּן, רַחֲמִים, רַחוּם and שִׂנְאָה are always used with a human patient and never with God as patient.

There is, however, a tendency for some elements to be dominated by one class of agent and also by one class of patient. Thus, for חַנּוּן— and also for רַחוּם—the dominating agent is God[1] (92.3% of the cases) and the dominating patient is human (100% of the cases). On the other hand, both *תַּחֲנוּן* and תְּחִנָּה tend to be dominated by a human agent (100% and 96.0% respectively) and by a divine patient (88.2% and 80.0% respectively). The dominant persons are both human for each of the derivatives of the root שׂנא—שׂוֹנֵא: 100% as agent, 87.2% as patient; שׂנא: 91.6% as agent, 90.2% as patient; שִׂנְאָה: 88.2% as agent, 100% as patient. This human dominance is slightly less in the derivatives of the root אהב—for אוֹהֵב: 100% as agent but only 46.4% as

---

1.   In all except two of the 13 occurrences of these elements they are together in a series combination—רַחוּם וְחַנּוּן three times and חַנּוּן וְרַחוּם eight times. Ten times this compound expression is an attribute of Yahweh, and some of the ancient versions have attempted to restore uniformity in the remaining case (Ps. 112.4) by adding their equivalent for Yahweh. Dahood (1970: 126-28) follows a different route to reach the same conclusion. He renders v. 4b as 'The Merciful and Compassionate and Just One' and says 'these divine appellations (see Ps. 111.4) stand grammatically in apposition with' אוֹר which he translates 'Sun', and claims that it designates Yahweh.

On the other hand, Briggs (1907: 384) paraphrases the psalm with 'the one that fears Yahweh' as subject throughout; like Weiser (1962: 702-704), he applies the three attributes in v. 4b to a man, not to God. This is also the view of Allen (1983: 93-98) who makes out a strong case by drawing attention to the close relationship between Psalms 111 and 112. The former he entitles 'God at Work' (p. 88) and the latter 'Godliness at Work'. 'Eleven terms or phrases have been taken over from Ps. 111, often with a different sense... No less than seven transfer to the righteous terms related to Yahweh or his law in Ps. 111'. This 'intentional counterpart of Ps. 111' urges 'that Yahweh's own characteristics detailed in the former psalm should be reflected in the life of the believer.' He also notes 'further stress upon godlike behavior, here a remarkable one : the credal statement of 111: 4... must find a moral echo in the life of the Yahwist.'

In our analysis, the agent of the compound expression in Ps. 112. 4 is to be understood as Man.

patient; for אהב: 80.7% as agent, 85.1% as patient; and for אֲהֲבָה: 76.9% as agent, 94.9% as patient.

The distributions of חֶסֶד, רַחֲמִים and רחם are strikingly similar; and some of the figures quoted in Subsection a above—those for Sections A (God is agent) and B (God is patient)—are repeated in Table 3.7. These percentages again emphasize the similarity of the distributions of חֶסֶד, רַחֲמִים and רחם; for the distribution figures of these elements are

1. fairly low but approximately equal when the agent is human: 24.9, 25.6 and 18.3 respectively (cf. 24.9, 25.6 and 16.3 in Section C); and
2. very high and of comparable magnitude when the patient is human: 95.1, 100 and 89.8 respectively.

The two aspects from which the statistics have been viewed in this and the preceding subsection both reveal a very close resemblance between the distributions of חֶסֶד, רַחֲמִים and רחם even though they differ in the contributions that they make to the distribution of their roots: whereas חֶסֶד predominates in Sections A and C, רַחֲמִים and רחם contribute in these sections amounts which are more nearly equal.

c. *Agent–Patient: God, Leader, Man, Woman*

The primary data, showing the occurrence of each element in each situation, are set out in Tables 3.8 and 3.9 and illustrated in Figures 3.5, 3.6 and 3.7 for the 19 elements listed in Table 3.7. Three preliminary points need to be made.

First, the information in Tables 3.8 and 3.9 is derived from PERDAT, the file that contains the data for all elements used in situations where both agent and patient are persons: in other words, either God or Human. Elements occurring in non-personal situations have been deleted.

Secondly, 11 other elements used less than 10 times in interpersonal situations have been omitted from Table 3.9, but their distribution is shown in Table 3.8.

AGENT	GOD					HUMAN																								OTH	TOTAL
						L	M	W	TOT	LEADER					MAN					WOMAN					HUMAN						
PATIENT	L	M	W	U	TOT	GOD				L	M	W	U	TOT	L	M	W	U	TOT	L	M	W	U	TOT	L	M	W	U	TOT		
ELEMENT																															
חָסִיד		1	1		2		28		28							1		1	2							1		1	2		32
חֶסֶד	16	162	5		183					4	9	1	2	16	2	28	3	8	41		3		1	4	6	40	4	11	61	1	245
חסד		2			2											1			1							1			1		3
TOTAL	16	165	6		187		28		28	4	9	1	2	16	2	30	3	9	44		3		1	4	6	42	4	12	64	1	280
חֲנִינָה		1			1																										1
חַנּוּן		12			12											1			1							1			1		13
חֵן	10	8			18					2	8	6		16	1	18	5		24				1	1	3	26	11	1	41	2	61
חנן	2	42			44	3	10		13		1			1	1	17			18	2				2	3	18			21	1	79
תְּחִנָּה		1			1	7	13		20	2				2	1	1			2						3	1			4		25
תַּחֲנוּן						1	14		15							2			2							2			2		17
TOTAL	12	64			76	11	37		48	4	9	6		19	3	39	5		47	2			1	3	9	48	11	1	69	3	196
רַחֲמָנִי																					1			1		1			1		1
רַחֲמִים	1	26	2		29						2			2		7			7		1			1		10			10		39
רַחוּם		12			12											1			1							1			1		13
רחם		31	5		36		1		1		2			2		5			5		1			1		8			8	4	49
TOTAL	1	69	7		77		1		1		4			4		13			13		3			3		20			20	4	102
אַהֲבָה		8	1		9		1	1	2			1		1		12	10		22		5			5		17	11		28		39
אהב	2	19	1		22	1	16		17		9	4		13	1	17	31		49		12	1		13	1	38	36		75		114
אוֹהֵב						2	13		15	1				1	1	10	1		12						2	10	1		13		28
אֲהָבִים																	1		1								1		1		1
TOTAL	2	27	2		31	3	30	1	34	1	9	5		15	2	39	43		84		17	1		18	3	65	49		117		182
שָׂנִיא																	1		1								1		1		1
שִׂנְאָה		2			2											12	3		15							12	3		15		17
שׂנא		5	1		6		7		7	1	4			5	3	32	16		51		2			2	4	38	16		58		71
שׂוֹנֵא							5		5						5	28			33			1		1	5	28	1		34		39
TOTAL		7	1		8		12		12	1	4			5	8	72	20		100		2	1		3	9	78	21		108		128
אָמְנָה							1		1							1			1							1			1		2
אָמֵן																														2	2
אָמוֹן							2		2							1			1		1			1		2			2		4
אמת	1	31		1	33	3	3		6	1	1			2	1	15	1	2	19						2	16	1	2	21	10	70
אֵמוּן							1		1																						1
אֱמוּנָה	3	20	1		24		3		3						1	15		1	17						1	15		1	17	4	48
אמן	4	5			9	2	24		26		4			4	6	7	1		14						6	11	1		18	7	60
אֹמֶן												1		1		3	1		4		2			2		5	2		7		7
אָמְנָה																	1		1								1		1		1
TOTAL	8	56	1	1	66	5	34		39	1	5	1		7	8	42	4	3	57		3			3	9	50	5	3	67	23	195
TOTAL	39	388	17	1	445	19	142	1	162	11	40	13	2	66	23	235	75	12	345	2	28	2	2	34	36	303	90	16	445	31	1083

Table 3.8. *Personal Distribution of Elements: Number of Occurrences of Each Element in Each Category* (Source: SRTKAP)

Table 3.9. Personal Distribution of Elements: Percentage of Occurrences of Each Element in Each Category (Source: Table 3.8)

AGENT	GOD					HUMAN																									OTH	TOTAL
PATIENT	GOD					GOD				LEADER					MAN					WOMAN					HUMAN							
ELEMENT	L	M	W	U	TOT	L	M	W	TOT	L	M	W	U	TOT	L	M	W	U	TOT	L	M	W	U	TOT	L	M	W	U	TOT		
		3.1	0.5	3.1	6.2		87.5		87.5	1.6	3.7	0.4	0.8	6.5		3.1		3.1	6.2		1.2		0.4	1.6		3.1	1.6	3.1	6.2	0.4	32
	6.5	66.1	2.0		74.7		10.0		10.0	1.4	3.2	0.4	0.7	5.7	0.7	10.7	1.1	3.2	15.7		1.1		0.4	1.4	2.4	16.3	1.6	4.5	24.9	0.4	245
TOTAL	5.7	58.9	2.1		66.8		10.0		10.0	3.3	13.1		9.8	26.2	1.6	29.5		8.2	39.3				1.6	1.6	4.9	42.6	18.0	1.6	67.2		280
	16.4	13.1			29.5	3.8	12.7		16.5	8.0	1.3			1.3	1.3	21.5			22.8	2.5			2.5	3.8	22.8			26.6	3.3	13
	2.5	53.2			55.7	28.0	52.0		80.0	8.0				8.0	4.0	4.0			8.0					12.0	4.0			16.0	1.3	61
						5.9	82.3		88.2							11.8			11.8						11.8			11.8		79
		4.0			4.0																									25
	6.1	32.7			38.8	5.6	18.9		24.5	2.0	4.6	3.1		9.7	1.5	19.9		2.6	24.0	1.0			0.5	1.5	4.6	24.5	5.6	0.5	35.2	1.5	17
TOTAL	2.6	66.7	5.1		74.4						5.1			5.1		17.9			17.9		2.6			2.6		25.6			25.6		196
		92.3			92.3	2.0			2.0	4.1				4.1		7.7			7.7							7.7			7.7		39
	63.3	10.2			73.5	1.0			1.0		3.9			3.9		10.2			10.2		2.0			2.0		16.3			16.3	8.2	13
TOTAL	1.0	67.6	6.9		75.5	0.9	14.0		14.9			2.6		2.6		30.8	25.6		56.4		2.9			2.9		43.6	28.2		71.8	3.9	49
	20.5	2.6			23.1	7.1	46.4		53.6	7.9	3.5			11.4	0.9	14.9	27.2	3.6	43.0	12.8	12.8	0.9		11.4	0.9	33.3	31.6		65.8		102
	1.8	16.7	0.9		19.3					3.6				3.6	3.6	35.7	3.6		42.9	10.5	10.5	0.9			7.1	35.7	3.6		46.4		39
										0.5	4.9		2.7	8.2	1.1	21.4	23.6		46.2	9.3	9.3	0.5		9.9	1.6	35.7	26.9		64.3		114
	1.1	14.8	1.1		17.0	1.6	16.4	0.5	18.7	1.4	5.6			7.0	4.2	45.1	22.5		71.8	2.8	2.8			2.8	5.6	53.5	22.5		88.2		28
TOTAL		11.8			11.8	9.9			9.9	1.4					12.8	71.8			84.6		2.6			2.6	12.8	71.8	2.6		87.2		182
	7.0	1.4			8.5	12.8			12.8																						17
	5.5	0.8			6.3	9.4			9.4	0.8	3.1			3.9	6.3	56.3	15.6		78.1	1.6	1.6	0.8		2.3	7.0	60.9	16.4		84.4		71
	1.4	44.3	1.4		47.1	4.3	4.3		8.6	1.4	1.4			2.9	1.4	21.4	1.4	2.9	27.1						2.9	22.9	1.4	2.9	30.0	14.3	39
	6.3	41.7	2.1		50.0	6.3			6.3		1.4				2.1	31.3		2.1	35.4						2.1	31.3		2.1	35.4	8.3	128
	6.7	8.3			15.0	3.3	40.0		43.3		6.7			6.7	10.0	11.7	1.7		23.3						10.0	18.3	1.7		30.0	11.7	70
TOTAL	4.1	28.7	0.5	0.5	33.8	2.6	17.4		20.0	0.5	2.6			3.6	4.1	21.5	2.1	1.5	29.2		2.8	2.6		3.1	4.6	25.6	2.6	1.5	34.3	11.8	195
TOTAL	3.6	35.8	1.6	0.1	41.1	1.7	13.1	0.1	15.0	1.0	3.7	1.2	0.2	6.1	2.1	21.7	6.9	1.1	31.9		2.6	0.2	0.2	3.1	3.3	28.0	8.3	1.5	41.1	2.9	1083

Thirdly, the original subdivision into Leader, Man and Woman has been retained for human agents and patients. The appropriate columns in Tables 3.8 and 3.9 reveal that the entries in the columns headed MAN are, with very few exceptions, greater than those in the columns headed LEADER and WOMAN. This is very significant and it is essential to beware of placing too much importance on it. There are two main reasons for this caveat: first, the relatively few cases that have been assigned to Leader and Woman as compared with those assigned to Man; second—and more importantly—Man has often been used in a generic sense, so that it frequently includes both leaders and women as well as men. This absorption of leaders and women is a necessary consequence of the definition of the former terms; the term Leader is rarely used except to refer to a named individual; and this is also true for a large number of cases that have been classified as Woman. There are, however, several exceptions to the latter: for example, the references in Deuteronomy to a man and his wife/wives. But of more interest are the terms used for the people of Israel. Very frequently masculine pronouns indicate that the people should be classified as Man; but, especially when reference is made to Israel in its state of apostasy, the feminine pronominal suffixes indicate that the people are properly classified as Woman. This aspect recurs later when a closer scrutiny is made of the terms used to refer to an activity or an attitude of God that is directed towards his unfaithful bride.

Figures 3.5, 3.6 and 3.7 were prepared after amending the percentages for חֶסֶד in Table 3.9 by reclassifying those cases which were originally unspecified. The unspecified cases for the other elements are shown below the zero-line in each section of the graph (where appropriate). The area represents the relative proportion of cases in which there is insufficient information to determine whether one of the persons involved is human or divine. There are no areas below the zero-lines in Figure 3.6, because the agent and the patient have been specified for all interpersonal occurrences of the elements derived from the roots רחם and אהב.

The graphs indicate that no element is almost always used in a situation that involves a specific agent or patient. However, further attention should be given to this aspect of the distribution of תְּחִנָּה and *תַּחֲנוּן. In a large proportion of their occurrences, these elements have God as patient; and it is clear from the graph of תְּחִנָּה in Section C that

3. *Distribution: Agent–Patient*

the human patient is very frequently a leader. In the light of the discussion at the end of Subsection B a on the usage of these two elements and also of the verb חנן, this raises a question slightly different from the one already posed—Is תְּחִנָּה almost always used in a situation where the patient is superior in status to the agent? And, if this is true, does it also apply to *תַּחֲנוּן and to חֵן? These questions cannot be answered simply by inspecting distribution data; instead, reference must be made to the actual passages in which the terms are used. This is not an appropriate place for such an investigation, but it will be taken up later.[1]

A key to the patterns used for the various combinations of agent and patient follows. The Agent is given in the top line, underlined; the Patient, not underlined, is in the column on the left.

	God	*Leader*	*Man*	*Woman*
God		▨	▦	▧
Leader	▨	▨	▨	▨
Man	▨	▨	▢	▨
Woman	▨	▨	▨	▨

Key to figures 3.5–3.7

---

1. See Section 5C in Chapter 8 below.

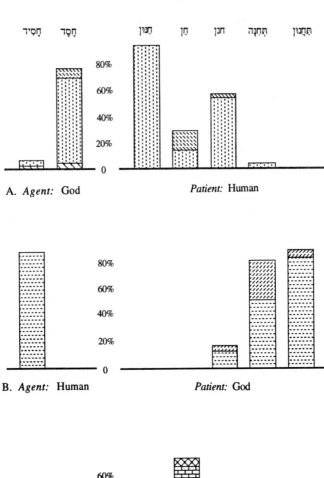

A. *Agent:* God   *Patient:* Human

B. *Agent:* Human   *Patient:* God

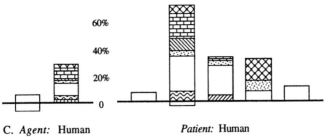

C. *Agent:* Human   *Patient:* Human

Figure 3.5. *Personal Distribution of* חסד *and* חנן *Elements*

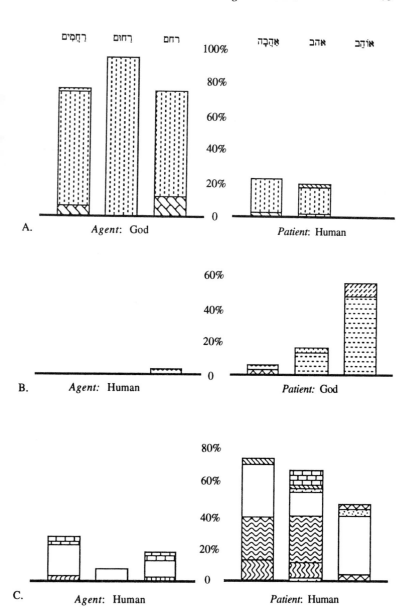

Figure 3.6. *Personal Distribution of* רחם *and* אהב *Elements*

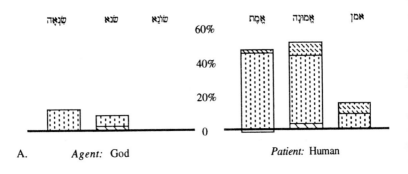

A.   *Agent:* God   *Patient:* Human

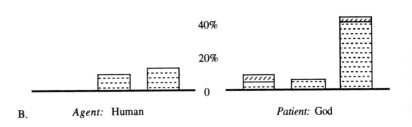

B.   *Agent:* Human   *Patient:* God

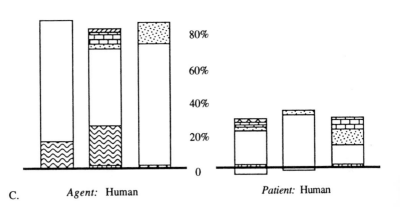

C.   *Agent:* Human   *Patient:* Human

Figure 3.7. *Personal Distribution of* שׂנא *and* אמן *Elements*

3. *Overview*

After giving preliminary attention to the occurrence of elements with a non-personal patient, this chapter has focused on the persons involved as agent and patient in the situations in which the various elements of the lexical field occur. Certain distinctive features have been noted, by means of which it is possible to distinguish between some of the elements. These features are set out in Table 3.10, where the symbols entered indicate the answers to the following questions:

1. Is the element used predominantly with God as agent (or patient)?
2. Is the element used predominantly with a human agent (or patient)?
3. Can the element be regarded as being restricted with respect to the agent (or patient)—that is, is it used almost exclusively with that agent (or patient)?
4. Is the root (or element) used significantly in a non-personal situation?

Element	AGENT			PATIENT			NONPERSONAL	
	God	Hum	Res	God	Hum	Res	Root	Elem
חָסִיד		+		+				
חֶסֶד	+			−	+	−		−
חַנּוּן	+		+	−	+	−		−
חֵן				−	+	−		
חנן				(+)	+		+	
תְּחִנָּה		+		+		+		
תַּחֲנוּן*		+		+		+		
רַחֲמִים	+		+	−	+	−		−
רָחוּם	+		+	−	+	−		−
רחם	+		+	−	+	−	−	−
אַהֲבָה		+			+	−		
אהב		+	−		+	−	+	+
אוֹהֵב	−	+						
שִׂנְאָה		+		−	+	−		
שׂנא		+		+	+	−	+	+
שׂוֹנֵא	−−	+		+	+	−		
אֱמֶת					+	−		+
אֱמוּנָה					+	−		
אמן		+					+	+

Table 3.10. *Distinctive Features*

A plus sign, +, indicates an affirmative answer to the question; a minus sign, –, indicates a negative answer; and a blank indicates that the feature is not relevant for the element. Note that the symbol (+) for חנן under God as patient signifies that this feature is significant for one derived stem only.

These distinctive features do not provide a means of distinguishing between the elements

1. תְּחִנָּה and *תַּחֲנוּן each of which has a positive sign in the same three columns, or
2. חַנּוּן ,רַחֲמִים ,רָחוּם and the verb רחם, each of which has a plus sign in the same three columns and a minus sign in three other columns, also the same for each element.

חֶסֶד differs from the latter group of elements, being used predominantly but not almost exclusively with God as agent whereas with each of the other elements God is both predominantly and almost exclusively the agent.

אֱמֶת and אֱמוּנָה differ from חֶסֶד when God is agent or patient. Whereas חֶסֶד is used predominantly with God as agent, this feature is not relevant for אֱמֶת and אֱמוּנָה. חֶסֶד is not used predominantly with God as patient, a feature which is again not relevant for אֱמֶת and אֱמוּנָה. A further difference is apparent in the non-personal use of these elements; אֱמֶת is used significantly in non-personal situations, חֶסֶד is not so used, and the feature is not relevant for אֱמוּנָה.

The third, NONPERSONAL, section of Table 3.10 shows that the root חנן is used significantly in non-personal situations. This feature is not relevant for the verb חנן but the element חַנּוּן is not used significantly in non-personal situations. On the other hand, because the root רחם is *never* used in a non-personal situation, it follows that its derivatives רַחֲמִים ,רָחוּם and the verb רחם can never be so used. The minus signs indicate that the root and the derivatives are not used significantly in non-personal situations. Again, the root אהב and the verb אהב are both used significantly in non-personal situations, as are the root and the verb אמן; one other derivative of this root—אֱמֶת—is also used significantly in these situations, but this feature is not relevant for אֱמוּנָה.

The table draws attention also to the contrasts between חֶסֶד and the derivatives of אהב. The agent is predominantly God when חֶסֶד is used, but predominantly human with the אהב derivatives. With חֶסֶד the patient is not predominantly God, but this feature is not relevant for the derivatives of אהב. The root and the verb אהב are both used significantly in non-personal situations, but חֶסֶד is not, and this feature is not relevant for the other derivatives of אהב.

Chapter 4

COLLOCATION PROFILES

Chapter 3 concentrated on the non-linguistic environment, giving particular attention to the persons involved as agent and patient in the various situations. Seven chapters will consider different aspects of the linguistic environment of members of the field. This and the following chapter concentrate on one aspect of the linguistic environment—that of the collocations of elements with each other and also with the additional lexemes listed in Table 2.2. These lexemes were not included in the computer analysis and only those cases which occurred within a certain near neighbourhood of an element have been selected for further examination.

In linguistics, the term 'collocation' applies to groups of lexical items that regularly, or habitually, occur together. Throughout this study the term will be used in a broader sense, to apply to the co-occurrence of any pair of the lexical items in a reasonably restricted linguistic environment—even though there may be only one such co-occurrence in the whole corpus. Firth (1957a: 180) holds that statements of meaning can be made at the collocational level for key words in a language. He appears to have had in mind the preparation of a 'collocational thesaurus', for he lists (p. 195) the four 'most productive preliminaries' for such a dictionary. Developing this idea, Sinclair (1966: 416) displays in a 'total environment table' the collocates of certain items that occur frequently in the record of a conversation. From such tables he proposes (p. 427) to obtain the lexical sets of the language, saying that these 'lexical sets parallel the categories of a thesaurus, but are linguistically arranged, and are the distillation of the massive evidence got, initially, from the study of collocations'.

Section 1 outlines the collection and recording of the collocations, and Section 2 describes the profiles that display the collocates of different lexical items. General features of the profiles are noted and the profile of חֶסֶד is compared with the profiles of some of the other elements, leading to a tentative definition of the formal meaning of six elements of the field in Section 3.

1. *Collecting the Collocations*

A. *The Lexemes*

Members of the lexical field are referred to as either members or elements, and the term 'lexeme' is uniformly applied to the additional lexemes that are not members of the field. The term 'lexical item' includes both elements and lexemes. Collocations of elements can be obtained directly from WIDATA, but the lexemes that collocate with any elements were discovered in a further search. Most of these lexemes had been noticed recurring occasionally in fairly close proximity to one of the field elements; others were included because they would probably be used in similar inter-personal situations, or because of a possible overlap in meaning with elements in the field; and a few more were added after considering all the derivatives of the roots already represented. The complete list of lexemes is given in Table 2.2, where details are given of the steps taken to find and record the occurrences of the lexemes.

B. *Types of Collocation*

The term 'collocation' has been applied to those sets of words which occur together in the neighbourhood, whether those words are elements or additional lexemes; but passages that repeat the same item have not been included unless another element or lexeme accompanies it. Three different relationships can be distinguished between words that collocate with each other. Sometimes the words occur in a parallel construction; sometimes they occur in a series (a group of two or more lexical items frequently joined by the conjunction ו but sometimes appearing asyndetically); or they may occur in neither of these special relationships, in which case the items are simply contiguous with each other. Collocations have been assigned to these various types and they are so recorded in the matrices displayed in the next section, using C for contiguous, P for parallel and S for series. Passages in which חֶסֶד occurs in parallel with some of the lexical items are discussed in Chapter 6, and the series expression חֶסֶד וֶאֱמֶת is investigated in Chapter 10.

C. *Recording Collocations*

There were many potential sources of error while the analysis was proceeding. Since the computer could not be used to collect the data, it was necessary to check the accuracy at each stage of the procedure. Such a check exists for the entries in a square array called a matrix, so it was decided to record the statistics in a series of square matrices. Each column of the matrix is headed by one of the lexical items (either a field element or an additional lexeme) which appears in the passage, and these items are used, in the same order, to label the rows of the matrix. The entry in each cell of the matrix indicates the number of times the item at the head of the column collocates with the item at the left of the row. These small matrices were eventually combined into a large matrix having 75 rows and 75 columns; 75 because 27 of the original 35 elements in the field appear in the collocations, as do all 48 of the additional lexemes. Further, the entries in the matrices must be symmetrical,[1] since if a word W_1 collocates n times with another word W_2 then W_2 also collocates n times with W_1. Hence the entries in each row, reading from left to right, will be the same as the entries in the corresponding column, reading from top to bottom. In addition, matrices that include repeated items must be consistent with those which have the same number of different (unrepeated) items.

In the following illustrations, each column and row has been sub-divided in order to distinguish the different types of collocation—Contiguous, Parallel and Series. Another column added at the right and another row at the bottom records the sums of the entries in each row and column respectively. It is important to bear in mind that there is only one column—and row—for each lexical item; this is indicated by the entries for the sums, since there is a single entry for each lexical item at the foot of the appropriate column and also at the end of each row.

Gen. 47.29 contains three field elements, חֵן and חֶסֶד וֶאֱמֶת. חֵן is

---

1. It had been hoped that this property of symmetry could be used as a basis for mapping the collocation pairs, using a distance factor defined as a function of the number of collocations between the pairs. It is possible to specify the position, in a plane, of any item relative to any other two items; but it soon became evident that it was not possible to place more than three items in positions such that the distance between any pair represented the number of collocations between them. Consequently this intention was abandoned, but it has been adapted for use in the collocation profiles introduced in Subsection 2A below.

contiguous with both חֶסֶד and אֱמֶת, and vice versa; and חֶסֶד is in series with אֱמֶת, and vice versa. These facts are shown in the following matrix:

		חֶסֶד		חֵן	אֱמֶת		Sum
		C	S	C	C	S	
חֶסֶד	C	–	–	1	–	–	
	S	–	–	–	–	1	2
חֵן	C	1	–	–	1	–	2
אֱמֶת	C	–	–	1	–	–	
	S	–	1	–	–	–	2
Sum		2		2	2		Total = 6

The entries in the first row agree with those in the first column, as do those in the second row and column, and also those in the third row and column. Further, the sum of the entries in any row is the same as that for the corresponding column. In addition, the sum of all the entries in the matrix can be readily determined by a simple formula: there are 3 rows, and the sum of the entries in each row is 2; so the total is $3 \times 2 = 6$.

Isa. 16.5 contains two field elements, חֶסֶד and אֱמֶת, in a parallel construction, and three additional lexemes; of these latter, צֶדֶק and מִשְׁפָּט are in parallel while שׁפט is contiguous with the other four items. חֶסֶד and also אֱמֶת are contiguous with both צֶדֶק and מִשְׁפָּט. This will be expressed in a 5×5 matrix in which the entries in each row and column add to a total of 4; consequently the sum of all the entries will be $5 \times 4 = 20$.

		חֶסֶד		אֱמֶת		צֶדֶק		שׁפט	מִשְׁפָּט		Sum
		C	P	C	P	C	P	C	C	P	
חֶסֶד	C	–	–	–	–	1	–	1	1	–	
	P	–	–	–	1	–	–	–	–	–	4
אֱמֶת	C	–	–	–	–	1	–	1	1	–	
	P	–	1	–	–	–	–	–	–	–	4
צֶדֶק	C	1	–	1	–	–	–	1	–	–	
	P	–	–	–	–	–	–	–	1		4
שׁפט	C	1	–	1	–	1	–	–	1	–	4
מִשְׁפָּט	C	1	–	1	–	–	–	1	–	–	
	P	–	–	–	–	–	1	–	–	–	4
Sum		4		4		4	4		4		Total = 20

Isa. 30.18-19 contains two field elements, חנן and רחם; the former occurs 3 times, once being in a parallel construction with רחם. There is also an additional lexeme, מִשְׁפָּט, which is contiguous with the other items. With 5 items altogether, the expected total of the entries in the

matrix is 20, as in the previous example. מִשְׁפָּט is contiguous with רחם
and also with each of the 3 occurrences of חנן; רחם is in parallel with
one occurrence of חנן and in contiguity with each of its other 2 occurrences as well as with מִשְׁפָּט; and each occurrence of חנן is contiguous
with its two other occurrences, that is, 6 times in all.

		חנן		רחם		מִשְׁפָּט	Sum
		C	P	C	P	C	
חנן	C	6	–	2	–	3	
	P	–	–	–	1	–	12
רחם	C	2	–	–	–	1	
	P	–	1	–	–	–	4
מִשְׁפָּט	C	3	–	1	–	–	4
Sum		12		4		4	Total = 20

The matrix above shows that the entries in each row agree with those
in the corresponding column, that the sums of rows and columns
agree, and that the total of the entries in all rows (and columns) is 20,
as expected.

The statistics for these three passages may now be combined in a
single matrix, which will have 8 rows and 8 columns (one for each
lexical item). Three of the items—חֶסֶד, אֱמֶת and מִשְׁפָּט—occur in two
of the passages. חֶסֶד and אֱמֶת both occur in the first matrix, where the
sum of the entries in each of their columns (and rows) is 2; they also
occur in the second matrix, where the entries in their columns (and
rows) add up to 4. Hence the sum of the entries in their rows and
columns in the combined matrix must be 6. מִשְׁפָּט does not occur in the
first matrix, but in each of the second and third matrices the sum of its
entries is 4; hence the sum of the entries for מִשְׁפָּט in the combined
matrix must be 8. The remaining five words occur in only one of the
matrices, so the entries in their columns and rows in the larger matrix
will agree with the entries in the smaller matrices. The entries in the
large matrix will be correct if

1. the sum of each row is equal to the sum of the corresponding
    column, and
2. the sum of all rows and the sum of all columns are both equal
    to the sum of all entries in the original three matrices, that is,
    46 (= 6 + 20 + 20).

If there is any discrepancy in these figures it is easy to locate the error
and to make the necessary correction.

D. *The Final Matrix*

There is no simple relationship between the entry in a given cell and the
number of occurrences of the item that heads the column; the entry
depends on the number of occurrences of both items that determine the
cell. As noted above, the entries in the first row of the third matrix
have been traceable to the triple occurrence of חָנַן; this repeated occurrence of חָנַן causes the entry 3 below מִשְׁפָּט, but this does not imply that
מִשְׁפָּט occurs three times in the passage. Again, when matrices are combined, the relationship between the entries and the number of occurrences of the item becomes even more complicated—because the entry
in each cell depends upon the number of occurrences of both items that
determine that cell. Obviously the sum of the entries in any column
cannot be directly related in any simple way to the number of times
the item occurs. For the same reason, it is not possible to make direct
quantitative comparisons between the collocations of different lexical
items. Also, it is of no value to replace the entries by a percentage as
was done when considering the distribution of the field elements; here
the actual figures recorded must be used as the basis for discussion and
for making comparisons between the different lexical items.

It is not practical to reproduce the 8 × 8 matrix here; and it is not
possible to show the final 75 × 75 matrix. The format of this final
matrix is not quite the same as that used in the illustrations above.
Each column is subdivided into four, to record the total number of
collocations as well as the numbers of contiguous, parallel and series
collocations; but the rows are not subdivided and the appropriate
entries are all made on the same line for each item. With this arrangement, the matrix fits conveniently on large sheets of graph paper ruled
in 5 mm squares, each square serving as a cell in the matrix. Further,
the collocations of each item with itself are omitted from the final
matrix. Inspection of this matrix reveals that 28 of the items collocate
less than 10 times with other items, while חֶסֶד and מִשְׁפָּט each enter into
approximately 300 collocations. So it was decided to examine more
closely those items that appear frequently in collocations. This
investigation is outlined in the following section.

2. *Examining the Collocations*

The matrix recording the number of collocations between the lexical .
items is too large to display. The alternative method adopted presents

the information relevant to 13 of the items in a set of diagrams called collocation profiles. These profiles display some general trends which form the basis of discussion in this section.

A. *Collocation Profiles*

Each collocation is a pair of lexical items, which is called a word-pair when there is no need to distinguish between field elements and additional lexemes. Only one word-pair enters into collocation more than 50 times: the pair חֶסֶד and אֱמֶת has a collocation frequency of 51. However, a total of 26 different word-pairs have a collocation frequency of at least 10, while 18 pairs enter into less than 20 collocations with each other. As the collocation frequency decreases below 10, the number of word-pairs involved in these collocations increases rapidly; for example, there are 17 word-pairs with a collocation frequency of 5, while 225 word-pairs collocate with each other only once. In the light of these facts, the collocations were divided into two categories—those which occurred more frequently (at least 10 times), and those which occurred less frequently (less than 10 times).

J.R. Firth (1951: 195-96) distinguishes between contextual meaning —'the functional relation of the sentence to the processes of a context of situation in the context of culture'—and meaning by collocation— 'an abstraction at the syntagmatic level [which] is not directly concerned with the conceptual or idea approach to the meaning of words. One of the meanings of *night* is its collocability with *dark*, and of *dark*, of course, collocation with *night*.' Sinclair (1966: 417) frames his definition of the formal meaning of a lexical item on the last sentence in this quotation: 'the *formal meaning* of an item A is that it has a strong tendency to occur nearby items B, C, D, less strong with items E, F, slight with G, H, I, and none at all with any other item'.[1]

Such considerations prompted the decision to present collocation profiles of several lexical items in diagrams based on a target or dartboard (see Figures 4.1–4.11). Each profile refers to a single lexical item, the keyword, and shows all the other items with which it collocates. The keyword is given in the inner circle or bull's-eye of

---

1.   Sawyer also advocates (1972: 31-32) dealing with the meaning of words from within the language : '... a word L... can be defined as associated with A, B, C (in the same language), opposed to D, influenced semantically by G because of frequent collocation with it in idiom I, and so on. This is the most reliable method of describing meaning, and must precede translation, not follow it.'

the profile diagram. Each of the four circles outside the bull's-eye is marked with a number—the largest number on the inner circle and the smallest on the outer circle. These numbers indicate the frequency with which the keyword collocates with other lexical items, and the profile is so arranged that it places nearest to the keyword those items which collocate with it most frequently, while those which enter into less frequent collocations with it appear further away.

Most keyword profiles are given in two parts. Those items with which the keyword collocates frequently (10 or more times) appear in the upper portion, while the lower portion contains those which collocate with it less than 10 times. The complete picture can be visualized by expanding the lower portion so that its inner circle (labelled 9) is slightly larger than the outer circle (labelled 10) of the upper portion. The expanded lower portion surrounds the upper portion, giving eight concentric circles around a single bull's-eye. This method of presentation would have required an outer circle with twice the present radius, resulting in a single profile occupying the space in which two can now be fitted. Another advantage of using the two portions is that the profiles of those keywords which enter into at most one frequent collocation can be displayed effectively using only the (reduced) outer portion.

The marks on the outermost circle indicate the radial lines to which the items of each word group have been assigned. The Hebrew roots from which the various groups of lexical items are derived, together with the lexeme בְּרִית, are set out in the appropriate positions in the key profile (see the fold-out, after p. 286), which may be compared with each of the profile diagrams in Figures 4.1–4.11. It will be noted that the field elements occupy the upper half of the diagram, with חֶסֶד in the 12 o'clock position, while the additional lexemes are in the lower half,[1] with שפט at 6 o'clock flanked on the right by צדק and on the left by נאף. Lexemes that appear to fit, at least partially, into the same semantic area have been placed in proximity; such as בְּרִית–בחר ('covenant'), ישׁר–טוב ('goodness') and נצל–ישׁע ('salvation') in the right-hand sector, and also in the left-hand sector זנה–נאף ('infidelity'), חוס–חמל ('compassion'), דוד–דבק–חבק–חשׁק–נשׁק (all of which suggest or presuppose the 'physical proximity' of two persons). The other member of the word-pair is entered on the appropriate radial line in a position that indicates approximately the number of times it collocates with the keyword.

---

1. These positions correspond with those of the lexemes in Table 2.2, as described in Section 4 of Chapter 2.

The items in the profiles include the 19 elements (listed in Table 3.6) used in situations that involve a personal agent and patient. There is one other element, *שָׂנֵיא, included in the profiles but not in Table 3.6 because it occurs only once in the corpus (Deut. 21.15), in an interpersonal situation where in the immediate context אהב is used three times, שׂנא four times and מִשְׁפָּט once. These 20 elements are distributed over the upper half of the diagram. Of the 48 lexemes in Table 2.2, 32 are distributed over the lower right-hand quadrant, while נמל and the 15 lexemes allocated to the 'infidelity', 'compassion' and 'physical proximity' areas appear in the lower left-hand quadrant. A position has been allocated to חבק, which occurs only twice—never with any of the items whose profiles are to be considered, but both times in series with נשׁק.

The 26 word-pairs that constitute the frequent collocations include only 11 field elements and 9 additional lexemes; but 11 of these lexical items (8 elements and 3 lexemes) occur in only one of the 26 word-pairs. Complete profiles are given for the remaining 9 items (3 elements and 6 lexemes) that enter into at least two of the frequent collocations. The upper diagram of these complete profiles show the items that collocate at least 10 times with the keyword, and the lower diagram shows all the other words that collocate with it. The outer (or less frequent) profile of another four items is also provided. These latter items enter into at most one frequent collocation, and so it is unnecessary to provide the inner (more frequent) profile.

The outer profiles of אֱמוּנָה and בְּרִית are given in Figure 4.1, and those of רַחֲמִים and אַהֲבָה in Figure 4.2. The complete profiles follow: מִשְׁפָּט (Figure 4.3), טוֹב (Figure 4.4), צְדָקָה (Figure 4.5), צֶדֶק (Figure 4.6), צַדִּיק (Figure 4.7), יָשָׁר (Figure 4.8), אֱמֶת (Figure 4.9), אהב (Figure 4.10) and חֶסֶד (Figure 4.11). Another diagram showing the relative positions of the Hebrew roots is provided as a fold-out at the end of the book. The diagrams have been placed at the end of the chapter in order that features mentioned in the discussion may be verified by referring to the diagrams.

B. *The Profile of* חֶסֶד

To simplify future reference to the profiles, a reasonably complete and detailed description of the profile of חֶסֶד is included here. The innermost circle is the boundary of the bull's-eye that contains the keyword. Around it are four more concentric circles; on a radial line between 2 and 3 o'clock a number alongside each circle gives the collocational frequency represented by the circles. The marks around the outer circle indicate the radial lines allocated to the various Hebrew roots, which are given in the fold-out key profile at the end of the book.

The upper section of the profile contains the items that collocate 10 or more times with חֶסֶד. There is one item in the inner ring; the element אֱמֶת collocates more than 40 times with חֶסֶד. Moving outwards along this radial line, אֱמוּנָה straddles the next circle indicating that it collocates 20 times with חֶסֶד. A clockwise movement around this circle shows רַחֲמִים collocating just over 20 times with חֶסֶד. Continuing to move clockwise leads to the lexeme בְּרִית just outside the circle; it collocates with חֶסֶד slightly less than 20 times. A little further round טוֹב is roughly midway between the two circles, showing that it collocates approximately 30 times with חֶסֶד. Nearing the 6 o'clock position are צְדָקָה and מִשְׁפָּט; the latter collocates slightly less than 20 times with חֶסֶד, but צְדָקָה, being further out, collocates with חֶסֶד less than מִשְׁפָּט does.

In the lower section, the radial line at about 2 o'clock shows three derivatives of חנן collocating with חֶסֶד. A counter-clockwise rotation reveals two derivatives of רחם in the inner ring (in addition to רַחֲמִים in the upper section). חָסִיד is next encountered in the outer ring, as the rotation continues, then three derivatives of אהב, and a derivative of שׂנא in the middle ring, and finally אמן, joining the two derivatives of this root already noted in the upper section. Only four lexemes are entered in the left-hand portion of the lower section, all near the outermost circle, and there are no entries in the same portion of the upper section; hence חֶסֶד collocates very rarely with items in the area of 'physical proximity' and never with those in the area of 'infidelity'.

Category	Interval	Symbol	Tendency
Most Frequent	40–80	7	very strong
Very Frequent	26–39	6	strong
More Frequent	20–25	5	not so strong
Frequent	10–19	4	moderate
Less Frequent	6–9	3	not so weak
Occasional	3–5	2	weak
Rare	1–2	1	very weak
Never	0	0	none

Table 4.1. *Collocational Categories and Tendencies*

Table 4.1 introduces the terms and symbols associated with the frequency ranges. The first four terms apply to the upper portion of the complete profile, while the next three terms refer to the lower portion of the complete profile, which is used also for profiles of items collocating less than ten times with other items. Most of these terms apply to a ring; the exception is the middle ring of the upper portion, which is subdivided between the terms 'More Frequent' and 'Very Frequent'. The collocational tendencies are used in defining formal meanings of some of the elements in Section 3 B, and the symbols are used in Table 4.5 to summarize these definitions. These terms help to ensure uniformity in the comparison of the profiles, and the symbols are particularly useful in the more detailed comparisons set out in Chapter 5.

Some of the information derived from the profile of חֶסֶד is repeated more precisely in the following paragraphs. The upper section of its profile reveals that חֶסֶד collocates more than 10 times with three elements and with four lexemes, while the lower section brings in 11 more elements and 26 more lexemes with which חֶסֶד collocates less than 10 times. Only four of the lexemes are in the left-hand sector of the profile. The derivatives of the root שׂנא are the elements with which חֶסֶד collocates least frequently; it collocates with שׂוֹנֵא only 5 times, and not at all with the verb שׂנא or with any of the other derivatives. This is not surprising, for שׂנא expresses an unfavourable inter-personal attitude and contrasts with the other roots. There are, however, only occasional collocations between חֶסֶד and אהב; but this aspect receives further consideration in Chapter 5 when the profiles of חֶסֶד and other items, including אהב, are compared.

The lexical items with which חֶסֶד rarely collocates are also significant when comparing its semantic domain with that of other elements and lexemes. Besides שׂנא and its derivatives, there are another five elements and 18 lexemes never found in collocation with חֶסֶד. Six more lexemes occur only once with חֶסֶד, and another six lexemes co-occur with it only twice. These significant items from both ends of the spectrum of the חֶסֶד-profile—those with which it collocates frequently as well as those with which it is rarely found in collocation—are listed below. חֶסֶד collocates

1. most frequently with אֱמֶת (51)[1]
2. very frequently with טוֹב (28)

1. Figures in brackets are the number of times the pairs of lexical items collocate.

3. more frequently with רַחֲמִים (21) and אֱמוּנָה (20)
4. frequently with מִשְׁפָּט and בְּרִית (18 each) and צְדָקָה (15).

On the other hand, חֶסֶד collocates

1. twice with בָּחִיר,[1] גּוֹאֵל, דַּעַת, פלא, שׁפט and חֶמְלָה, as well as with חָסִיד;
2. once with בחר, פֶּלֶא, חוס, נשק, חשק and גמל;
3. but never with the elements תְּחִנָּה, *תַּחֲנוּן, שׂנא, שְׂנָאָה and *שָׂנִיא
4. and never with the lexemes צדק, מֵישָׁרִים, מִישׁוֹר, יֹשֶׁר, ישׁר, נֶאְלָה, and its derivatives, חמל, נְשִׁיקָה, חבק, דבק, דָּבֵק and דּוֹד.

These rare collocates of חֶסֶד have been indicated in the profiles of the other elements and lexemes by using three thicknesses of underlining. Items that collocate twice have light underlining; those which collocate once with חֶסֶד have medium underlining; and those never found with חֶסֶד have heavy underlining.

3. *Comparing the Profiles*

This section discusses some of the more general features of the collocation profiles, concentrating on the broader areas of comparison and contrast between the חֶסֶד profile and the profiles of other elements. The similarity of the distributions of חֶסֶד, רַחֲמִים and רחם, and also the contrasts between חֶסֶד and each of אַהֲבָה, אהב, אֱמֶת and אֱמוּנָה, have been noted[2] previously. Are these distributional similarities and contrasts reflected in the collocational profiles?

A. *General Features of Profiles*
Table 4.2 sets out the number of elements and lexemes collocating with the keywords, which are ranked according to the total number of lexical items collocating with them. The lexemes are allocated to two columns; those in the left-hand column belong to the groups 'infidelity', 'compassion' and 'physical proximity' and appear in the bottom left-hand sector of the profiles. The final row of the table gives the TOTAL number of elements and lexemes; the *hapax legomenon* *שָׂנִיא is added to the 19 elements listed in Tables 3.6, 3.7 and 3.9.

----

1. These lexemes are listed clockwise in the order of their appearance on the lower half of the profile.
2. See Subsections 2B a and b in Chapter 3.

KEYWORD	ELEMENTS	LEXEMES		TOTAL
		Left	Right	
חֶסֶד	14	4	26	44
מִשְׁפָּט	17	4	23	44
טוֹב	16	8	19	43
אהב	14	9	15	38
אֱמֶת	12	1	20	33
בְּרִית	15	3	13	31
צְדָקָה	11	0	20	31
רַחֲמִים	10	2	17	29
צַדִּיק	15	1	13	29
יָשָׁר	14	0	15	29
צֶדֶק	12	2	15	29
אַהֲבָה	9	6	10	25
אֱמוּנָה	6	0	17	23
TOTAL	20	15	33	68

Table 4.2. *Keywords, Showing Number of Items Collocating with Each*

Most of the keywords collocate with more than half of the elements; two keywords collocate with more than three-quarters of the elements, yet none of them collocates with all 20 elements. Only חֶסֶד collocates with three-quarters of the lexemes allocated to the right-hand column, but seven keywords collocate with more than half of these lexemes. On the other hand, eight keywords collocate with less than one-quarter of the lexemes in the left-hand column.

The tabulation makes plain some features that are not obvious in the profiles; these include:

1. צַדִּיק is the only keyword that collocates with more elements than lexemes;
2. four lexemes collocate with more elements than חֶסֶד does— מִשְׁפָּט with 17, טוֹב with 16, בְּרִית and צַדִּיק with 15; חֶסֶד, אהב and יָשָׁר all collocate with 14 elements.

The tabulation emphasizes a feature already noted while comparing the profiles, that most keywords collocate with only a few lexemes in the left-hand quadrant. אהב, טוֹב and אַהֲבָה collocate with more of these lexemes than the other keywords do; צְדָקָה, יָשָׁר and אֱמוּנָה never collocate with any of them, while אֱמֶת and צַדִּיק occur with only one of them, and רַחֲמִים and צֶדֶק both collocate with two of these lexemes. חֶסֶד and מִשְׁפָּט each collocates with four, and בְּרִית with three of these lexemes. None of these lexemes appears in the upper (or inner) portion of the profiles, and most of those which do appear are towards the outer rim of the lower portion of the profiles. Four lexemes are found in collocation with חֶסֶד; two belong to the 'physical proximity' area and the other two to the 'compassion' area. חֶסֶד never collocates with any of the lexemes in the 'infidelity' area, but אהב is found with four of the 'infidelity' lexemes—six times with one of them, and three times with another; אַהֲבָה also collocates with one lexeme from this area. מִשְׁפָּט collocates with three of the lexemes in the 'infidelity' area—five times with one of them; and בְּרִית also collocates with one of these lexemes.

B. *Profiles of* חֶסֶד *and Other Elements*
The distribution of חֶסֶד is in many respects similar to those of רַחֲמִים and רחם[1] and in contrast with those of אֱמֶת, אהב, אַהֲבָה and אֱמוּנָה, especially with regard to the agent.[2] The profiles of five of these elements (the profile of רחם has not been provided) are examined, comparing their profiles with that of חֶסֶד concentrating on the two ends of the חֶסֶד spectrum. Profiles of אַהֲבָה, אֱמוּנָה and רַחֲמִים are in Figures 4.1 and 4.2, and those of אֱמֶת and אהב are in Figures 4.9 and 4.10. The numerical values of the collocational frequencies of different word-pairs have a limited value when comparing the profiles of lexical items, since these frequencies depend on the number of occurrences of each item in the collocating pair. Nevertheless, they may be used to indicate general trends.

a. *Frequent Collocates of* חֶסֶד

Item	חֶסֶד	רַחֲמִים	אהב	אַהֲבָה	אֱמֶת	אֱמוּנָה
חֶסֶד		21	4	6	51	20
אֱמֶת	51	6	6	–		2
טוֹב	28	3	15	6	15	2
רַחֲמִים	21		–	1	6	4
אֱמוּנָה	20	4	1	–	2	
מִשְׁפָּט	18	5	17	4	24	9
בְּרִית	18	3	1	3	6	2
צְדָקָה	15	3	4	2	11	7

Table 4.3. *Frequent Collocates of* חֶסֶד: *Number of Collocations with Other Elements*

1. See Subsection 2B a in Chapter 3.
2. See Table 3.7 in Chapter 3.

Table 4.3 ranks the seven items in the inner (upper) portion of the
חֶסֶד profile in the order of their collocational frequencies with חֶסֶד.
The remaining columns show the frequency of their collocations with
the other five elements. A dash (–) indicates that the item does not
enter into collocation with the element. These items do not collocate
very often with any elements besides חֶסֶד, so that from this aspect
רַחֲמִים and the other elements all contrast with חֶסֶד. This contrast is
most noticeable in the collocations of these elements with אֱמֶת, רַחֲמִים,
אֱמוּנָה and בְּרִית and is also significant with צְדָקָה.

אֱמֶת and אהב are the only elements that collocate more than 10 times
with any of the listed items. Since the expression חֶסֶד וֶאֱמֶת accounts for
almost half the collocations of these elements, it is conceivable that
many of the collocations of אֱמֶת with מִשְׁפָּט, טוֹב and צְדָקָה may occur in
the presence of the compound expression. The detailed investigation
of the collocations of חֶסֶד, אֱמֶת and חֶסֶד וֶאֱמֶת in Section 2 of Chapter
10 show that this is not the case; consequently there are grounds for
asserting that in its collocations with these three lexemes אֱמֶת
resembles חֶסֶד. Similarly, אהב resembles חֶסֶד in its collocations with
טוֹב and מִשְׁפָּט. But the total picture of the frequent collocates of חֶסֶד
provides evidence that each of these elements contrasts with חֶסֶד. The
contrast is greatest for רַחֲמִים and אַהֲבָה, not so pronounced for אהב, and
least for אֱמֶת.

b. *Rare Collocates of* חֶסֶד
At the other end of the spectrum, seven items collocate twice with חֶסֶד;
they are חָסִיד, בָּחִיר, גּוֹאֵל, דַּעַת, פלא, שפט and חֶמְלָה. Most of these enter into
collocations with no more than two of the remaining five elements of
Table 4.3, and then only once or twice with the element. The
exception is שפט, which collocates once with רַחֲמִים, five times with both
אהב and אֱמוּנָה, and six times with אֱמֶת.

Of the six lexemes that collocate once with חֶסֶד, בחר is the only one
to enter into collocations with more than two of the remaining
elements; it collocates once with each of רחם, אַהֲבָה and אֱמֶת, and four
times with אהב. Here again אהב apparently contrasts with חֶסֶד. חוס
collocates three times with רחם, thus justifying its inclusion in the area
of 'compassion'.

	רַחֲמִים	אהב	אַהֲבָה	אֱמֶת	אֱמוּנָה
תַּחֲנוּן*	1	1	–	–	1
שׂנא	–	44	2	4	–
שִׂנְאָה	–	2	8	–	–
מִישׁוֹר	–	–	–	1	1
נאף	–	6	1	–	–
נְשִׁיקָה*	–	2	1	–	–
דבק	1	5	1	–	–
דוד	–	2	1	–	–

Table 4.4. *Items Collocating with Two or More Elements but not with* חֶסֶד

Six of the items that never occur in close proximity with חֶסֶד never collocate with the other elements listed; they are גְּאֻלָּה, תְּחִנָּה, חבק, זְנוּנִים, שׁוֹפֵט and דְּבַק, but each of them collocates either with other elements not in the list or with other lexemes. Table 4.4 includes the items that collocate with at least two of the elements listed but never with חֶסֶד, showing the number of collocations with each element.

Nine other items never found with חֶסֶד collocate with only one of these elements; they are—

1. זוֹנָה four times with אהב;
2. מֵישָׁרִים, שָׂנִיא* and תַּזְנוּת each three times with אהב;
3. צדק twice with אֱמֶת, and חמל twice with רחם;
4. ישׁר and זנה each once with אהב, and יָשָׁר once with אֱמֶת.

אהב again stands in contrast with חֶסֶד, since it collocates at least three times with seven of the lexical items that never occur in close proximity with חֶסֶד.[1]

c. *Summary*

This section has concentrated on the profiles of six field elements. Drawing upon information presented in the profiles, the schema suggested by Sinclair is adapted to formulate a tentative definition of the formal meanings of these six elements. The same set of lexical items is included with each of the elements, so that comparisons may be readily made between their collocational tendencies.[2]

1. Three of these are shown in Table 4.4 above, and the remaining four are mentioned in lines 1. and 2. above.
2. These 'definitions' are summarized in Table 4.5 below.

The tendency of חֶסֶד to collocate with

1.   אֱמֶת is very strong;
2.   טוב is strong;
3.   אֱמוּנָה and רַחֲמִים is not so strong;
4.   צְדָקָה, מִשְׁפָּט and בְּרִית is moderate;
5.   אהב is weak; and
6.   חֶסֶד has no tendency to collocate with שׂנא and lexemes in the area of 'infidelity'.

The tendency of רַחֲמִים to collocate with

1.   חֶסֶד is not so strong;
2.   אֱמֶת and מִשְׁפָּט is not so weak;
3.   טוב, בְּרִית, אֱמוּנָה and צְדָקָה is weak; and
4.   רַחֲמִים has no tendency to collocate with שׂנא, אהב and lexemes in the 'infidelity' area.

The tendency of אהב to collocate with

1.   שׂנא is very strong;
2.   טוב and מִשְׁפָּט is moderate;
3.   אֱמֶת and נאף is not so weak;
4.   זוֹנָה, צְדָקָה, חֶסֶד and תַּזְנוּת is weak;
5.   בְּרִית, אֱמוּנָה and other lexemes in the 'infidelity'[1] area is very weak; and
6.   אהב has no tendency to collocate with רַחֲמִים.

The tendency of אַהֲבָה to collocate with

1.   אהב, חֶסֶד and טוב is not so weak;
2.   מִשְׁפָּט and בְּרִית is weak;
3.   צְדָקָה, שׂנא and רַחֲמִים is very weak; and
4.   אַהֲבָה has no tendency to collocate with אֱמוּנָה, אֱמֶת and lexemes in the 'infidelity' area.

The tendency of אֱמֶת to collocate with

1.   חֶסֶד is very strong;
2.   מִשְׁפָּט is not so strong;
3.   טוב and צְדָקָה is moderate;
4.   אהב, רַחֲמִים and בְּרִית is not so weak;

---

1.   Three of these have already been mentioned in lines 3. and 4. above.

5. שׂנא is weak;
6. אֱמוּנָה is very weak; and
7. אֱמֶת has no tendency to collocate with the lexemes in the 'infidelity' area.

The tendency of אֱמוּנָה to collocate with

1. חֶסֶד is not so strong;
2. צְדָקָה and מִשְׁפָּט is not so weak;
3. רַחֲמִים is weak;
4. טוֹב, בְּרִית, אֱמֶת and אהב is very weak; and
5. אֱמוּנָה has no tendency to collocate with שׂנא and the lexemes in the 'infidelity' area.

	חֶסֶד	רַחֲמִים	אהב	אַהֲבָה	אֱמֶת	אֱמוּנָה
חֶסֶד		5	2	3	7	5
רַחֲמִים	5		0	1	3	2
אהב	2	0		3	3	1
שׂנא	0	0	7	1	2	0
אֱמֶת	7	3	3	0		1
אֱמוּנָה	5	2	1	0	1	
בְּרִית	4	2	1	2	3	1
טוֹב	6	2	4	3	4	1
צְדָקָה	4	2	2	1	4	3
מִשְׁפָּט	4	3	4	2	5	3
Infidelity	0	0	2	0	0	0

Table 4.5. *Formal Meanings of Six Elements, in Terms of Collocational Tendencies with Other Lexical Items*

7	very strong	3	not so weak
6	strong	2	weak
5	not so strong	1	very weak
4	moderate	0	none

Table 4.5 facilitates the comparison of collocational trends between the elements given in the top line. The numbers are the collocational tendencies defined in Table 4.1. In order to decide whether the collocational trends of the various elements resemble each other, the tendencies will be called similar when they are in adjacent regions (i.e., the symbols differ by one), and they will be said to contrast when the difference between the symbols is greater than one. The first row of the table indicates that אֱמֶת tends to collocate very strongly with חֶסֶד, in contrast with the other elements; רַחֲמִים and אֱמוּנָה have a similar

(fairly strong) tendency, and they also contrast with אהב and אַהֲבָה, which have a similar (rather weak) collocational tendency with חֶסֶד. Subsequent rows show that חֶסֶד has a much stronger tendency than the other elements to collocate with רַחֲמִים, אֱמֶת and אֱמוּנה; and also that its tendency to collocate with טוֹב is stronger than that of each of the other elements. אהב has a much stronger tendency than the other elements to collocate with שׂנא, and it is the only element that collocates with members of the infidelity group. All elements except אַהֲבָה are similar to חֶסֶד in their collocation tendencies with מִשְׁפָּט.

It does not necessarily follow that consideration of collocates should support the conclusions obtained when examining situational distributions, since these are two independent avenues of investigating the field. The similarities and contrasts that exist between the collocational habits of חֶסֶד and the other keywords are not as pronounced as in the case of their distributions. When considering items that collocate frequently with חֶסֶד, the contrast with חֵמָ is greatest for רַחֲמִים and אַהֲבָה, and least for אֱמֶת. However, the collocational tendencies of רַחֲמִים, אֱמֶת and אֱמוּנָה with lexemes in the area of 'infidelity' are similar to those of חֶסֶד, since none of these elements is ever found in close proximity with these lexemes. The next chapter examines the collocations more closely, taking note of the lexical items involved.

4. *Overview*

This chapter has commenced the examination of the linguistic environment of the elements. It investigates the collocations into which the elements enter with each other and with the additional lexemes. A few distinguishing features discerned in the previous chapter when considering distributions have been supported by the investigation of collocations. The distributional trends of חֶסֶד and רַחֲמִים are similar in some respects, as are those of אהב and שׂנא, but the distributions of these two pairs contrast with each other. This contrast of אהב and שׂנא with רַחֲמִים is supported by their collocational tendencies with חֶסֶד; but חֶסֶד and רַחֲמִים also contrast in their collocations with most of the lexical items considered in this chapter.

The collocational trends of חֶסֶד have been compared with those of other elements, with results that differ at the two ends of the חֶסֶד spectrum.

With items that collocate frequently with חֶסֶד, the contrast with the collocational trends of חֶסֶד is

1. greatest with רַחֲמִים and אַהֲבָה and
2. least with אֱמֶת.

With items that collocate rarely with חֶסֶד, the tendencies of

1. רַחֲמִים, אֱמֶת and אֱמוּנָה are similar to those of חֶסֶד and
2. אהב contrast with those of חֶסֶד.

Thus, while the distribution of אֱמֶת contrasts with that of חֶסֶד, its collocational tendencies show more similarities to those of חֶסֶד; that is, אֱמֶת seems closer to חֶסֶד in terms of their common collocations than it does in terms of their situational distributions.

The collocation trends of these six elements have been summarized by suggesting a definition of the formal meaning of each of them. Further refinement in detail is provided by considering collocation patterns in the next chapter.

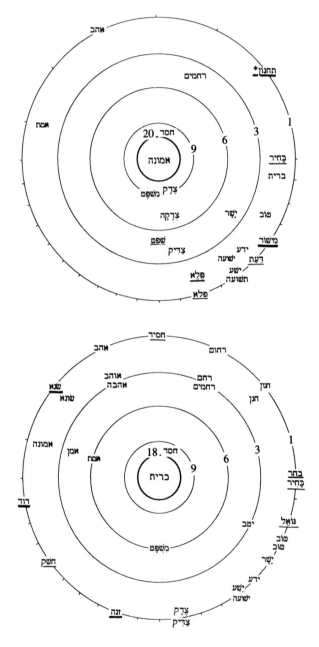

Figure 4.1. *Outer Profiles of* בְּרִית *and* אֱמֶתָה

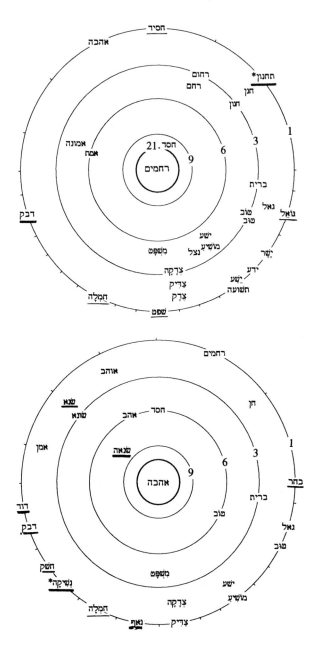

Figure 4.2. *Outer Profiles of* רַחֲמִים *and* אַהֲבָה

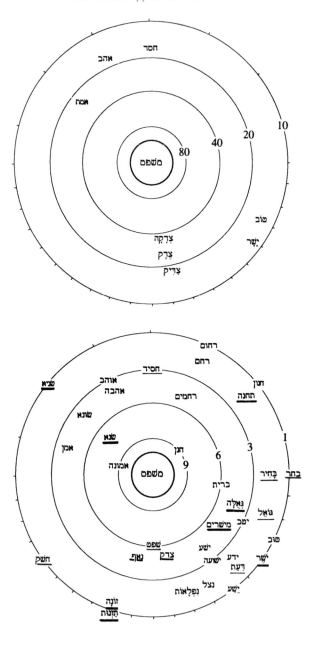

Figure 4.3. *Complete Profile of* מִשְׁפָּט

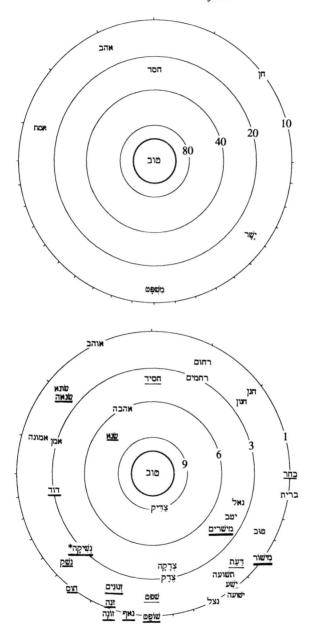

Figure 4.4. *Complete Profile of* טוב

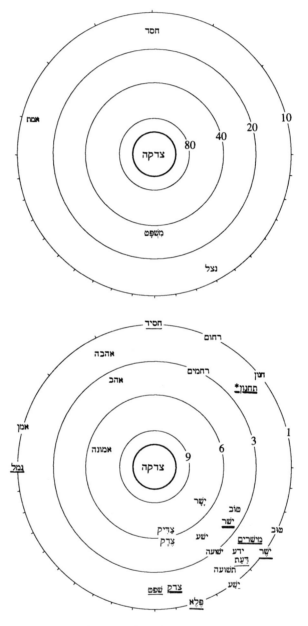

Figure 4.5. *Complete Profile of* צְדָקָה

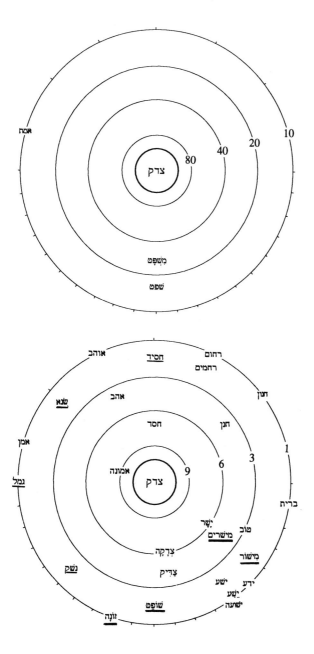

Figure 4.6. *Complete Profile of* צֶדֶק

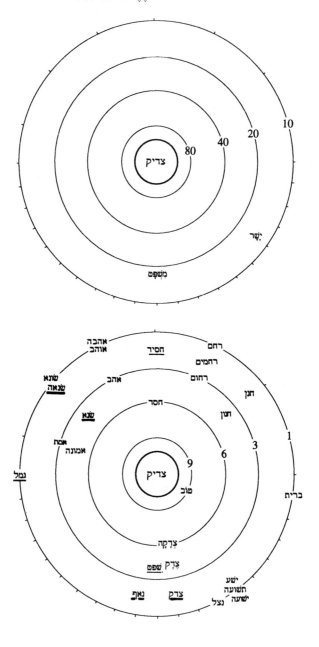

Figure 4.7. *Complete Profile of* צַדִּיק

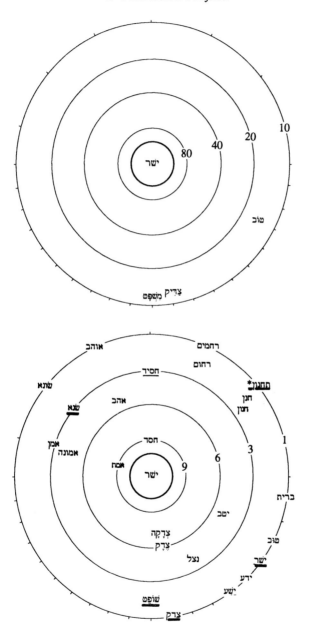

Figure 4.8. *Complete Profile of* יָשָׁר

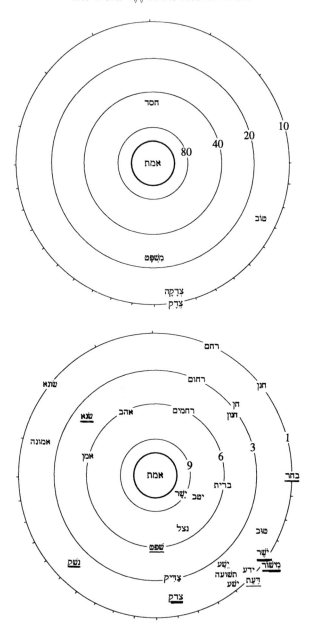

Figure 4.9. *Complete Profile of* אֱמֶת

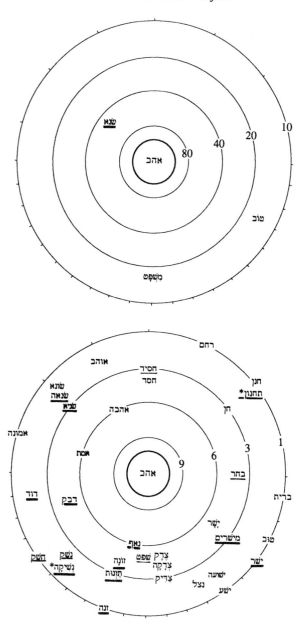

Figure 4.10. *Complete Profile of* אהב

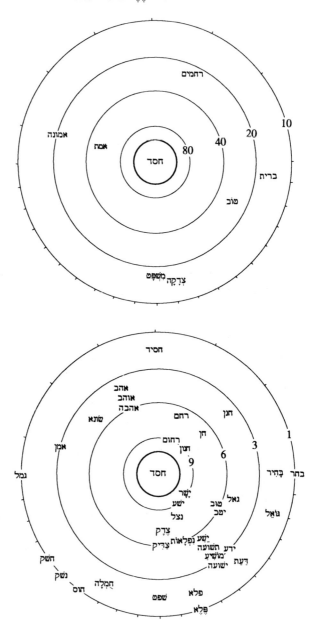

Figure 4.11. *Complete Profile of* חֶסֶד

Chapter 5

COLLOCATION PATTERNS

Comparisons have been made between the 13 keywords, based on the considerable amount of information derived from the collocation profiles of six elements and seven additional lexemes. These comparisons have taken a broad view of general features of the profiles; collocations of the keywords with individual lexemes have not been emphasized, since attention has been centred on the general areas to which some of the lexemes have been allocated, although four of the lexemes that collocate frequently with חֶסֶד are included in Table 4.3 in order to compare the collocational trends of חֶסֶד with those of five other elements. Trends that have become apparent in the relationships between the elements, particularly with regard to their resemblances and contrasts, have been expressed in the definition of the formal meanings of the elements.

1. *Rearrangement of Material*

The material has been rearranged, making it easier to compare the keywords in their collocation with all items in the same area, for example, with all derivatives of the same root, or with all lexemes assigned to the same semantic group. The two main parameters in the profiles are the lexical items and the frequencies with which various word-pairs enter into collocation with each other. The lexical items have been reduced by eliminating some of them and then considering the 15 groups into which they have already been arranged. Instead of the actual frequencies (ranging from 0 to 51), the frequency intervals for the various rings in the profiles produce 8 different categories.

A. *The Word-Groups*

Twelve lexical items were eliminated. Two items (the element חסד and

the lexeme חבק) do not appear in any of the 13 profiles. Also, since
the focus is on the element חֶסֶד rather than on the חסד group, חָסִיד has
been eliminated; it occurs in 10 of the profiles but only in the two
lowest frequency intervals. Another three elements are excluded—
תְּחִנָּה and תַּחֲנוּן* appear only in the lowest frequency range, the former
in one and the latter in five profiles. The other element is the *hapax
legomenon* שְׂנִיא* occurring in two of the profiles but only on the two
outermost rings,[1] and its omission does not greatly affect the patterns
of the שׂנא elements in each profile. After eliminating these, the
remaining elements form five groups each containing three items.

The lexemes eliminated include the three members of the פלא group
occurring in only four of the profiles, in the lowest frequency interval
in all except one. Three more lexemes appear almost always in the
lowest frequency interval; גמל (occurring in four profiles), דַּעַת (in six
profiles) and ידע (in nine profiles) have been eliminated. The remaining
41 lexemes are arranged in 10 groups. There are three lexemes in
each of five groups—'covenant', גאל, טוב, שׁפט and 'compassion'; four
lexemes in the צדק group; five lexemes in the ישׁר and 'infidelity'
groups; and six lexemes in the two groups labelled 'salvation' and
'physical proximity'.

B. *The Frequency Intervals*
Table 4.1 shows the frequency intervals, and the term and symbol
used for each. The intervals are based on the rings of the profile
targets, one ring being divided into two categories: More Frequent
and Very Frequent. It was a purely arbitrary decision to use four
rings in each section of the profile—any number other than four could
have been adopted, and there is no reason why the same number
should be used in both sections. However, this proved to be a convenient choice, since the rings in the profiles are not over-crowded
when the lexical items are placed in their appropriate positions.

C. *The Profile Patterns*
The profile patterns provide pictorial representations of the collocations into which each keyword enters with the word-groups in 15
sectors of its profile. The framework for the patterns is a pair of
perpendicular axes; the eight frequency intervals are represented by

---

1. שְׂנִיא* appears in the profiles of אהב and מִשְׁפָּט. See Section 2A in Chapter 4
above.

the numbers 0 to 7 at equidistant points on the horizontal axis, and the members of the word-group are placed at equidistant points on the vertical axis. The pattern is obtained by plotting the points that represent the frequency interval for each member of the word-group, then joining these points by straight line segments, starting at the point on the highest level and moving down to the points on each level in succession. These patterns, in Figure 5.1, make it easier to compare patterns made by different lexical items with the members of each word-group. The patterns in each row represent the collocational frequencies of the same lexical item (the keyword in the left-hand column is the lexical item shown in the bull's-eye of the appropriate profile) with the members of the various word-groups. Each column is allocated to a word-group that is identified at the head of the column; by concentrating on one column at a time it is possible to compare the way in which each keyword collocates with the same word-group. For example, the second column contains the profile patterns for the רחם word-group, which consists of the three members רחם, רַחֲמִים and רחוּם; these elements have been arranged in this order, reading downwards.[1] A pattern is not provided for a lexical item that is a member of the word-group under consideration; thus, there is no pattern for רַחֲמִים in the column for the רחם group to which it belongs.

Careful thought was given to the effect various changes in presentation would have on the patterns—for example, arranging frequency intervals in the reverse order along the horizontal axis, altering the arbitrarily determined cut-off points for the frequency intervals, and changing the order on the vertical axis of the items in each group. Since the aim of the exercise is to compare the patterns חֶסֶד and the other lexical items make with the same word-group, the items in each word-group are arranged in such a way that the חֶסֶד patterns all have a characteristic shape—a V-shape, open either to the left or to the right. Using a few simple rules it is easy to make consistent and objective decisions when comparing the slopes of corresponding line segments in different patterns, and hence to classify the patterns as *similar*, *opposite*, or *different*.

1. This information—the members of the word group, and the order in which they are arranged—is given in the first paragraph of the appropriate subsection of Sections 2 and 3, where the profile patterns are discussed. For the רחם group, see Section 2B below.

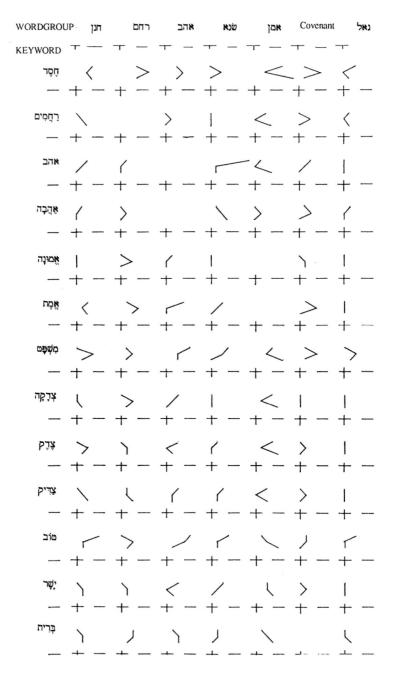

Figure 5.1. *Profile Patterns*

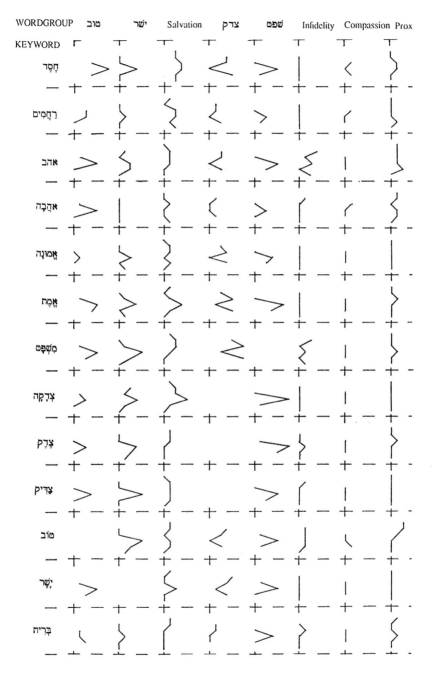

Figure 5.1. *Profile Patterns (Continued)*

Some patterns are *identical* with that of חֶסֶד, being translations of the same pattern; often one keyword does not, while another keyword does, collocate with all the items in the group. For example, with the רחם group, the patterns of חֶסֶד and אֱמוּנָה are identical, but אֱמוּנָה collocates with only one element of the רחם group, while חֶסֶד collocates with all three. With the same רחם group, אֱמֶת and מִשְׁפָּט both have patterns that are similar to that of חֶסֶד; both אֱמֶת and מִשְׁפָּט are found in close proximity to all three elements, as also is חֶסֶד. Hence, from the point of view of their collocational trends, both אֱמֶת and מִשְׁפָּט are closer to חֶסֶד than אֱמוּנָה is; and of all the keywords, אֱמֶת is closest to חֶסֶד in this particular word-group, while מִשְׁפָּט may be classed as 'close' or 'near' to חֶסֶד. The term 'closest' is intended to sum up all the features involved in the collocation patterns. Numerical values are not assigned to any of these features, but together they simplify the comparison of the collocation patterns of חֶסֶד and the different keywords.

2. *Word-Groups—Elements*

Attention is first directed to each of the triads into which the field elements have been grouped, considering in turn the שׂנא, אהב, רחם, חנן and אמן word-groups. The order in which the elements are arranged on the vertical axis is specified before proceeding to compare the חֶסֶד pattern with the patterns of the other lexical items.

A. *The* חנן *Group*
The elements are arranged, reading from the top downwards, in the order חַנּוּן, חֵן, חנן.

The pattern of אֱמֶת alone is *similar* to that of חֶסֶד; they are in fact *identical*, since each point in the אֱמֶת pattern is in the frequency interval that is one below the corresponding חֶסֶד point. אֱמֶת is also *closest* to חֶסֶד in its collocational trend with the חנן group.

The patterns of מִשְׁפָּט and צֶדֶק are *opposite* to that of חֶסֶד.

טוב has one point of its pattern in a higher frequency interval than the points in the חֶסֶד pattern. צְדָקָה, אַהֲבָה, יָשָׁר and בְּרִית, as well as אֱמוּנָה (which *never* collocates with any members of this group) have all points in lower frequency intervals than any point in the חֶסֶד pattern, while רַחֲמִים, אהב and צַדִּיק each has a single point in the lowest frequency interval of the חֶסֶד pattern but no points in any higher frequency interval than this.

In summary:

1. חֶסֶד collocates with each element in the חנן group more
    frequently than all other items except מִשְׁפָּט, צֶדֶק and טוֹב;
2. the collocational pattern of אֱמֶת is closest to that of חֶסֶד.

B. *The* רחם *Group*

The elements are arranged in the order רַחוּם, רַחֲמִים, רחם reading
downwards.

Several patterns are *similar* to that of חֶסֶד—מִשְׁפָּט, אֱמֶת, אֱמוּנָה, אַהֲבָה,
צְדָקָה and טוֹב; but of these only אֱמוּנָה is *identical,* having each of its
points three frequency intervals below those of חֶסֶד.

No patterns are *opposite* to that of חֶסֶד.

All patterns have all points in lower frequency intervals than any
point of the חֶסֶד pattern, with the exception of אֱמֶת which has one point
in the lowest frequency interval for חֶסֶד.

In summary:

1. חֶסֶד collocates more frequently than any of the other items
    with each element in the רחם group;
2. the collocational pattern of אֱמֶת is closest to that of חֶסֶד.

C. *The* אהב *Group*

The elements are arranged in the order אוֹהֵב, אַהֲבָה, אהב reading
downwards.

רַחֲמִים provides the only pattern *similar* to that of חֶסֶד in this group;
in fact these patterns are *identical* with each point in the רַחֲמִים pattern,
being two frequency intervals below the corresponding חֶסֶד point.

Both צֶדֶק and יָשָׁר, whose patterns are identical, are *opposite* to חֶסֶד.

מִשְׁפָּט, טוֹב and אֱמֶת all collocate with אהב in a higher frequency
interval than חֶסֶד does. But, while all the lexical items collocate with at
least one member of this group, רַחֲמִים and אֱמוּנָה have all points in a
lower frequency interval than any of the חֶסֶד points. צַדִּיק, צֶדֶק, צְדָקָה,
and יָשָׁר are all in the same frequency interval as חֶסֶד for אהב, and בְּרִית
is in the same frequency interval as חֶסֶד for אוֹהֵב; but the other points
of the patterns of these six lexemes are in lower intervals than the חֶסֶד
points.

In summary:

1. מִשְׁפָּט and טוֹב are the only items which appear in the Frequent
    interval, both with אהב;

2.   אֱמֶת also collocates with אהב more frequently than חֶסֶד does;
3.   the pattern of רַחֲמִים is identical with that of חֶסֶד, but אַהֲבָה is
     the only element in the group with which it collocates—and
     then only rarely. Hence none of the lexical items collocates
     with this group in a pattern similar to that of חֶסֶד.

D. *The* שׂנא *Group*

The elements are in the order שׂנא, שׂוֹנֵא, שִׂנְאָה reading downward.

1.   No pattern is *similar* to that of חֶסֶד.
2.   No pattern can be classed as *opposite* to חֶסֶד.
3.   אֱמוּנָה, רַחֲמִים and צְדָקָה *never* collocate with any member of this
     group.

The disparities between the חֶסֶד pattern and many of the other patterns
in this group stem from the fact that חֶסֶד collocates with only one of
the elements; consequently most of the profiled items collocate more
frequently than חֶסֶד does with at least one, and sometimes two, of the
elements in the group—but never with all three. Thus, צַדִּיק, אַהֲבָה, אהב
and טוב all collocate more frequently with both שׂנא and שִׂנְאָה, with which
חֶסֶד never collocates; and אֱמֶת, מִשְׁפָּט, צֶדֶק, יָשָׁר and בְּרִית all collocate with
שׂנא. It is therefore not possible to decide which pattern is closest to
that of חֶסֶד by applying the same principles as in the previous sections.
It may be argued that the items that never enter into collocation with
the elements of this group are also close to the חֶסֶד pattern.

In summary, this word-group highlights the disparity between חֶסֶד
and all the other lexical items.

E. *The* אמן *Group*

The elements are arranged in the order אֱמֶת, אמן, אֱמוּנָה reading
downwards.

Seven patterns (צֶדֶק, צְדָקָה, מִשְׁפָּט, אהב, רַחֲמִים and צַדִּיק) are *similar* to
that of חֶסֶד.

The pattern of אַהֲבָה is *opposite* to that of חֶסֶד.

All points in the אַהֲבָה pattern are in lower frequency intervals than
any point in the חֶסֶד pattern.

In summary:

1.   the מִשְׁפָּט pattern is closest to that of חֶסֶד, followed by the
     identical patterns of צְדָקָה and צֶדֶק.
2.   no item collocates with אֱמוּנָה and אֱמֶת as frequently as חֶסֶד does;

3.   no item collocates with any member of this group in a higher
frequency interval than חֶסֶד does.

3. *Word-Groups—Lexemes*

A. *The 'Covenant' Group*

The lexemes are arranged in the order בָּחִיר, בְּרִית, בחר reading
downwards.

Seven patterns are *similar* to that of חֶסֶד: מִשְׁפָּט, אֱמֶת, אַהֲבָה, רַחֲמִים,
צֶדֶק צַדִּיק, and יָשָׁר; these last three are identical, since each lexeme
collocates only with בְּרִית in the Rare interval.

No patterns are *opposite* to that of חֶסֶד.

צְדָקָה *never* enters into collocations with any of the lexemes in this
group.

חֶסֶד is the only item whose collocations enter the Frequent interval—
with בְּרִית; and אהב alone collocates more frequently than חֶסֶד with any
lexeme (בחר).

In summary:

1.   מִשְׁפָּט has the pattern which is closest to that of חֶסֶד;
2.   no item collocates with any of these lexemes in a higher
frequency interval than חֶסֶד does with בְּרִית.

B. *The נאל Group*

The order of the lexemes is גּוֹאֵל, נִגְאָלָה, גָּאַל reading downwards.

רַחֲמִים alone has a pattern *similar* to that of חֶסֶד.

The pattern of מִשְׁפָּט is *opposite* to that of חֶסֶד, גּוֹאֵל being in the same
frequency interval for both חֶסֶד and מִשְׁפָּט.

Seven items (צַדִּיק, צֶדֶק, צְדָקָה, אֱמֶת, אֱמוּנָה, אהב) צַדִּיק and יָשָׁר) *never* collocate
with any of these three lexemes.

מִשְׁפָּט and טוֹב each have one point in the highest frequency interval of
the חֶסֶד pattern.

In summary:

1.   רַחֲמִים has the closest pattern to that of חֶסֶד, and טוֹב is also very
close;
2.   no point is in any frequency interval higher than Occasional;
3.   the only lexemes in the Occasional interval are נאל (with חֶסֶד
and טוֹב) and נִגְאָלָה (with מִשְׁפָּט).

C. *The* טוב *Group*

The lexemes are in the order יטב, טוֹב, טוּב reading downwards.

Nine patterns (צַדִּיק and יָשָׁר) צֶדֶק, צְדָקָה, מִשְׁפָּט, אֱמֶת, אַהֲבָה, אֹהֵב, אֱמוּנָה) are *similar* to that of חֶסֶד.

צַדִּיק alone has a pattern *identical* with that of חֶסֶד, but it collocates only with טוֹב.

There are no patterns *opposite* to that of חֶסֶד; and each item collocates with at least one of the lexemes in this group.

All items collocate in a lower frequency interval than חֶסֶד with each of the lexemes.

In summary:

1. חֶסֶד collocates with each lexeme in a higher frequency interval than any of the other lexical items;
2. the identical patterns of מִשְׁפָּט and יָשָׁר are closest to that of חֶסֶד.

D. *The* ישר *Group*

The five lexemes in this group are arranged in the order ישר, יָשָׁר, יָשָׁר, מִישׁוֹר, מֵישָׁרִים, reading downwards.

The patterns are more complex because the group contains more members than those considered previously. None of the patterns is *identical* with that of חֶסֶד, but three (בְּרִית, צַדִּיק and רַחֲמִים) are *similar*.

אַהֲבָה *never* collocates with any of these lexemes.

צַדִּיק, מִשְׁפָּט and טוֹב are all in a higher frequency interval than חֶסֶד with יָשָׁר, and מִשְׁפָּט and טוֹב both collocate more frequently than חֶסֶד with two of the other lexemes.

In summary:

1. צַדִּיק has the pattern which is closest to that of חֶסֶד.

E. *The 'Salvation' Group*

The six lexemes in this group are in the order תְּשׁוּעָה, נצל, ישׁע, יָשַׁע, יְשׁוּעָה, מוֹשִׁיעַ reading downwards.

The patterns are again complex.

None of the patterns can be classed as *opposite* to that of חֶסֶד.

Seven items (טוֹב, צַדִּיק, צֶדֶק, אֱמוּנָה, אַהֲבָה, אֹהֵב and בְּרִית) have all points in lower frequency intervals than any points in the חֶסֶד pattern, while מִשְׁפָּט, רַחֲמִים and יָשָׁר have some points in the lowest חֶסֶד frequency interval but none in any higher interval than this.

צְדָקָה collocates with נצל in a higher frequency interval than חֶסֶד, while אֱמֶת collocates in the same frequency interval as חֶסֶד with נצל.
In summary:

1. חֶסֶד collocates with each lexeme of this group in a higher frequency interval than almost all the other lexical items;
2. the exceptions are רַחֲמִים (with מוֹשִׁיע in the same interval), אֱמֶת (with נצל in the same interval), and צְדָקָה (with יְשׁוּעָה in the same interval and נצל in the next higher interval).

F. *The* צדק *Group*

The four lexemes are in the order צְדָקָה, צדק, צֶדֶק, צַדִּיק reading downwards.

The patterns of רַחֲמִים and אהב are both *similar* to that of חֶסֶד.

No pattern is *opposite* to the חֶסֶד pattern, and there are no keywords that *never* collocate with any of the lexemes in this group.

Each point in the מִשְׁפָּט pattern is in a higher frequency interval than the corresponding point in the חֶסֶד pattern; and אֱמֶת and יָשָׁר both have points in, but not above, the highest חֶסֶד frequency interval.

Three points in the חֶסֶד pattern are in a higher frequency interval than the corresponding points in the pattern of each of אַהֲבָה, רחמים, אהב and בְּרִית; the fourth point is in the Never interval for each of these five items.

In summary:

1. מִשְׁפָּט collocates with each lexeme in a higher frequency interval than חֶסֶד;
2. חֶסֶד collocates with each lexeme in a non-lower frequency interval for each of the four keywords listed in the previous paragraph;
3. the pattern of אֱמוּנָה is closer than those of רַחֲמִים and אהב to the חֶסֶד pattern.

G. *The* שפט *Group*

These three lexemes are in the order שׁפט, מִשְׁפָּט, שׁוֹפֵט reading downwards.

This column is unique in that all the patterns are *similar* to that of חֶסֶד.

Each point in the צֶדֶק pattern is in a higher frequency interval than the corresponding חֶסֶד point, while both אֱמֶת and צְדָקָה have at least one point in a higher frequency interval than the corresponding point(s) in the חֶסֶד pattern.

In summary:

1. צֶדֶק collocates in a higher frequency interval than חֶסֶד with each lexeme, and אֱמֶת likewise with two of the lexemes;
2. the closest patterns to that of חֶסֶד are the identical pair of אהב and צַדִּיק, followed by those of טוֹב and צְדָקָה.

H. *The 'Infidelity' Group*

The order of these five lexemes, reading downwards, is זוֹנָה, זנה, נאף, תַּזְנוּת, זְנוּנִים.

חֶסֶד *never* collocates with any of these lexemes, nor do אֱמוּנָה, רַחֲמִים, אֱמֶת, צְדָקָה and יָשָׁר; their patterns are therefore *similar* to that of חֶסֶד.

The patterns which show greatest variation from that of חֶסֶד are those of אהב and מִשְׁפָּט.

In summary:

1. חֶסֶד is never found with any of the lexemes in this group;
2. אהב, on the other hand, collocates in the Rare interval with זנה, in the Occasional interval with both זוֹנָה and תַּזְנוּת and in the Less Frequent interval with נאף; it thus presents the strongest contrast with חֶסֶד.

I. *The 'Compassion' Group*

The three lexemes are in the order חוס, חמל, חָמְלָה reading downwards.

None of the patterns is *similar* to that of חֶסֶד.

Nine of the items *never* collocate with any of the lexemes.

In summary:

1. אַהֲבָה, רַחֲמִים and טוֹב are closest to the חֶסֶד pattern.

J. *The 'Physical Proximity' Group*

There are six lexemes in this group; their order, reading downwards, is דָּבַק, דבק, חשק, נשק, נְשִׁיקָה*, דּוֹד.

None of the patterns is *similar* to that of חֶסֶד.

The four items צְדָקָה, אֱמוּנָה, צַדִּיק and יָשָׁר *never* collocate with any of these lexemes.

טוֹב has two points, and אהב one point, in a higher frequency interval than any points of the חֶסֶד pattern. The points in all other patterns, including that of חֶסֶד, are confined to the two lowest frequency intervals.

In summary:

1. אהב shows the greatest variation from the חֶסֶד pattern;
2. אֱמֶת and צֶדֶק (with identical patterns) and מִשְׁפָּט are closest to the חֶסֶד pattern.

4. *Profiles and Patterns*

The preceeding sections have compared the pattern of חֶסֶד with those of the other keywords, considering one word-group at a time. Attention is now directed, first, to the number of members in each group with which חֶסֶד enters into collocations. חֶסֶד and other items collocate on different levels with the same word-group; these are noted, and suggestions are made regarding the semantic implications of these differences. Finally, lexical items whose patterns resemble those of חֶסֶד in more than one area are considered, again noting the semantic implications of these resemblances.

A. *The* חֶסֶד *Profile*

Previous discussion of the profile of חֶסֶד concentrated on the frequency with which this element collocates with each of the other lexical items. Such an approach makes it possible to fill in the details of a statement like that suggested by Sinclair. But no attempt was made previously to group the items together as has been done in the patterns. The element חֶסֶד collocates with each member of seven of the word-groups: חנן, רחם, אהב, אמן, 'covenant', טוב and 'salvation'; it is also found with all except one member of four other groups: גאל, שפט, צדק and 'compassion'.

B. *Profile Pattern Comparisons*

When the profile pattern of חֶסֶד is compared with the patterns made by other keywords with the same word-group, it is seen that חֶסֶד is

1. in a higher frequency interval than all the other keywords with each member of the רחם group;
2. in at least as high a frequency interval as all the other keywords with members of the טוב group, where אֱמֶת collocates with יטב in the same interval as חֶסֶד, and also with members of

the אמן group, where מִשְׁפָּט ,טוֹב, יָשָׁר and בְּרִית all collocate with
אמן in the same interval as חֶסֶד;

3. in at least as high a frequency interval as all except one of the
    keywords with members of the 'salvation' group (צְדָקָה is in a
    higher interval than חֶסֶד with נצל; אֱמֶת is in the same interval
    as חֶסֶד with נצל, as are רַחֲמִים with מוֹשִׁיעַ and both מִשְׁפָּט and
    צְדָקָה with יְשׁוּעָה) and with members of the 'covenant' group
    (אהב is in a higher interval than חֶסֶד with בחר; אֱמֶת ,אַהֲבָה,
    מִשְׁפָּט and טוֹב are all in the same interval as חֶסֶד with בחר, as
    are both אֱמוּנָה and מִשְׁפָּט with בָּחִיר).

However, חֶסֶד collocates with few of the lexemes in four groups. חֶסֶד is
never found in close association with any of the five lexemes in the
'infidelity' group. Eight other keywords are in the same situation,
never being found with these lexemes; but both אהב and מִשְׁפָּט are found
in collocation with most of the lexemes in this group, and this
highlights the fact that the patterns of these keywords contrast with
that of חֶסֶד. All other keywords collocate with these lexemes in the
lowest (Rare) interval, which again emphasises that אהב and מִשְׁפָּט
contrast with חֶסֶד. חֶסֶד also collocates with only one of the five lexemes
in the יָשָׁר group, one of the three in the שׂנא group and two of the six
in the 'physical proximity' group.

The previous statement of the formal meaning of the element חֶסֶד
may now be expanded by asserting that it collocates

1. more frequently than all other keywords with each element
    in the רחם group;
2. at least as frequently as all other keywords with members of
    the אמן and the טוֹב groups;
3. more frequently than most other keywords with members of
    the 'covenant' and the 'salvation' groups;
4. less frequently than אהב ,אַהֲבָה, and טוֹב with at least two
    lexemes in the 'physical proximity' group;
5. never with any lexeme in the 'infidelity' group, in contrast
    with both אהב and מִשְׁפָּט.

C. *Resemblances to the* חֶסֶד *Patterns*

This section draws together the resemblances of some keyword
patterns with the חֶסֶד patterns. The term 'resemblance' is being used
here to include both *like* and *unlike* patterns; under *like* are included

'identical' and 'similar' as well as 'closest' and 'near', all introduced previously. The last two terms distinguish between the similar patterns and take into account both the shape of the pattern and the number of members of the group with which the keyword collocates. The patterns with the אהב group show that the בְּרִית pattern (classified as 'different' on account of its vertical line segment) is closer to the חֶסֶד pattern than the 'identical' רַחֲמִים pattern, since רַחֲמִים is found with only one of the three אהב members whereas בְּרִית is found with all three and is in the same frequency interval as חֶסֶד with אוֹהֵב; hence the בְּרִית pattern is classed as 'closest' to that of חֶסֶד. There is a fine line of distinction between 'closest' and 'near'; the latter term is used when several patterns are all very close to that of חֶסֶד, and it indicates those that are not as close as others. The term *unlike* includes patterns that have been classed as 'opposite' as well as those which are in 'contrast' with the חֶסֶד pattern; 'contrast' applies to the patterns of אהב with each of the שׂנא, 'infidelity' and 'physical proximity' groups.

Patterns of nine keywords (five elements and four lexemes) are *like* those of חֶסֶד with two or more groups; and three of these (two elements and one lexeme) have patterns which are *unlike* those of חֶסֶד with two or more groups. Details for these nine keywords are set out below in a decreasing order of likenesses.

1. רַחֲמִים is *identical* with חֶסֶד in the אהב group, *closest* to חֶסֶד in both the גאל and 'compassion' groups, and *near* to חֶסֶד in the שׂנא, 'salvation' and צדק groups.

2. אֱמֶת, being *identical* with חֶסֶד in the חנן group, is also *closest* to חֶסֶד in the חנן as well as in the רחם and 'physical proximity' groups, and *near* to חֶסֶד in the טוב group.

3. טוֹב is *closest* to חֶסֶד in the 'compassion' group, and *near* to חֶסֶד in both the גאל and שׁפט groups.

4. צַדִּיק is *identical* with חֶסֶד in the טוב group, and *closest* to חֶסֶד in both the ישׁ and שׁפט groups.

5. אֱמוּנָה is *identical* with חֶסֶד in the רחם group, *closest* to חֶסֶד in the צדק group, and *near* to חֶסֶד in the שׂנא group.

6. צְדָקָה is *near* to חֶסֶד in both the שׂנא and שׁפט groups.

7. מִשְׁפָּט is *closest* to חֶסֶד in the אמן, 'covenant', טוב and 'physical proximity' groups; but it is *opposite* to חֶסֶד in both the חנן and גאל groups, and in *contrast* in the 'infidelity' group.

8. אהב is *closest* to חֶסֶד in both the שׁפט and 'salvation' groups; but it is in *contrast* with חֶסֶד in both the שׂנא and 'infidelity' groups.

רַחֲמִים is *like* חֶסֶד in six of the groups, although the identity between the patterns of רַחֲמִים and חֶסֶד in the אהב group has little significance, since רַחֲמִים collocates with only one of the אהב elements. אֱמֶת is *like* חֶסֶד in four groups; here the identity between the patterns is important because both elements collocate with all three members of the חנן group. צַדִּיק, טוֹב and אֱמוּנָה are all *like* חֶסֶד in three groups, although the identities for both צַדִּיק and אֱמוּנָה are open to question for the same reason as רַחֲמִים. צְדָקָה is *like* חֶסֶד in two groups. On the other hand, מִשְׁפָּט is *like* חֶסֶד in four groups but it is *unlike* חֶסֶד in three other groups. Similarly, אהב is *like* חֶסֶד in two groups but *unlike* חֶסֶד in two other groups. It is not possible to devise an arithmetical method of simplifying the 'likes' and 'unlikes'; but the order in which the items have been listed above correctly displays the degree of resemblance between חֶסֶד and each of the keywords.

Comparison of the collocation patterns with that of חֶסֶד thus separates the remaining lexical items into four sections. Three items (אֱמֶת, רַחֲמִים and טוֹב) have the greatest number of patterns resembling that of חֶסֶד; another three items (צְדָקָה, צַדִּיק and אֱמוּנָה) have fewer patterns resembling that of חֶסֶד; four more (צֶדֶק, יָשָׁר, בְּרִית, אַהֲבָה) have at most one pattern like that of חֶסֶד, while the remaining two (אהב and מִשְׁפָּט) have both likenesses and contrasts with חֶסֶד. This may indicate that the semantic affinities with חֶסֶד are greater for אֱמֶת, רַחֲמִים and טוֹב than for צַדִּיק, אֱמוּנָה and צְדָקָה, whereas the affinities of the remaining items with חֶסֶד are much smaller.

5. *Contrasts between* חֶסֶד *and* אהב

While investigating contrasts between חֶסֶד and some of the other elements, it has been found that אהב and its derivatives have different patterns from חֶסֶד in their distribution between various agents and patients,[1] and also in their collocations,[2] where the contrasts have been most pronounced in the usage of these elements with the lexemes in the 'covenant', 'physical proximity' and 'infidelity' groups. The significance of these contrasts will now be considered by examining passages which contain these lexemes and either חֶסֶד or אהב, noting the verb אהב and also אַהֲבָה and אֹהֵב. In each section a tabulation gives the number of times each lexeme in the group collocates with each of the

1. See Chapter 3, noting especially Sections 2A and B.
2. See Section 3B of Chapter 4 and Sections 3H and J above.

elements, showing also whether the keyword is used with God or a
human as the agent. The figures presented do not always tally with
those in the corresponding collocation tables because the actual
number of occurrences, as distinct from collocations, is given.

A. *The 'Covenant' Group*

חֶסֶד occurs more than once in the one passage where it collocates with
בָּחִיר and also in at least one passage containing בְּרִית as well as חֶסֶד. בְּרִית
also occurs more frequently with חֶסֶד than with the derivatives of the
root אהב, while the opposite is the case with בחר. The lexemes in this
group are found with חֶסֶד, and also with the verb אהב, more frequently
when God is agent than with a human agent; but the agent is more
frequently human when they are used with אַהֲבָה and אוֹהֵב.

Lexemes	חֶסֶד		אהב		אַהֲבָה		אוֹהֵב	
	God	Human	God	Human	God	Human	God	Human
בחר	1	–	4	–	1	–	–	2
בָּחִיר	*1	–	–	–	–	–	–	–
בְּרִית	*13	1	2	–	1	2	–	3

Table 5.1. *The 'Covenant' Group*
The asterisk (*) indicates that the element is repeated in some passages.

a. *Human Agent*
When both the agent and the patient are human with חֶסֶד and אַהֲבָה,
בְּרִית is used once with each of these elements, and the covenant is also
between two humans—David and Jonathan. 1 Sam. 18.1-3, 1 Sam. 20.8
and 1 Sam. 20.14-17 will be considered.

The first passage records David's meeting with Jonathan shortly
after David defeated Goliath, and of Jonathan's love for David which
preceded the covenant between them. This covenant is based on and
prompted by Jonathan's love for David (18.3). The other passages are
set against the background of Saul's jealous attempts to kill David
(1 Sam. 18.10-11; 19.2, 10-18; 20.3). Fearing for his life, David
decides to absent himself from Saul's table and, reminding Jonathan of
their solemn covenant (בְּרִית יהוה—20. 8), asks him to bring news of
Saul's reaction—describing Jonathan's response to his request as an act
of חֶסֶד. David's request for חֶסֶד is reinforced by a reference to the
covenant (20. 8) which in turn is based on Jonathan's love for David.
Jonathan tells David how he intends to convey this information to him
and, apparently sensing that it will not be good news, he also asks

David to show חֶסֶד יהוה to him and his posterity (20.14-15). Moreover, in making his request, he insists that David renew his vow in view of Jonathan's love for him (20.17).

Both Glueck (1967: 46-48) and Sakenfeld (1978: 82-88) link these passages together. Although 1 Sam. 18. 3 does not include the central word of their studies, it is there—as Sakenfeld points out on p. 83— that the establishment of the בְּרִית between David and Jonathan is recorded.

Glueck, while discussing 1 Sam. 20.8, refers to this passage in a footnote, to justify his statement that the bonds of friendship already united David and Jonathan. He insists, however, that there was a sacred covenant between them, concluded in the name of Yahweh so that each had a 'solemn obligation to take care of the welfare and safety of his friend'.[1] On 1 Sam. 20.14-15, Glueck asserts that although the text is mutilated the meaning is clear—namely, Jonathan entreats David to preserve his life and that of his descendants.

Sakenfeld finds that both incidents in 1 Samuel 20 fit into the pattern that she has already discerned in the secular use of חֶסֶד. By referring to himself in v. 8 as 'your servant', David acknowledges that he is the subordinate party. Again, Jonathan considers that their בְּרִית places him under an obligation even though, humanly speaking, he would be free to ignore David's request. After sorting out the textual problems, she summarizes the content of vv. 14-15 as Jonathan's request for David to express his חֶסֶד by preserving Jonathan's lineage when he comes to power. While in the existing relationship David is the subordinate party, there will be a role reversal before he is able to express his חֶסֶד to Jonathan. David's action will then 'be the free act of a superior to an inferior performed in compliance with a specific political (and humanly personal) obligation'.

The main interest of both Glueck and Sakenfeld is in the covenantal basis for an expression of חֶסֶד, and they find this in 1 Samuel 18, which Sakenfeld mentions in her introduction to these incidents. Alluding to the frequent use of 'love' words in political contexts, both in the ancient Near East and in biblical writings, she thinks that the narrator may be referring to a political relationship rather than to a purely personal friendship; but she immediately adds that it is most unlikely that the king's son would enter into such a political pact with

---

1. Glueck acknowledges Kraetzschmar, *Die Bundesvorstellung im Alten Testament* (Marburg, 1896: 20), for this quotation.

a young unknown warrior at their first meeting. Her emphasis, as she discusses the sequel (1 Sam. 20.14-15), is on the political rather than the personal obligation. One of her reviewers[1] observes that Sakenfeld refuses to allow the acts associated with חֶסֶד 'to be limited to a formal covenant relationship'; but this is one occasion on which she fails to take advantage of the opportunity to press the point home. Is there, of necessity, an allusion to a formal political covenant in 1 Samuel 18? Sakenfeld herself suggests that she has reservations about the significance of the verb אהב when it is used in political contexts. Thompson (1974) also is hesitant in his claims that derivatives of the root אהב carry political overtones in the David–Jonathan narratives. There is a possibility of political implications when these derivatives are used. Similarly, it is possible that the word בְּרִית carries political implications, but this does not amount to certainty. Is there a more satisfactory way of accounting for the facts in the David–Jonathan narratives?

Glueck (1967: 46) draws attention to the bond of friendship between David and Jonathan, and this provides a more reasonable approach to the use of the word בְּרִית in this context. The בְּרִית here can hardly be a document drawn up in a strict legal manner to ensure that both parties are bound by the terms of their agreement and answerable to each other in case of default. This is not to deny that there is an agreement, moreover a binding agreement, recognized and accepted by both David and Jonathan—an agreement which may not set out any specific terms and conditions, but in which each accepts the obligation and the responsibility to take care of the welfare and the safety of the other. Such an agreement, in which each pledges his loyalty to the other, overcomes Sakenfeld's objection (1978: 83) that a political covenant is an unlikely outcome of the first meeting of Jonathon and David. Yet even the word 'loyalty' carries political implications—at least in modern western civilization, if not in the ancient Near Eastern culture. Perhaps 'commitment' expresses more clearly the essential element in the friendship of David and Jonathan; it is no casual friendship, but is from its very beginning a lasting, an enduring friendship, a commitment to each other in which each recognizes—and intends to observe—his moral obligations to the other. And Yahweh is the witness to this commitment which, in 1 Sam. 20.8, is called a בְּרִית יהוה.

The ancient Near Eastern treaties recovered from Hittite archives

1.   See Pardee 1980: 244.

have increased our knowledge of the biblical covenants; but it is not wise to import all this background into every use of the word בְּרִית in the Old Testament. Nor is it legitimate to insist that every use of the אהב derivatives carries the full weight of political implications, even in the David–Jonathan pericope. The foregoing account of this covenant avoids weaknesses inherent in the treatments of both Glueck and Sakenfeld, who appear to have read more into the text than is necessary; at the same time it provides for the acts of חֶסֶד a context that is not as wide as Sakenfeld (1978: 3) claims Glueck's relationship is, for he leaves the impression that secular חֶסֶד could be done in any relationship with the possible exception of open enmity.

In Isa. 56.6, אַהֲבָה and בְּרִית appear in collocation also with עֶבֶד. Here it is the love which Yahweh expects from his loyal covenant partners. The people involved are foreigners; provided that they love his name, serve him and keep his covenant,[1] Yahweh will accept them as his own people (v. 3). Such a possibility was unacceptable to the author of the book of Jonah, yet it is implicit in Yahweh's calling of Abram in Gen. 12.3, where Yahweh's blessing is not confined to Abram and his descendants but is to be extended to all the families of the earth.

b. *God as Agent*
The lexeme בְּרִית frequently occurs in close association with the element חֶסֶד when God is agent; on each occasion the reference is to Yahweh's covenant. Deut. 7.7-13 is important in this connection, but it will be more appropriate to consider this passage as a whole later in the chapter, since other lexemes also appear in it. Verse 9 contains the words 'keeping covenant and חֶסֶד' which also occurs in five other passages as the opening invocation of a prayer; in each case the expression is used as an attribute of Yahweh. Prayers that confess the sins of the people of Israel and beseech Yahweh to forgive them are recorded in Neh. 1.5-11 and Dan. 9.4-19; both invocations include this expression from Deut. 7.9 and also the words that follow it. The interceders are aware that Yahweh is no longer obliged to honour his covenant promises because his people are not expressing their love to him by obeying his commandments; yet they anticipate that Yahweh will forgive his rebellious people when they repent and return to him and obey him (Neh. 1.9; Dan. 9.13). There is in neither passage a

1. The final colon sums up what has been specified in the preceding cola.

direct link between Yahweh's חֶסֶד and his forgiveness. Sakenfeld (1978: 135) regards Neh. 1.9 as restating the basis for חֶסֶד given in Deut. 7.9; and she points out (p. 137) that in Dan. 9.18 the interceder calls on God to act because of his great רַחֲמִים. Do these two intercessory prayers suggest that Yahweh's covenant is, like that of David and Jonathan, a solemn commitment to his people, a commitment that endures even when they fail to love and obey him?

This same expression occurs also in another public confession of sin (Neh. 9.32) in a very abbreviated form, with no mention of those who are the recipients of חֶסֶד. In Solomon's prayer at the dedication of the temple—1 Kgs 8.23 // 2 Chron. 6.14—it is used again, but here the ascription to Yahweh replaces 'those who love him and keep his commands' (used in the original expression) by 'keeping covenant and חֶסֶד with your servants who walk wholeheartedly before you'. Perhaps the narrator introduces the word 'servants', which is used commonly in secular treaties to refer to the vassals, to emphasize the relationship existing between Yahweh, the suzerain, and Israel. Perhaps he is simply anticipating the repeated use of the word with reference to David (8.24-26 // 6.15-17). In any case, the alternatives have the same meaning: those who love Yahweh and those who are his servants are both required to obey his commandments. Moreover, Sakenfeld observes (p. 138) that following his prayer Solomon exhorts his people to live by God's decrees and obey his commands (8.61), thus completing the theme of Deut. 7.9-11; which is evident also in the invocation. In addition, here the infinitive construct לָלֶכֶת serves to link this exhortation with the invocation in v. 23.

Glueck barely mentions the passages noted in this subsection, but he frequently lists these and other passages in footnotes. He uses them (1967: 47) to support his statement that when חֶסֶד and בְּרִית occur together they are not entirely synonymous but are 'mutually contingent upon one another'. They form the basis of his assertion (p. 89) that 'those who love God, serve Him faithfully, keep His commandments and His covenant, and who pray to Him and wholly trust in Him, can confidently expect His חֶסֶד'.

Other passages containing both the element חֶסֶד and the lexeme בְּרִית associate divine חֶסֶד with Yahweh's covenant. In Ps. 25.5-10, חֶסֶד, which occurs three times, is available to those who keep Yahweh's covenant. In Ps. 89.29 God's חֶסֶד appears in parallel with the enduring בְּרִית he has made with David, and Ps. 106.45 states that when his people cry to him in their distress Yahweh remembers his covenant with them and provides relief for them according to the richness of his חֶסֶד.

Isa. 54. 7-10 uses חֶסֶד and בְּרִית in close association. It contains חֶסֶד twice and also three derivatives of the root רחם: רַחֲמִים and two forms of the verb רחם. These verses form the climax to a section in which the restoration of Israel is described in terms of taking again a wife who had been rejected (cf. Sakenfeld 1978: 200). Although it is not specifically stated here, Glueck (1967: 84) asserts that Israel has been 'chastened by expulsion', thus implying that Yahweh's rejection of Israel is prompted by its unfaithfulness—its failure to keep its covenant obligations. Hence, from Yahweh's point of view the covenant is no longer in existence, and yet his great compassion moves him to gather Israel again to himself. This persistence of Yahweh's compassion points again to his deep commitment to his people even when they reject him; it is a commitment that leads him first to punish and then to restore his wayward people, establishing with them his covenant of peace which, like his חֶסֶד, will be more enduring than the mountains and hills.

c. בחר *and* בָּחִיר

In a speech attributed to Moses, Deut. 4.37 contains the sentence 'he loved your fathers and chose their descendants after them', of which the subject is clearly Yahweh (v. 35). Yahweh's love for the ancestors plainly precedes his choosing of their descendants. A similar statement occurs in Deut. 10.15, where חשק is closely associated with אַהֲבָה, emphasizing the special nature of Yahweh's love that leads to his choice, while Deut. 7.7-8 asserts that his love is the reason for Yahweh's choice. This thought appears to lie behind two passages— Ps. 47.5 and Ps. 78.68—where אהב and בחר occur together, and it seems to be present also in the collocation of אוֹהֵב with בחר in Isa. 41.8. אֹהֲבִי, used in apposition with Abraham in this speech attributed to Yahweh, certainly refers to Abraham's love for Yahweh, but it also serves as a reminder of Yahweh's love for, and his choice of, both Abraham and his grandson Jacob.

בָּחִיר occurs with בְּרִית and with a double occurrence of חֶסֶד in Ps. 89.2-4. These verses also contain אֱמוּנָתְךָ, where the suffix refers to Yahweh, in parallel with חֶסֶד each time it occurs; the בְּרִית is specifically that of Yahweh with David, who is described as his בָּחִיר and his servant. The psalmist stresses the אֱמוּנָה that undergirds Yahweh's relationship with David—a relationship in which Yahweh's commitment to David is a prominent feature.

d. *Summary*

Much of the discussion in this section can be summarized by considering Deut. 7.7-13. The lexical items under consideration appear in a significant sequence. In vv. 7-11 אוֹהֵב–חֶסֶד–בְּרִית–אַהֲבָה–בָּחַר–חָשַׁק occur in that order; with all except the last, God is the agent. Yahweh's relationship with Israel commences in his deep, yearning love, a love that longs for a close attachment and expresses itself in a lasting devotion—a love that is anticipated in v. 6 where Israel is Yahweh's precious possession. Such love Yahweh expresses by choosing Israel; and the speaker emphasizes that the choice is not influenced by anything the people themselves contribute; they are not a great or mighty nation, but Yahweh chooses them simply because he loves them. Sakenfeld agrees, for she comments (1978: 134) that God's love and choice—not any special merit on Israel's part—provides the reason why he continues to act in accordance with his covenant. Yahweh goes on loving them, remaining faithful to their ancestors and to the promises he made to them, and leading to the establishment of the covenant relationship between Yahweh and his people—a relationship that places them under the obligation to love him and to obey him. Verses 12-13 reiterate and summarize what has already been said, starting with the obedience of the people to their obligation; if they are faithful to Yahweh, he will be faithful to them and to the covenant; he will go on loving them and expressing that love by fulfilling the promises he made to their ancestors. The relationship that Yahweh establishes and seeks to maintain with his people is founded securely on his love for them—a committed, enduring love. The covenant in which he formulates this relationship expresses his loving commitment to them—a commitment that persists even in the face of their unfaithfulness.

Bowen (1938: 32-34) regards vv. 9 and 12 as 'freely expanded interpretations of the second commandment of the decalogue'. The first 'noteworthy addition to the thought of Exod. 20.5' is Yahweh's love for the faithful (v. 12), which 'is not found elsewhere in the Pentateuch', and Bowen expresses surprise that the Deuteronomist 'stresses Isarel's responsibility to love Yahweh' without giving 'more attention to the thought of its being mutual'. The second addition is the intimate relationship between חֶסֶד and בְּרִית, which the writer makes explicit. Bowen quotes with approval the entire comment on v. 12 by Glueck (1967: 73-74), where he associates this verse, in a footnote, with the group of passages discussed at the beginning of Subsection b above, and he asserts that Yahweh's covenant with the ancestors has חֶסֶד as a consequence. Moreover, חֶסֶד is 'the content of every בְּרִית as well as every covenantal relationship'. In another footnote at the end of the quotation, Glueck adds that no other word or phrase in the Old Testament expresses as definitely as חֶסֶד 'the closest partnership relation between God and his faithful'. However, nowhere does Glueck mention the commitment of Yahweh to his people that underlies both his covenant and his חֶסֶד.

These passages in which חֶסֶד collocates with lexemes in the 'covenant' group point to the underlying relationship between Yahweh and his people, a relationship best described as his deep enduring commitment to them.

B. *The 'Physical Proximity' Group*

Table 5.2 shows the lexemes that collocate with חֶסֶד. The passages in which these lexemes occur will now be considered, taking the lexemes in the order of their appearance in the Table.

| | חֶסֶד | | אהב | | אַהֲבָה | | אוֹהֵב | |
Lexemes	God	Human	God	Human	God	Human	God	Human
חָמְלָה	*1	–	–	–	1	–	–	–
חוס	1	–	–	–	–	–	–	–
נשק	1	–	–	*1	–	–	–	–
נְשִׁיקָה*	–	–	–	*1	–	1	–	1
חשק	1	–	1	–	1	–	–	1
דבק	–	–	–	5	–	1	–	–
דֶּבֶק	–	–	–	–	–	–	–	1
דוד	–	–	–	*1	–	1	–	–

Table 5.2. *The 'Physical Proximity' Group*
The asterisk (*) indicates that the element is repeated in (some of) the passages.

Isa. 63.7-9, the introduction to an extended petition, acknowledges Yahweh's past acts of חֶסֶד before requesting his renewed assistance. The writer regards the people as totally undeserving, drawing attention to their rebelliousness (v. 10) and their hardness of heart, which they consider has been inflicted by Yahweh (v. 17). The hopelessness of his people's condition leads the writer to use several field elements and additional lexemes in the introductory verses—חֶסֶד twice, once in parallel with רַחֲמִים (v. 7); מוֹשִׁיעַ (v. 8) followed by the verb יָשַׁע (v. 9) and חֶמְלָה in series with אַהֲבָה as well as the verb נָאַל; in each case, Yahweh is the agent. He remembers that Yahweh is their father (v. 16), and this is the basis of his appeal on their behalf. Sakenfeld (1978: 207-208) concludes her comment on this passage thus:

> The fact of the particular relationship of the people to Yahweh provides a ground for hope for future salvific acts. The hope that he will continue to recognize the relationship and act from a sense of responsibility for his people is held in tension with the recognition that there can be no claim on him.

She does not specifically mention the covenant here, but this seems to be the 'particular relationship' to which she refers. However, this is another instance in which Yahweh's commitment to his people even in their rebellion provides a sufficient basis for a renewal of his חֶסֶד when they return to him in response to his רַחֲמִים, his אַהֲבָה and his חֶמְלָה. In this passage, חֶמְלָה is closely associated with אַהֲבָה both by being in series and also in relative proximity. Likewise, חֶסֶד is more closely associated with רַחֲמִים—they are in parallel as well as in proximity—than with חֶמְלָה.

Neh. 13.22 records the brief prayer at the end of the section in which Nehemiah describes what he did to restore the proper sabbath observance. It contains the verb חוס alongside the expression רֹב חֶסֶד. חוס is very frequently used with the negative particle—as when the people of Israel are enjoined to apply the full penalties of the law to those who transgress,[1] and when the prophets[2] warn the people of the strict application of Yahweh's sanctions on those who persist in their infidelity to him. It is used once in a purely human situation, without the negative—in 1 Sam. 24.11, when David reveals to Saul that the king placed his life in jeopardy by entering the cave at Engedi. The closest approach to Nehemiah's use, without the negative, is in Joel 2.17, where the priests entreat Yahweh to spare his people; but Nehemiah's entreaty is on his own behalf, and this is the only occasion on which the patient is an individual when the agent is Yahweh.

1. Deut. 13.9; 19.13, 21; 25.12.
2. Especially in Ezek. 5.11; 7.4, 9; 8.18; 9.5, 10; 24.14.

Glueck (1967: 94-95) hints at the mutuality and reciprocity of חֶסֶד, noting that Nehemiah (v. 14) uses the term חֲסָדַי to refer to the pious deeds that have proved his devotion to God, and (v. 22) asks God to 'be gracious to him in accordance with the fullness of his חֶסֶד, as Nehemiah had done'. Glueck concludes that he formulates this prayer, 'Show compassion to me according to the greatness of your חֶסֶד, in such a way that it 'expresses not only the deep religiosity and reverence of Nehemiah toward God, but also the understanding that the covenant, and the corresponding חֶסֶד which God grants to His faithful, emanates ultimately from his mercy'. Nehemiah's 'pious deeds' were indeed associated with the keeping of the covenant; but a more satisfactory explanation of this incident is in terms of Yahweh's commitment to his people—a commitment that enables Yahweh to extend both mercy and חֶסֶד to his people, including Nehemiah.

Ps. 85.11 is the only passage in which נשק occurs in proximity with חֶסֶד; the verb, in the second half of the parallelism, is not closely related to חֶסֶד, which is in the first colon. Each colon contains a compound subject followed by a plural verb; the verse stresses the close relatedness of four attributes of Yahweh—חֶסֶד and אֱמֶת on the one hand, and צֶדֶק and שָׁלוֹם on the other.

These lexemes occur, in purely human situations, in close association with derivatives of the root אהב.

נשק and *נְשִׁיקָה, as well as דּוֹד, all occur with the verb אהב (twice) in Song 1.2-4. דּוֹד is also found with אַהֲבָה in Song 5.8.

*נְשִׁיקָה also occurs with both אַהֲבָה and אוֹהֵב in Prov. 27.5-6. Here 'open rebuke' and 'hidden love' are contrasted in the first verse, and 'the wounds of a friend' and 'the kisses of an enemy' in the following verse.

דָּבֵק collocates with אוֹהֵב in Prov. 18.24. Similarly, the verb דבק collocates in human situations, first with אהב in Gen. 34.3, where both verbs have the same agent—Shechem—and the same patient—Dinah—and then with אַהֲבָה in 1 Kgs 11.2, the agent here being Solomon and the patient(s) being the wives he had taken from the nations with which intermarriage had been forbidden. In each of these passages דבק and each of the אהב derivatives carry overtones of physical attraction rather than physical proximity, and the disapproval of each author is evident.

There are, however, four other passages in which the collocation of

דבק with אהב has the approval of the author because here the patient for both verbs is Yahweh. Blessings that will attend the people of Israel when they obey the command to love Yahweh and to hold fast to him follow the collocations in Deut. 11.22 and Deut. 30.20. In Deut. 13.4-5 and Josh. 22.5 the collocation occurs in an exhortation to obedience. Each time this word-pair collocates, אהב precedes דבק; it seems that the speaker is trying to make sure that his hearers have a better understanding of what it means to 'love Yahweh'. This love is not merely an emotion or an attitude towards Yahweh; it is an emotion that is expressed in activity—an activity which is variously expressed as walking in his ways, keeping his commandments, obeying his voice, serving him wholeheartedly.

C. *The 'Infidelity' Group*

The following table brings out clearly the point previously emphasized—that חֶסֶד never collocates with members of the 'infidelity' group; and it also indicates that the elements, but not the lexemes, are usually repeated when members of this group occur with אהב and אַהֲבָה. Three passages apply these lexemes to Israel, in its faithlessness.

	חֶסֶד		אהב		אַהֲבָה		אוֹהֵב	
Lexemes	God	Human	God	Human	God	Human	God	Human
נאף	–	–	–	*1	*1	*1	–	–
זנה	–	–	–	1	–	–	–	–
זוֹנָה	–	–	–	*2	–	–	–	–
תַזְנוּת	–	–	–	*1	–	–	–	–

Table 5.3. *The 'Infidelity' Group*
The asterisk (*) indicates that the element is repeated in (some of) the passages.

Ezek. 16.35-38 is part of an extensive word of Yahweh to Israel, which is addressed as זוֹנָה (v. 35). תַזְנוּת also occurs in this passage, as does the verb נאף; the verb אהב occurs three times—twice referring to Israel's lovers and once to Israel's attitude to her paramours. An account follows of the punishment that Yahweh is preparing for his wayward people, but this concludes on a note of hope. Although Israel has broken the covenant (בְּרִית, v. 59), Yahweh promises to remember the covenant of earlier days and to establish an everlasting covenant with his people (v. 60). The absence of the word חֶסֶד from this account of Israel's apostasy is not surprising; but there is no mention of Yahweh's compassion or mercy either. His willingness to restore his unfaithful people depends only on their response to his punishment, administered in accordance with his commitment to them, with the sole purpose of bringing them to their senses and causing them to return to him.

Hos. 3.1 contains Yahweh's instruction to the prophet to love an adulteress. Besides אַהֲבָה, with Yahweh as agent and Israel as patient, and the Piel feminine participle of נאף, there are three forms of the verb אהב in this verse. Twice this verb is used of human love, of a man for a woman, and once it is associated with the cultic practices being adopted in Israel's apostasy—their love for the sacred raisin cakes. Here, again, the persistent love of Yahweh for his people is evident—even in their apostasy.

Prov. 29.3 uses אהב in close association with זוֹנָה in a purely human situation, where the son who loves wisdom is contrasted with the companion of prostitutes. This passage does not increase an understanding of the relationships between the lexical items being considered.

D. *Summary*

Contrasts have been noted in the usage of the elements חֶסֶד and אַהֲבָה with the three collocational groups 'covenant', 'physical proximity' and 'infidelity'.

When the covenant is between human partners:

1. the covenant is founded on אַהֲבָה, and the request for חֶסֶד is based on the existing covenant relationship;
2. בְּרִית refers to an agreement between the partners;
3. it is most unlikely that there was a formal document specifying each party's rights and obligations;
4. yet each partner accepted the binding agreement to preserve the welfare and safety of the other.

When Yahweh initiates the covenant:

1. his choice of those with whom he establishes his covenant is based on his אַהֲבָה for them;
2. he expects אַהֲבָה—but never חֶסֶד—from his covenant partners;
3. he is always ready to extend חֶסֶד to his people; even when they are rebellious his punishment is so moderated by his חֶסֶד that it prompts them to return to him.

In both the 'physical proximity' and 'infidelity' groups:

1. the lexemes are more closely associated with the אהב derivatives than with חֶסֶד.

6. *Overview*

Sections 2, 3 and 4 discuss the comparisons between חֶסֶד and other lexical items. The salient features have been drawn together in Table 5.4, which lists four elements and four lexemes that have been mentioned very frequently. Three columns are concerned with the collocations of these lexical items with חֶסֶד; the first gives the symbol for the frequency interval in which the keyword collocates with חֶסֶד; the second column shows how many members of the group to which the keyword belongs collocate with חֶסֶד; and the third column indicates the relative level of the collocation of חֶסֶד with the group. The symbols used in this latter column have the following significance:

+   חֶסֶד collocates with each member of this group in a higher frequency interval than all other keywords;

+ *n* =   *n* items collocate with members of this group in the same frequency interval as חֶסֶד, but חֶסֶד is in a higher interval than all other keywords;

±   חֶסֶד collocates with members of this group in a higher interval than some of the keywords and in a lower interval than other keywords.

The remaining five columns list the number of times the pattern of the keyword resembles that of חֶסֶד, that is, whether the patterns are *identical* (here * indicates that חֶסֶד collocates with all members of the group but the keyword does not), *closest*, *near*, *opposite* or in *contrast*.

ITEM	COLLOCATION			RESEMBLANCE				
	Freq	Mem	Level	Ident	Close	Near	Opp	Cont
רַחֲמִים	5	3/3	+	1*	2	3		
אהב	2	3/3	±		2			2
אֱמוּנָה	5	3/3	+ 4=	1*	1	1		
אֱמֶת	7	3/3	+ 4=	1	3			
טוֹב	6	3/3	+ 1=		1	2		
צַדִּיק	3	3/4	±	1*	2			
צְדָקָה	4	3/4	±			2		
מִשְׁפָּט	4	2/3	±		4		2	1

Table 5.4. *Profile Pattern Comparisons with* חֶסֶד

חֶסֶד has a greater affinity for the elements אֱמוּנָה ,רַחֲמִים and אֱמֶת than for אהב and the affinity of טוֹב for חֶסֶד is greater than that of the other lexemes צַדִּיק, צְדָקָה and מִשְׁפָּט.

1.   אֱמֶת, אֱמוּנָה, רַחֲמִים and טוֹב all collocate with חֶסֶד in the higher frequency intervals; צַדִּיק, צְדָקָה and מִשְׁפָּט are in intervals in the medium range, while אהב is in one of the lower intervals.
2.   The four elements and טוֹב belong to word-groups whose members all collocate with חֶסֶד; but one member of the groups to which צַדִּיק, צְדָקָה and מִשְׁפָּט belong does not collocate with חֶסֶד.

When the collocations of חֶסֶד are compared with those of other keywords with the same word-group,

1.   חֶסֶד is in a higher frequency interval than the other keywords with all the members of the group to which רַחֲמִים belongs;
2.   חֶסֶד is in at least as high an interval as the other keywords with all the members of the groups to which אֱמוּנָה and אֱמֶת, and טוֹב belong;
3.   with the groups to which צַדִּיק, אהב and צְדָקָה, and מִשְׁפָּט belong, חֶסֶד falls in the middle of the range: members of these groups collocate with some keywords in a higher frequency interval than חֶסֶד and in a lower frequency interval than חֶסֶד with other keywords.
4.   With regard to resemblances between their profile patterns and those of חֶסֶד, רַחֲמִים has a total of 6 *like* patterns, אֱמֶת has 4, אֱמוּנָה and טוֹב each have 3; צַדִּיק also has 3 and צְדָקָה 2 *like* patterns; מִשְׁפָּט has 4 *like* and 3 *unlike* patterns; and אהב has 2 *like* and 2 *unlike* patterns.

All of this information can be used—as in fact some has already been used—to describe the formal meaning of חֶסֶד. Can it also be used to compare the extent to which each of the items attracts חֶסֶד to its own semantic areas?

Section 5 has looked more closely at the collocations into which חֶסֶד and the derivatives of אהב enter with members of three different groups. Tables 5.1 and 5.2 have revealed that, when חֶסֶד collocates with the lexemes in the 'covenant' and 'physical proximity' groups, it is almost invariably in a situation where God is the agent. However, when the derivatives of אהב collocate with these lexemes, the agent is more often human; this is also the case with the אהב derivatives in Table 5.3.

Table 5.5 presents statistics similar to those in Tables 5.1 to 5.3 for the derivatives of other roots when they collocate with חֶסֶד. For the field elements, the total number of occurrences in PERDAT with God or a human as agent have been extracted from Table 3.8; these latter figures are not available for the additional lexemes. The figures for נצל have been included with those of the derivatives of ישׁע, which is used here as an abbreviation for the 'salvation' group.

	חֶסֶד		TOTAL	
	God	Human	God	Human
חסד			187	92
חנן	12	2	76	117
רחם	17	2	77	21
אהב	9	–	31	151
אמן	38	11	66	106
גאל	4	1		
טוב	20	7		
ישר	5	–		
ישע	23	1		
צדק	14	4		
שפט	8	6		

Table 5.5. *Usage of Roots with God/Human Agent*

The collocations with חֶסֶד of each of the roots included in Table 5.5 show the same trend as the lexemes in Tables 5.1 and 5.2; most of the collocations occur when חֶסֶד is used with God as agent. The figures in the last two columns place a greater emphasis on this trend, for חסד and רחם are the only roots whose elements are used more frequently with God as agent than with a human agent. As for the elements derived from חנן, אהב and אמן, the greater number of their collocations with חֶסֶד is drawn from the smaller portion of their overall usage, that in which God is agent; for example, the collocations of אמן with חֶסֶד account for more than half the occurrences of this root with God as agent. The number of collocations with חֶסֶד shown in Table 5.5, like those given in Tables 5.1 and 5.2, have been obtained by counting the actual number of times the derivatives occur in these collocations, and they have not been inflated by multiple occurrences of חֶסֶד in any of the passages. It is true that חֶסֶד itself occurs much more frequently when God is agent—183 times—than with a human agent—61 times. It is therefore more likely to collocate with another lexical item when God is agent; but that it does so with all the items considered is hardly due to chance distributions of the items.

One explanation is that the elements and the lexemes selected are biased towards collocation with חֶסֶד when God is agent; but this factor was certainly not a criterion for selecting the lexemes. A more plausible explanation is that there is an affinity between these items and חֶסֶד when it is used with God as agent, an affinity that results in חֶסֶד attracting these items to itself, or these items attracting חֶסֶד to themselves; or, alternatively, the fact that God is agent may produce the attraction between חֶסֶד and the other lexical items.

The outstanding contribution made in this section is the discovery of a more satisfactory basis for the expression of חֶסֶד, which is not to be confined to a bipartisan relationship that depends upon a formal agreement, a בְּרִית, between the two parties. The expression of חֶסֶד is appropriate to, and is often based in, a deep, enduring, persistent commitment of each party to the other. This commitment is characteristic of instances in which חֶסֶד is expressed between two human parties and also when Yahweh expresses his חֶסֶד to his people. Indeed, it appears that such a commitment is an essential factor in Yahweh's renewal of the covenant relationship with his wayward but now repentant people.

Chapter 6

PARALLEL CONSTRUCTIONS

Parallelism is a long-recognized characteristic feature of Hebrew poetry. Attempts had been made to use the metrical principles of classical poetry to account for the poetical cadences of Hebrew, but the studies of Robert Lowth in the eighteenth century showed that Hebrew poetry is based on a parallelism of thought rather than of sound or of rhythm. According to Harrison (1970: 966), Lowth maintained that Hebrew poetry consisted of measured lines and that these individual verses contained two or more components; the thought expressed in the first of these cola was frequently repeated in the second, possibly with some variation. This produced a parallelism of literary units; but, as Barr (1968: 278 with n. 1) points out, it does not follow that the lexical items used in the parallel literary units have the same meaning. Kaddari (1973: 175) asserts that 'Biblical poetry does not necessarily presuppose semantic parallelism', but the parallelism provides a 'peculiarly constructed environment' for its constituent members so that it has 'considerable relevance to the sense' of these members (p. 167). Parallelism must be established without reference to semantic features of its components before valid conclusions can be made about semantic relationships between the lexical items that comprise the literary units. Among other things, both cola must have: 1. a common semantic area (that is, both must deal with the same theme) and 2. an identical syntactic structure. If, after considering the content and the formal and grammatical (non-semantic) features, all components of both cola can be placed in a parallel series—$A_1B_1C_1...// A_2B_2C_2...$—then semantic relationships can be discovered between corresponding components. However, these relationships can only be expressed in very general terms, such as (p. 172) saying that the parallel lexical items share a common semantic field, or their occurrence in parallel emphasizes their common features. Only by making further investigations is it possible 'to establish the inner semantic relation between the parallel pairs, i.e., to disclose the relationship between semantic units belonging to a common field'. Following his careful study of the Psalms and the poetic portions of some of the prophetic literature, Kaddari (1973: 172-73) describes various possible semantic relationships between lexical items that occur in parallel pairs. Parallel semantic units sometimes cover a common area in the semantic field; sometimes the overlap is complete, as in the case of synonyms, or partial, as when one of the parallel portions covers a larger section than the other. Or semantic units cover neighbouring sections of their common semantic field.

Kaddari states the main application of this approach to parallelism (p. 172)—'if we can define precisely one colon on the basis of the regular meaning of the words included in it, problematic and poly-semic constituents of the other can be elucidated by analogy'. However, these insights will be utilized here in attempting to define more precisely the sections of the semantic field covered by חֶסֶד and other lexical items that occur in parallel with it. There are 39 passages to examine; most are in the Psalms, although six come from the prophetic literature. All except six occur with God as the agent. Field elements found most frequently in parallel with חֶסֶד are אֱמוּנָה (8 times), אֱמֶת (5 times) and רַחֲמִים (4 times); these are examined in Section 1. Additional lexemes צְדָקָה (4 times) and יְשׁוּעָה (3 times) that occur in parallel with חֶסֶד are discussed in Section 2.

1. חֶסֶד *in Parallel with Elements*

This section examines passages containing חֶסֶד and another element in parallel applying Kaddari's principles. All occurrences of the same element are grouped together, and passages in which the elements occur in close proximity but not in parallel are also examined in an endeavour to obtain more information about the area that each element occupies in the semantic field.

A. חֶסֶד *in Parallel with* רַחֲמִים
רַחֲמִים is found with חֶסֶד more frequently in contiguity than in parallel. However, in the four cases where these elements are in parallel, they always refer to attributes of God. The relevant passages are Isa. 63.7, Ps. 51.3, Ps. 69.17 and Lam. 3.22.

רַחֲמִים precedes חֶסֶד only in the Isaiah passage, and here—as well as in the verse from Lamentations—the plural of חֶסֶד is used. These points will be discussed later.

Each passage has a *single theme*: Yahweh's goodness to Israel (Isa. 63), a plea for forgiveness (Ps. 51), an urgent request for an answer (Ps. 69), and Yahweh's compassion for his people during their captivity (Lam. 3). Investigating the *syntactic structure* reveals:

The focal semantic units in Isaiah 63 are רַחֲמִים and רֹב חֲסָדִים where רֹב, by drawing attention to the multitude of Yahweh's חֲסָדִים, serves to emphasize חֶסֶד which predominates over רַחֲמִים in the thought of the prophet.[1] Each unit has prefixed כְּ and a pronominal suffix referring to Yahweh, and they are both adverbial modifiers of the verb גמל, which occurs in the first colon only.

The relevant semantic units in Psalm 51 are חֶסֶד and רֹב רַחֲמִים[2] where רֹב again gives emphasis, but this time to רַחֲמִים, which here predominates over חֶסֶד in the psalmist's thought. Again each unit has a prefixed כְּ and a pronominal suffix referring to Yahweh, and each is an adverbial modifier of the verb in its colon.

The focal semantic units in Ps. 69. 17 (the verbless sentence containing חֶסֶד and the expression רֹב רַחֲמִים) and in Lam. 3.22 (חַסְדֵי יהוה and רַחֲמִים) fulfil different functions in their respective cola and do not satisfy Kaddari's criteria. The two passages that do satisfy these criteria—Isa. 63.7 and Ps. 51.3—indicate that חֶסֶד and רַחֲמִים share a common semantic field. Since these elements also occur in contiguity, the parallelism emphasizes their common features and suggests that the units cover a common area in the semantic field. Four passages in which the two elements are contiguous contain a variant of the expression חֶסֶד וְרַחֲמִים; they are Jer. 16.5, Hos. 2.21, Ps. 25.6 and Ps. 103.4. All these passages draw attention to the intimate connection between the two elements but do not provide any means of distinguishing between the semantic areas that each covers.

Other passages besides those mentioned above have one or other of the elements prefixed by what Gesenius (1966: 375-76, §118*s*) refers to as the comparative particle, כְּ. One of the many meanings of this particle is 'according to', although 'in accordance with', which possibly

---

1. The expression כְּרֹב חֲסָדָיו occurs in Ps. 106.45 and Lam. 3.32; in both cases, the consonantal text has the singular form of חֶסֶד but the vocalized text indicates that the plural חֲסָדָיו should be read.

2. This expression occurs only here and in Ps. 69.17; see below.

implies 'as a consequence of', as well as conveying the notion of con-
formity of kind, is an acceptable rendering of the prepositions
'entsprechend' and 'gemass' given under כְּ in KB (1958: 417). It is not
possible to distinguish between רַחֲמִים and רֹב חֶסֶד in Isa. 63.7, where
these words are linked with the great goodness that Yahweh has
granted to his people Israel. The psalmist (Ps. 25.6-7) first links very
closely together the רַחֲמִים and חֶסֶד that have always been characteristic
of Yahweh and then beseeches Yahweh to overlook his youthful sins
and to remember him in accordance with his חֶסֶד. In Ps. 51.3, the
psalmist seeks God's mercy in accordance with his חֶסֶד and, being very
conscious that he has sinned against Yahweh (vv. 5-6), asks that his
transgressions may be blotted out in accordance with his רֹב רַחֲמִים.
In deep distress (Ps. 69.17), but knowing that Yahweh's חֶסֶד is good,
the psalmist beseeches him to turn towards him in accordance with his
רֹב רַחֲמִים. Several times in Ps. 119 the psalmist requests that he may
live—in accordance with Yahweh's חֶסֶד in v. 159, but in accordance
with Yahweh's רַחֲמִים in v. 156 and also in Ps. 119.77. In Neh. 9.27-28
Yahweh delivers rebellious but repentant Israel from its enemies in
accordance with his abundant רַחֲמִים.

The particle בְּ is also prefixed occasionally to these elements in what
appears to be its instrumental use (GKC 1966: 380, §119*o*), representing 'the means or instrument (or even the personal agent), as something *with which* one has associated himself in order to perform an
action'. The two elements (Hos. 2.21-22) form part of a chain of
similar qualities by means of which Yahweh promises to betroth Israel
to himself when she repents and returns to him (vv. 16-19); their
usage here serves to underline the intimate connection between חֶסֶד
and רַחֲמִים without providing any means of distinguishing between
them. There is a distinction between them in Isa. 54.7-8, where רַחֲמִים
is the means by which Yahweh gathers Israel to himself after having
momentarily forsaken her, while חֶסֶד is the means which prompts him
to have compassion on her after momentarily hiding his face from
her. The repetition of 'momentarily' in each of these verses suggests
that the רחם action in the latter verse includes, but is not necessarily
restricted to, the רַחֲמִים of the former verse. Here רַחֲמִים is an expression
of חֶסֶד which may therefore be regarded as the motivating force
behind these examples of Yahweh's רַחֲמִים.

Neh. 9.19 and 9.31 represent רַחֲמִים רַבִּים as instrumental in pre-
venting Yahweh from forsaking his rebellious people; v. 31 adds

emphasis by attributing this to אֵל־חַנּוּן וְרַחוּם. A similar expression in
v. 17, where the speaker quotes from Yahweh's self-revelation (Exod.
34.6-7) affirms that God is ready to forgive and does not forsake his
people even when they rebel against him.

Another clear allusion to Yahweh's revelation of himself to Moses
at Mount Sinai (Ps. 145.8) is followed immediately by the affirmation
that Yahweh is good to all and extends his רַחֲמָיו to כָּל־מַעֲשָׂיו. To what
does this last term refer? It may well apply to every *thing* which he
has made; but in that case this is the only occasion on which any
derivative of the root רחם has a non-personal patient. In the creation
story, the verb עשׂה is used more than once with God as subject; one
such occasion is when he says, 'Let us make man...' So all that he
made includes persons as well as things, and it is reasonable to conclude that the psalmist does not merely include persons but that he
specifically refers to persons. But, whereas v. 8 applies to the people
of Israel, v. 9 is not so restricted—it applies to people of all nations.
There is thus evidence for universal רַחֲמִים and restricted חֶסֶד.

Daniel (Dan. 9.4) addresses Yahweh as the God who extends חֶסֶד to
those who love and obey him, alluding to Exod. 20.5-6 which is
echoed in Deut. 7.9, 12 and also in Ps. 25.10. Daniel later (Dan. 9.9)
asserts that even though Israel has rebelled and disobeyed Yahweh the
people are still experiencing his רַחֲמִים and forgiveness, for the
calamities that he has allowed to befall them have not resulted in their
destruction but are designed to cause them to seek his favour and to
turn from their sins.

Jer. 16.5 ties חֶסֶד and רַחֲמִים closely together. Yahweh has taken away
from Israel his חֶסֶד and רַחֲמִים because they have rejected him; the
result will be their violent expulsion from the land that he had given
them (vv. 10-13). The possibility that Yahweh may take away both his
חֶסֶד and his רַחֲמִים is known also to the psalmist who claims to be
obedient to Yahweh and to have made public proclamation of
Yahweh's חֶסֶד וֶאֱמֶת (Ps. 40. 9-11). He requests Yahweh not to remove
his רַחֲמִים but to continue his חֶסֶד וֶאֱמֶת towards him (Ps. 40.12). Deeply
distressed, the psalmist feels that God has forsaken him, causing him
to query (Ps. 77.9-10) whether Yahweh has cut off both his חֶסֶד and
his רַחֲמִים.

The prophet speaks on behalf of rebellious Israel (Isa. 63.15),
asserting that Yahweh has withheld, temporarily, his רַחֲמִים; but in
Lam. 3.22 the poet, a representative of the people exiled from their

land and separated from their God, claims that Yahweh's רַחֲמִים never comes to an end. Isa. 54.10 records Yahweh's promise that his חֶסֶד shall not be removed from his people whom he has gathered again to himself, and in Ps. 89.34 Yahweh makes a similar promise, this time specifically to David.

Yahweh's רַחֲמִים is thus intimately connected with his חֶסֶד, and there is an almost bewildering complexity in the relationship between these two elements. On the one hand, they are frequently so closely connected that it is difficult to distinguish between them; this evidence supports the hypothesis that the two elements cover the same region in the semantic field. Instances of this intimate relationship between חֶסֶד and רַחֲמִים may be summarized as follows:

1. they are both taken away when rebellious Israel rejects Yahweh (Jer. 16.5);
2. their removal is suspected by one who feels forsaken by God (Ps. 77.9-10);
3. their continuance is requested by one of the faithful (Ps. 40.12);
4. their enduring nature is asserted by the poet (Lam. 3.22).

Further, each element is associated with similar requests: 1. for the preservation of life by the writer of Psalm 119 (חֶסֶד in Ps. 119.159, and רַחֲמִים in Ps. 119.77, 156), 2. for Yahweh to remove from his sight and memory the sins of the psalmist: חֶסֶד in Ps. 25.7, and רַחֲמִים in Ps. 51.3.

On the other hand, there is also evidence that indicates that the regions of the semantic field covered by חֶסֶד and רַחֲמִים do not overlap completely. Ps. 145.8-9 refers to חֶסֶד as an attitude peculiar to the relationship between Yahweh and Israel, while רַחֲמִים is not so restricted but is extended by Yahweh to people of other nations as well as to Israel. Again, in Isa. 54.7-8 רַחֲמִים enables Yahweh to gather faithless Israel to himself, but חֶסֶד enables him to show this compassion. This suggests that חֶסֶד is the basic, the primary, quality that is expressed as רַחֲמִים. Those who distinguish between the application of the singular and the plural forms of חֶסֶד support this idea. Thompson (1963: 312) regards the singular חֶסֶד as referring to 'a permanent attitude of magnanimity and devotion', whereas the plural denotes 'a number of specific acts in which חֶסֶד is displayed'. In passages where חֶסֶד and רַחֲמִים both occur, the singular חֶסֶד normally precedes רַחֲמִים

and the writer implies that חֶסֶד is being shown in certain concrete ways. However, the plural חֲסָדִים follows רַחֲמִים only in Isa. 63.7 and Ps. 25.6 where, Thompson says, 'the חֲסָדִים and the רַחֲמִים were both regarded as specific examples' of חֶסֶד יהוה.[1] The plural חֲסָדִים occurs relatively rarely, always referring to instances, or manifestations, of חֶסֶד; such concrete expressions of חֶסֶד may also be referred to as רַחֲמִים.

Daniel 9 provides further evidence that the semantic regions of חֶסֶד and רַחֲמִים do not completely overlap; here it is stated that חֶסֶד is extended to those who love and obey Yahweh (Dan. 9.4), but that rebellious Israel is still experiencing רַחֲמִים (Dan. 9.9). These statements seem to conflict with Jer. 16.5, which refers to Yahweh's removal of both חֶסֶד and רַחֲמִים from rebellious Israel. This is the only occasion on which Yahweh withholds חֶסֶד, but there are several passages in which he withholds רַחֲמִים from his people—Isa. 63.15 has been noted above, and the verb רחם with negative occurs in Isa. 9.16, 27.11, Jer. 13.14, Hos. 1.6 and Zech. 1.12. Since חֶסֶד is the basic quality expressed as רַחֲמִים, חֶסֶד is not only extended to, but is also experienced by, those who love and obey Yahweh—they have, as it were, an expectation that they will experience Yahweh's חֶסֶד—and those who are rebellious towards Yahweh are unaware that חֶסֶד is also being extended to them. But, because of the רַחֲמִים that is an expression of his חֶסֶד, Yahweh has allowed them to be punished in order to remind them that they have sinned against him and also that he is ready to pardon them and to restore them when they return penitently to him. In this way the insights gained from Isa. 54.7-8, Jer. 16 and Daniel 9 can be reconciled. But the relationship between חֶסֶד and רַחֲמִים is far too complex to be reduced to a simple and uniform pattern. All that can be asserted is that the regions of the semantic field covered by חֶסֶד and רַחֲמִים overlap considerably but do not coincide.

All passages considered above have been concerned with Yahweh's חֶסֶד and רַחֲמִים expressed towards human parties. In Ps. 106.45-46, divine חֶסֶד is contiguous with human רַחֲמִים; it is possible, but by no means certain, that Yahweh's חֶסֶד permits and also produces the רַחֲמִים that their captors feel when Yahweh's people cry to him. Two more passages (Zech. 7.9 and Dan. 1.9) use both terms to refer to the attitude of one

---

1.   Bowen (1938: 109) agrees with this opinion; referring to Isa. 63.7, he says that the plurals 'suggest specific acts rather than a general attitude'. So, too, Dumortier (1972: 178 n. 1), referring to Ps. 89.2.

human party to another. Neither of these passages affords any insight into semantic distinctions between חֶסֶד and רַחֲמִים. Glueck's comment (1967: 62) on the first of these passages draws attention to the closeness of חֶסֶד to רַחֲמִים but he notes that they are distinguished by the obligatory aspect of חֶסֶד that is entirely absent from רַחֲמִים.

However, other passages referring to human רַחֲמִים provide evidence that this is a deeply-seated emotion aroused spontaneously, often when one becomes aware of another's need or distress. Eichrodt (1961: 237-38) describes divine רַחֲמִים as 'a quite spontaneous expression of love, evoked by no kind of obligation', and Morris (1981: 85-86) sees this as an appropriate description of human, as well as divine, רַחֲמִים. In human situations it frequently issues in tangible and practical aid to the needy one, even though there is not necessarily any commitment between the parties. One example is found in Gen. 43.30, when Joseph speaks to his brother Benjamin. Joseph knows beforehand that Benjamin has come with his brothers (v. 16), but he apparently does not anticipate that his emotional reaction, termed רַחֲמִים, will be both so spontaneous and beyond his ability to control. The wider context provides ample evidence of Joseph's commitment to all the members of his family, but there is no evidence of any commitment on the part of the brothers; they are over-awed and full of fear in the presence of this high-ranking foreign official. רַחֲמִים is also the motivation for the extra portions Joseph sends from his table to Benjamin (v. 34).

Again, Neh. 1.11 records a prayer for רַחֲמִים and the following verses (2.1-8) tell how the prayer is answered. As soon as the king perceives the sadness of his cupbearer, his concern is immediately aroused, and without hesitation he authorizes Nehemiah's journey to Jerusalem. Although Nehemiah's commitment to serve the king faithfully is apparent, there is no evidence for the king's commitment to his cupbearer.

To summarize: חֶסֶד and רַחֲמִים are frequently very closely associated, and it is difficult to differentiate between them in many passages. They cover a common region in the semantic field, but their individual regions do not completely overlap, for:

1. רַחֲמִים can be seen as a motivating force that leads to the expression of Yahweh's חֶסֶד (Isa. 54.7-8);
2. חֶסֶד is peculiar to the relationship between Yahweh and Israel, but רַחֲמִים is not so restricted (Ps. 145.8-9);

3. חֶסֶד is experienced by those who fear Yahweh, but רַחֲמִים is extended also to rebellious Israel (Dan. 9.4; 9.9).

These are but a few of the facets of the very complex relationship existing between these two elements. They often collocate with each other and also have similar collocational trends with other lexical items. Also, Yahweh's persistent commitment to Israel[1] can be associated with his רַחֲמִים, which is still operative in his relationship with his people in their apostasy. Even though he is no longer acting in חֶסֶד towards them, he is holding it temporarily in abeyance and will renew it to them when they return to him.

B. חֶסֶד *in Parallel with* אֱמוּנָה

חֶסֶד and אֱמוּנָה occur in parallel eight times in seven passages—Pss. 36.6-7; 88.12; 89.2-3, 34; 92.2-3; 100.5; and Prov. 20.6. In several of the verses from the Psalms the reference is clearly to the חֶסֶד—and also the אֱמוּנָה—of Yahweh, and the context indicates that this is also true in the other passages from the Psalms. The terms occur five times in chiastic parallelism. The passage in Proverbs, however, plainly refers to human חֶסֶד and אֱמוּנָה. It follows, therefore, that while the same terms are used in all these passages, they do not always apply to what Kaddari (1973: 170) calls the same semantic unit, which is not necessarily the same as the lexical unit; this can only be determined by closely inspecting the context in which the lexical unit occurs. The semantic units in the following passages may be defined as 'חֶסֶד + God as agent' and 'אֱמוּנָה + God as agent' in the Psalms, and 'חֶסֶד + human agent' and 'אֱמוּנָה + human agent' in Proverbs.

The *same theme* is expressed in both cola in these passages from the Psalms, where חֶסֶד and אֱמוּנָה appear in parallel. These themes vary from passage to passage. The cola also have in each case an *identical syntactic structure*. This is not immediately apparent in Ps. 89.34, where בֶּאֱמוּנָתִי could be an adverbial modifier. However, such an analysis cannot be reconciled with the rest of the sentence, nor indeed with other sentences in which a form of the expression שֶׁקֶר בְּ occurs.[2] In each of these cases the preposition is associated with the verb rather than with the following noun, rendering the expression as 'to be false to', 'to betray', with the noun as direct object. Thus, in this passage,

---

1. See discussion in Subsection 5A b of Chapter 5.
2. See Lev. 19.11 and Ps. 44.18.

both חֶסֶד and אֱמוּנָה fulfil the same function—as the direct object of the verb.

The two cola of Prov. 20.6 differ in surface structure, since one is a statement and the other is a question. But Kaddari (1973: 171 n. 25) allows legitimate transformations to be included when identifying syntactic structure, citing Active–Passive as an example. Hence the question may be transformed into a statement incorporating the expected answer which is, presumably, 'No one' (in the worst case), or 'Very few' (in the most favourable case). The verse may then be rephrased as: 'Many make the claim X but few in fact are Y', where X includes the expression אִישׁ חֶסֶד and Y includes אִישׁ אֱמוּנִים. Then both cola have the same syntactic structure, and the relationship between the parallel members X and Y includes the following alternatives:

a. X and Y are synonyms, covering the same area in the semantic field;
b. X and Y are related as part to whole, with one covering a larger section than the other in their common area of the semantic field;
c. X and Y cover non-overlapping neighbouring areas in the semantic field.

The most suitable alternative is b, with אִישׁ חֶסֶד as the whole and אִישׁ אֱמוּנִים as the part—indeed, an essential part of the whole; an appropriate paraphrase is: 'A man cannot claim to be אִישׁ חֶסֶד unless he is אִישׁ אֱמוּנִים'.

The validity of this conclusion cannot be tested, since this is the only passage in which the elements collocate in a purely human situation. As noted above, 'חֶסֶד + God as agent' is a different semantic unit from 'חֶסֶד + human agent'; hence it is not possible to validate the argument by referring to the other passages listed. However, the hypothesis that when God is agent אֱמוּנָה is an essential component of חֶסֶד may be examined using the passages from the Psalms listed at the beginning of this section as well as other passages in which the two elements occur in close collocation; for example, חֶסֶד and אֱמוּנָה are contiguous in Ps. 89.50, they are in series in Ps. 89.25, and in these two verses both words refer to attributes of Yahweh.

חֶסֶד and אֱמוּנָה with God as agent appear as parallel members seven times in the passages noted above. The frequency with which they occur together thus points to the close association of these attributes of

Yahweh in the thought of the Hebrew poets and suggests that the
elements חֶסֶד and אֱמוּנָה cover areas that are in close proximity in the
semantic field. However, these passages do not afford any means of
relating these areas to each other. Both elements are used several times
in Psalm 89, and Glueck draws attention to their inter-relatedness; his
comments (1967: 76) include—

1. Yahweh swears by his אֱמוּנָה to show חֶסֶד to David (vv. 50, 25
    and 34);
2. Yahweh commits himself to show חֶסֶד to David and his
    descendants, and this חֶסֶד is one with his אֱמוּנָה (vv. 2, 3, 25,
    34, 50 and 15);
3. Yahweh promises not to withhold his חֶסֶד or break his אֱמוּנָה
    with David's descendants (v. 34).

Verses 2, 3 and 34 of Psalm 89 do not provide any means of distinguishing between the elements, nor does the statement וֶאֱמוּנָתִי וְחַסְדִּי עִמּוֹ
in v. 25, although it confirms that these attributes of Yahweh are
frequently associated closely with each other in the mind of the
psalmist. However, חֶסֶד and אֱמוּנָה both occur also in v. 50 where they
are neither in series nor in parallel according to Kaddari's criteria.
The expression נִשְׁבַּע בְּ is used in two different ways: either to introduce the name of the God who is invoked as a witness and guarantor
of the oath,[1] or to indicate something of value by which the oath is
guaranteed and which will be forfeited if the oath is not kept—thus,
Yahweh in Ps. 89.36 guarantees his oath by his holiness and this verse
may be paraphrased either positively as 'Since I am holy I will keep
my promise' or negatively as 'If I do not keep my promise you may
say that I am not holy'. Similarly, God guarantees his oath by his אֱמוּנָה
in v. 50, paraphrased as 'If I do not keep my promised חֶסֶד for David
you may say that I am not faithful'. In this case, Yahweh's אֱמוּנָה is not
only the guarantee that he will keep his promise; it is also what may
be termed the motivator for the promised חֶסֶד, and as such it is so
intimately related to that חֶסֶד that it may be regarded as a component
part of חֶסֶד יהוה. Thus Ps. 89.50 provides evidence in favour of the
hypothesis that אֱמוּנָה is an essential component of חֶסֶד יהוה; and this may
be part of the reason why these two elements appear in parallel so
frequently in situations where the agent is God.

1. Thus Abimelech requests Abraham to swear by אֱלֹהִים in Gen. 21.23, and
Rahab in Josh. 2.12 asks the spies to swear by יהוה; cf. also Deut. 6.13.

חֶסֶד and אֱמוּנָה are contiguous in other passages in the Psalms. Semantic differences between them cannot be discerned in Ps. 98.3 and Ps. 119.75-76. However, Ps. 33.4-5 associates Yahweh's אֱמוּנָה with all his work, which includes his work of creation (vv. 6-9) as well as his oversight of the affairs of human beings (vv. 10-17)—and this includes people of other nations besides Israel. But the psalmist sees the people of Israel—those who fear Yahweh—as the ones who both desire and experience his חֶסֶד (vv. 18-22). The scope of אֱמוּנָה is here less restricted than that of חֶסֶד, which Yahweh directs towards his own people.

In Ps. 143.1 חֶסֶד and אֱמוּנָה are again closely related, but אֱמוּנָה is more basic, leading on to חֶסֶד—the psalmist says that because he is a God of אֱמוּנָה, therefore Yahweh can be relied upon to extend his חֶסֶד to his servant.

חֶסֶד and רַחֲמִים are enduring attributes of Yahweh in Lam. 3.22, and these qualities are closely related to his אֱמוּנָה in the following verse. For the poet as well as for the psalmist, אֱמוּנָה is more basic and results in Yahweh's expression of his חֶסֶד; also, experiences of Yahweh's חֶסֶד remind the poet of the אֱמוּנָה of Yahweh. This passage emphasizes the very close relationship between Yahweh's חֶסֶד and his אֱמוּנָה but it does not define more precisely the nature of this close relationship.

The intimate connection between חֶסֶד and רַחֲמִים in Hos. 2.21-22 provides no means of distinguishing them. Yahweh desires his faith-less people's return to him (vv. 14-16) and he addresses Israel as his bride. The purpose and effect of the repeated 'I will betroth you to myself' is apparent in BHS, where the clause commences three successive lines. For Yahweh's part, the betrothal will be permanent (v. 21a); חֶסֶד and רַחֲמִים (v. 21b) are among 'the gifts which he intends to bring into the marriage as a kind of purchase price' (Glueck 1967: 83; cf. Eichrodt 1961: 238). But to whom is this price to be paid? David uses the same expression in 2 Sam. 3.14 to introduce the bride price that he paid to Michal's father, Saul; but it cannot be the intention of Yahweh to make such a payment to the father of his own people Israel. However, in Gen. 24.50-53, Abraham's servant gives valuable presents to Rebecca as well as to Laban and to her mother, after it has been agreed that Rebecca will become Isaac's wife. It thus seems more appropriate to regard Yahweh's 'bride price' as his gifts to his bride; he directs them to his people in the expectation that they will direct them towards each other—for, as Glueck rightly points out (1967: 83

n. 105), Israel cannot practise רַחֲמִים towards God.[1] So Hosea (2.21-22)
first emphasizes the permanency of the new relationship between
Yahweh and Israel ('for ever'), then he lists the gifts to the bride that
are also instrumental in establishing this relationship (including חֶסֶד
and רַחֲמִים between human partners), and he finally sums up by stating
that this betrothal is an expression of the אֱמוּנָה of Yahweh. Yahweh
desires that his people should know him; his betrothal and the betrothal
gifts, which are to be exercised on the human level, enable his people
to know him. His gifts to his bride are instrumental in establishing the
new relationship between Yahweh and Israel; thus human חֶסֶד is one of
the factors that contributes to the expression of Yahweh's אֱמוּנָה. But
this אֱמוּנָה undergirds his persistent commitment to his wayward people,
moving him to woo them back to himself and opening the way for
him to express his חֶסֶד—divine חֶסֶד—to them again.

It is frequently difficult to discover features that distinguish between
חֶסֶד and אֱמוּנָה; but the following differentia have been noted:

1. human חֶסֶד in Hos. 2.21-22 is a factor that contributes to the
   expression of Yahweh's אֱמוּנָה, which in turn leads on to his
   expression of his חֶסֶד to his restored people;
2. חֶסֶד is directed towards Yahweh's own people, but אֱמוּנָה is
   extended (like רַחֲמִים) to people of other nations also (Ps.
   33.4-5);
3. when God is agent, אֱמוּנָה is an essential component of חֶסֶד (Ps.
   89.50);
4. אֱמוּנָה is sometimes seen as more basic than חֶסֶד and leads on to
   the expression of Yahweh's חֶסֶד (Ps. 143.1).

Hence the regions covered by these elements in the semantic field
overlap but do not coincide completely. This is in harmony with
previous observations that

1. Yahweh has committed himself to his people and this commitment is dependent on his אֱמוּנָה as well as his רַחֲמִים;
2. אֱמוּנָה and רַחֲמִים have a similar tendency to collocate with חֶסֶד;

---

1. This has been confirmed by analysing the usage of the element רַחֲמִים; and
חֶסֶד is never directed by a human agent towards God. Compare Eichrodt's comment
(1961: 244-45, his emphasis) on this passage, that the prophet envisages 'the
purpose of these gifts as… *the establishment of those godlike features in its inner life*
which befit the character of the covenant people'.

3.   the profile patterns of אֱמוּנָה and רַחֲמִים with other lexical items show similar collocation trends to those of חֶסֶד.

C. חֶסֶד *in Parallel with* אֱמֶת

The elements חֶסֶד and אֱמֶת collocate with each other very often, mostly in contiguity or in the series expression חֶסֶד וֶאֱמֶת. They are in parallel five times, each time with God as agent—once in the prophecy of Micah (7.20) and four times in the Psalms (26.3; 57.11; 108.5; 117.2).

The *same theme* is expressed in both cola in which the parallel elements חֶסֶד and אֱמֶת occur. The *syntactic structure* of the cola also is identical in all cases except Psalm 26, where חֶסֶד is the subject of a verbless sentence but אֱמֶת occurs in an adverbial modifier of the verb in the second colon. Hence four of these passages may be examined to discover semantic relationships between the elements.

Yahweh extends אֱמֶת to Jacob and חֶסֶד to Abraham (Mic. 7.20); but the term 'our fathers' indicates that the writer makes no distinction between Abraham and Jacob; consequently this passage cannot be used as a basis for distinguishing between חֶסֶד and אֱמֶת. Nor is it reasonable to delineate the distinctions between 'the heavens' and 'the clouds' in the parallel passages (Ps. 57.11 and Ps. 108.5) and to use these distinctions to distinguish חֶסֶד from אֱמֶת. Likewise differences between גֶּבֶר and עוֹלָם in Ps. 117.2 do not entail semantic distinctions between חֶסֶד and אֱמֶת. On the other hand, it cannot be concluded that חֶסֶד and אֱמֶת are synonyms; rather, it is necessary to examine other passages in order to discover semantic relations between the elements.

Although חֶסֶד collocates with אֱמֶת more than 50 times, they are in parallel only in these five passages. Over 20 passages contain a form of the series collocation חֶסֶד וֶאֱמֶת, which is examined in Chapter 10. The closely linked elements suggest that these attributes of Yahweh are closely associated in the thought of the writers; hence they will probably not yield any information to distinguish between the semantic areas covered by חֶסֶד and אֱמֶת. This leaves only the instances where the elements occur in contiguity; but these are not very numerous because the figures for contiguous collocations are inflated by examples like those[1] in which חֶסֶד occurs three times and אֱמֶת twice, giving a total of six collocations between the elements.

---

1.   Josh. 2.12-14 and Ps. 25.5-10.

אֱמֶת is contiguous with חֶסֶד in six passages, being used attributively in Josh. 2.12-14, Zech. 7.9 and Ps. 69.14-17. Solomon speaks of David's upright walk before Yahweh (1 Kgs 3.6), claiming that the אֱמֶת of David and the חֶסֶד that Yahweh extends to David are inter-related; but this does not form a basis for conclusions about the divine חֶסֶד and אֱמֶת found in the passages listed at the head of this section. If it is Yahweh who establishes the throne (Isa. 16.5), then divine חֶסֶד and human אֱמֶת are juxtaposed here. Alternatively, the reign is established by the king's חֶסֶד which enables him to judge in אֱמֶת, so that אֱמֶת is an expression, or a manifestation, of the king's חֶסֶד. The semantic units are human חֶסֶד and human אֱמֶת, with אֱמֶת being an essential component of חֶסֶד.

The people recall some of the rebellious acts that marred Israel's relationship with Yahweh. They recognize (Neh. 9.31-33) that God is merciful and keeps his covenant and חֶסֶד, and they acknowledge that he has been just in all that has happened to them; he has acted faithfully, but they have done wrong. Here are juxtaposed חֶסֶד with God as agent and אֱמֶת referring to God's acts. Why is the word אֱמֶת used here? The verb עשׂה is used frequently with חֶסֶד but very rarely with אֱמֶת. Indeed, this is the only place where a form of עשׂה אֱמֶת occurs with God as subject.[1] The leader seems to be thinking of חֶסֶד, yet he substitutes אֱמֶת. A previous study[2] has shown that חֶסֶד יהוה 'issues in well-being...for Israel, Yahweh's covenant people'. Ultimately, the retributive hardships suffered by the people of Israel—with Yahweh's knowledge and permission, and at his instigation—were for their well-being, which is emphasized by the statement that Yahweh did not annihilate his rebellious people. But the hardships were caused by their wicked acts and so they are not attributed to the חֶסֶד of Yahweh; instead Yahweh's אֱמֶת accounts for his just dealings with his people.

This passage confirms that in the semantic field חֶסֶד and אֱמֶת cover areas that are very close together, as elicited from the parallel passages noted above. It also provides a means of distinguishing between them, since not חֶסֶד (which produces human well-being) but אֱמֶת is here associated with the punishment of those who have rebelled against Yahweh. Neh. 9.33 is not an example of parallelism from which semantic conclusions may be drawn. However, in both lines of the metrical display (in BHS) the first component refers to God,

1.   The expression also occurs in Ezek. 18.9, where it applies to human conduct.
2.   See Clark 1976: 189-93.

linking צַדִּיק with אֱמֶת, while the second component refers to the people. The pleonastic אֲנַחְנוּ emphasizes the contrast between God and his people and links his אֱמֶת with their wickedness.

Thus, חֶסֶד and אֱמֶת are very close together in the semantic field. Alternatives for representing the regions occupied by these elements include the possibility that the areas covered by חֶסֶד and אֱמֶת are

a.   neighbouring without any overlap;
b.   adjacent without overlap;
c.   overlapping.

The third alternative, c, best accounts for the facts that have been noted. This is certainly so for these elements when they refer to human attributes, where אֱמֶת has been seen as an essential part of חֶסֶד which is the whole. When the reference is to divine attributes, the two elements are distinguished from each other by the association of אֱמֶת with the punishment and hardship that is designed to result in the well-being associated with חֶסֶד. However, אֱמֶת cannot be considered as lying wholly within the semantic area of חֶסֶד; there is an area common to both elements, and each of them covers a region that it does not share with the other. Features—such as the very strong tendency of אֱמֶת to collocate with חֶסֶד, and the similar trends observed in the profile patterns of אֱמֶת and חֶסֶד—support the suggestion that the semantic regions covered by חֶסֶד and אֱמֶת are very close together. Further, in the commitment of human parties to each other and also of Yahweh to his people, אֱמֶת plays an important role, as do רַחֲמִים and אֱמוּנָה.

2. חֶסֶד *in Parallel with Additional Lexemes*

Each passage has been carefully examined to determine whether it satisfies Kaddari's criteria, but, where there is no special reason for stating the reasons which led to the decision, the passages satisfying the criteria are simply listed.

A. חֶסֶד *in Parallel with* יְשׁוּעָה

חֶסֶד is used with God as agent in 2 Sam. 22.51; Pss. 18.51; 13.6. The song that celebrates David's deliverance from his enemies is recorded in Psalm 18 as well as in 2 Samuel 22. There are many problems in the Hebrew text of the books of Samuel; one such problem occurs in the first word of 2 Sam. 22.51, where the consonantal text differs from that of Ps. 18.51. The Masoretes have taken both passages into account, allowing the two readings to influence each other. The vowels that are more appropriate to one form are, in both cases, applied to the other form where they are less appropriate. Retaining the vocalisation מַגְדִּל in Psalm 18 and inserting the same vowels in מַגְדִּיל in 2 Samuel 22 produces in both places the Hiphil participle,[1] and the identical syntactic structure of the cola is preserved in each verse.

In these passages, חֶסֶד and יְשׁוּעָה share a common semantic field; moreover, they are both experienced by the same person—by the anointed king in David's song and by the psalmist in Ps. 13.6. The words also occur contiguously in Ps. 98.2-3, where the house of Israel experiences Yahweh's חֶסֶד while his יְשׁוּעָה is made known to the nations of the earth. The psalmist repeats, in both verses, that Yahweh's יְשׁוּעָה is being revealed, and he makes it clear that this revelation is not only to Israel. חֶסֶד occurs at the beginning of v. 3, between the two references to Yahweh's יְשׁוּעָה, and it is here joined in series with אֱמוּנָה. There is a close connection between Yahweh's חֶסֶד and his יְשׁוּעָה. Possibly יְשׁוּעָה is here a manifestation of חֶסֶד יהוה—the former but not the latter being evident to the nations, while Israel is in fact experiencing both חֶסֶד and יְשׁוּעָה.[2] A similar thought occurs in Ps. 106.1 and Ps. 118.1 and 29—'Give thanks to Yahweh, for he is good; his חֶסֶד endures for ever'. Both psalms keep Yahweh's חֶסֶד clearly in view as they recall many of his mighty deeds on behalf of his people—including his יְשׁוּעָה in Ps. 106.4 and in Ps. 118.14, 15, 21. The sentence repeated at the beginning and end of Psalm 118, and also the second colon echoed in vv. 2-4, effectively bring Yahweh's חֶסֶד vividly into focus throughout the psalm. Again, this חֶסֶד is expressed, made manifest, in the acts of Yahweh and especially in his יְשׁוּעָה.

Thus חֶסֶד and יְשׁוּעָה share a common semantic field, and many passages in which they are contiguous do not provide any means of distinguishing between the regions they cover. However, in Psalms 98, 106

---

1. Without venturing further into a discussion of textual emendation, it should be noted here that LXX uses the same form of the same participle in both passages.

2. Sakenfeld (1978: 223) comments that in these verses from Pss. 13 and 98 'the nuances of power or ability to deliver and that of deliverance itself are not clearly distinguishable... Either deliverance itself or the power which gives deliverance may here [in Ps. 98.1-3] be understood as the expression of God's faithfulness'. Glueck (1967: 73) also sees יְשׁוּעָה and צְדָקָה as 'acts by which Yahweh shows his חֶסֶד and אֱמוּנָה in history'.

and 118, יְשׁוּעָה is a manifestation of Yahweh's חֶסֶד; and while his people experience and are aware of his חֶסֶד and יְשׁוּעָה, the latter alone is evident to the people of other nations.

B. חֶסֶד *in Parallel with* צְדָקָה

חֶסֶד and צְדָקָה are parallel members in Ps. 36.11 and Ps. 103.17-18. These two passages satisfy Kaddari's criteria for semantic parallelism, and in both the pronominal suffixes refer to Yahweh.

Hos. 10.12 and Ps. 143.11-12 have also been examined, but they do not have the required identical syntactic structure. Much thought was given before including Ps. 103.17-18. One problem is the length of v. 17;[1] but the text in the selected corpus must be dealt with as it stands. The two verses together form a verbless sentence. The subject in the first colon of v. 17 is חֶסֶד יהוה; the predicate contains an objective, 'on those who fear him', naming those who benefit from חֶסֶד and echoing a statement already present in v. 11; between the subject and the predicate is the expression 'from everlasting to everlasting' which will be considered shortly. The second colon consists of subject, his צְדָקָה, and objective, 'children's children'. Verse 18 may be designated as either an adjectival construction that describes the objective more exactly, or as a nominal construction in apposition to the objective; the sense is the same whichever alternative is adopted. But to which objective does v. 18 refer—to that of the second colon, to that of the first colon, or to both? The repeated לְ provides an audible link with 'children's children', and this link is reinforced by the proximity of the verse to the phrase. Without doubt the statement is true—that those who keep his covenant and obey his commandments benefit from Yahweh's צְדָקָה. But there is also a very frequent link between fearing Yahweh and keeping his covenant and/or obeying his commandments.[2] Hence the statement is true, that those who fear Yahweh are expected to obey his commandments and keep his covenant. The psalmist deliberately brings together both those who fear Yahweh and also the succeeding generations, and reminds them of the necessity to obey his laws and keep his covenant in order that they may experience his

---

1.   The syllable count advocated by Freedman (1980: 45) to determine the length of the line shows that this verse contains 25 syllables, whereas most of the other verses in Ps. 103 have between 15 and 21 syllables. Three verses fall outside this range—v. 9 at the lower end, and vv. 10 and 27 at the upper end.

2.   See Deut. 6.2, 24; 10.12-13; 17.19; 31.12; also Jer. 32.40 and Dan. 9.4.

blessings. Thus the effect of v. 18 is to bind together both those who benefit from Yahweh's חֶסֶד and those who experience his צְדָקָה.

The two cola of v. 17 have identical syntactic structure as far as subject and objective are concerned. But what of the first colon with the additional expression 'from everlasting to everlasting'? Possibly the poet's intention was not to restrict its application to the first colon, but to apply it, without repeating it, to both cola. He thus stresses the enduring nature of Yahweh's חֶסֶד and also the enduring nature of his צְדָקָה, and he emphasizes this by using v. 18 to bind both cola together. Hence the two cola in Ps. 103.17 have identical syntactic structure.

In these two passages, then, חֶסֶד and צְדָקָה share a common semantic field. They also occur together in several other passages, including Jer. 9.23 and Ps. 88.12, which confirm the closeness of the lexical items to each other without providing any basis for distinguishing between them. Two other passages use both of the lexical items with the prefix בְּ; but the context is such that this particle cannot be construed as introducing the means or instrument.[1] It rather indicates that the outcome is an expression of the attribute. For example, Ps. 5.8-9 can be paraphrased as 'because you are rich in חֶסֶד, you allow me to come into your house to worship you', and the psalmist then asks, expectantly, that Yahweh will express his צְדָקָה by leading (נחה) him. There are instances where חֶסֶד is substituted for צְדָקָה (v. 9) in this construction with נחה. Abraham's steward (Gen. 24.27) acknowledges that Yahweh has expressed his חֶסֶד וֶאֱמֶת by leading him to his master's kinsfolk. Again, Yahweh's חֶסֶד is expressed by leading Israel out of Egypt (Exod. 15.13). These passages underline the closeness of חֶסֶד to צְדָקָה but do not provide a means of distinguishing semantically between them.

The expressions בְּחַסְדְּךָ and בְּצִדְקָתְךָ are also used in this manner in Ps. 143.1 and Ps. 143.11-12, but there is no basis for arguing that Yahweh's חֶסֶד is distinguished from his צְדָקָה. Again, צְדָקָה (Ps. 98.2-3) is closely associated with יְשׁוּעָה which is a manifestation of חֶסֶד.[2] Yahweh reveals his צְדָקָה to the nations but he expresses his חֶסֶד and his אֱמוּנָה to the people of Israel. Hence both צְדָקָה and יְשׁוּעָה are manifestations of Yahweh's חֶסֶד. However the people of Israel experience Yahweh's חֶסֶד and are made aware of it as they benefit from his

---

1. This has been noted in Section 1A above.
2. See Section 2A above.

צְדָקָה and יְשׁוּעָה, but the surrounding nations are made aware only of the more tangible expression of חֶסֶד יהוה as יְשׁוּעָה and צְדָקָה. This passage appears to conflict with Jer. 9.23, where Yahweh directs his חֶסֶד—and his צְדָקָה—to the inhabitants of the earth; but this conflict is more apparent than real, for the people of Israel are also inhabitants of the earth. Rather, the effect of the two passages is to highlight the richness of the content of חֶסֶד.

חֶסֶד and צְדָקָה also occur contiguously in Ps. 33.5, where the psalmist distinguishes between the nations of the earth (vv. 8-10, 13-17) and the people whom Yahweh has chosen (vv. 12, 18-22). There is again[1] a close link between חֶסֶד and those who fear Yahweh (v. 18). The צְדָקָה which Yahweh loves is seen in people's actions towards one another; it is therefore human צְדָקָה. This is in fact an expression of divine צְדָקָה, since Yahweh is himself the source of justice and therefore the צְדָקָה manifested between humans emanates from the divine צְדָקָה. When people express Yahweh's צְדָקָה towards each other, the earth is filled with Yahweh's חֶסֶד; and thus the psalmist confirms the distinction noted above—that צְדָקָה is a manifestation of חֶסֶד.

חֶסֶד and צְדָקָה also occur in close contiguity in 1 Kgs 3.6 and Ps. 106.1, 3—where the חֶסֶד is divine and the צְדָקָה is human—and Hos. 10.12, where both חֶסֶד and צְדָקָה are human qualities.

This section has been concerned with the חֶסֶד and the צְדָקָה of Yahweh. Ps. 36.11 and Ps. 103.17-18 satisfy Kaddari's criteria for semantic parallelism and support the conclusion that חֶסֶד and צְדָקָה share a common semantic field. Jer. 9.23, Ps. 5.8-9, 88.12-13 and 143.11-12 do not provide evidence for semantic distinctions between חֶסֶד and צְדָקָה. The closeness of the two items in these six passages suggests that they cover a common region in the semantic field. Ps. 98.2-3, however, provides two distinguishing features:

1. Yahweh's חֶסֶד is especially for his chosen people, whereas people of other nations also may experience his צְדָקָה;
2. צְדָקָה is a manifestation of Yahweh's חֶסֶד; this also finds support in Ps. 33.5.

Hence the regions covered by חֶסֶד and צְדָקָה overlap but do not completely coincide.

---

1. See above, on Ps. 103.11, 17.

3. *Overview*

Passages in which חֶסֶד is used in parallel with other elements and lexemes provide sufficient evidence to assert that the region covered by each of these lexical items overlaps but does not coincide completely with the region covered by חֶסֶד. Moreover, some of the items share a feature that distinguishes each of them from חֶסֶד as noted in the following summary.

The relationship between חֶסֶד and רַחֲמִים is very complex—so complex, indeed, that sometimes these elements seem to be interchanged in certain contexts. Yet there are features that distinguish רַחֲמִים from חֶסֶד. The following is not an exhaustive list of differences between the various word-pairs, and these distinctions cannot always be found on every occasion when the words are used together.

1. Several times Yahweh's חֶסֶד is especially directed towards his own chosen people, but רַחֲמִים, as well as אֱמוּנָה, is sometimes also extended to people of other nations.
2. On the other hand, Yahweh's יְשׁוּעָה and his צְדָקָה are sometimes evident to other nations, at the same time as the people of Israel are aware that these are manifestations of Yahweh's חֶסֶד which they are also experiencing.
3. רַחֲמִים and אֱמוּנָה are factors that contribute to Yahweh's expression of חֶסֶד to his people.
4. אֱמוּנָה is an essential component of חֶסֶד in a human situation and also when God is the agent.
5. אֱמֶת also is an essential part of חֶסֶד in relationships between humans.
6. אֱמֶת is on one occasion associated with Yahweh's punishment of Israel, in contrast with חֶסֶד, which results in the people's well-being.

It is significant that the conclusions obtained from the examination of field elements used in parallel with חֶסֶד (Section 1) are in line with those obtained earlier, when considering the collocation profiles of these elements (Section 3B in Chapter 4) and their collocation patterns (Section 4 in Chapter 5). Some additional light has also been thrown on the relationship between the parties involved in an expression of חֶסֶד—a relationship that is described (Section 5 in Chapter 5) as a deep and enduring personal commitment to each other.

Chapter 7

SYNTAGMS—ELEMENTS WITH עשׂה

Previous chapters have been related to the syntagmatic axis, centring on the co-occurrences of various word-pairs that occur together in a restricted neighbourhood. This and the next two chapters investigate other sets of words that also occur together in a near neighbourhood, but these syntagms were selected by noting verbs and prepositions used with חֶסֶד in interpersonal situations. The verb חסד occurs much less frequently than the verb forms of the other roots from which the lexical field has been drawn—only three times[1] in the whole corpus. The members of each syntagm are a verb (e.g. עשׂה) that takes חֶסֶד as its object, and (where it exists) the preposition (e.g. עִם) used to introduce the patient. Further, verb forms related to lexemes that replace חֶסֶד appear occasionally in an interpersonal situation with one of the prepositions already found, for example, יטב עִם. Since this verb performs the same function as the expression עשׂה טוֹב, this and similar cases are also investigated. Even-Shoshan's *New Concordance of the Bible* has greatly simplified the search for appropriate syntagms containing these additional lexemes; its special and unique features include a list of syntagms in which each entry word appears.[2]

עשׂה, used more than 40 times with חֶסֶד, also occurs with some of the additional lexemes. This chapter examines syntagms containing עשׂה and either חֶסֶד or another field element. חֶסֶד syntagms are discussed in Sections 2 to 4, while Section 5 investigates עשׂה syntagms with other elements. Other verbs used with חֶסֶד and with other

---

1. Two of these occurrences are in the parallel passages 2 Sam. 22.26 and Ps. 18.26.

2. This concordance is based primarily on the text of the edition of Koren Publishers, but versions using the Leningrad Codex have also been consulted. It has therefore provided a reliable guide to the text of *BHS* upon which the present study depends.

elements include זכר, נטה, נשׂא, נתן, עזב and שׁמר; these and מצא חֵן בְּעֵינֵי, a commonly occurring syntagm, are investigated in Chapter 8. Chapter 9 examines syntagms with another lexeme replacing חֶסֶד, directing attention to the paradigmatic axis. Examining these syntagms throws light on meaning relations between the lexical items in the paradigm.

1. *The* עשׂה *Syntagms*

A. *Statistics for* עשׂה *Syntagms*

Table 7.1 shows the number of times each syntagm occurs, classifying them according to the nature of the agent—usually the subject of the verb. The relevant lexical items appear in the first three columns; the preposition introduces the patient, the person to whose advantage the action takes place; the nouns, which with the verb complete the statement of the action, are in the column headed OBJECT; יטב itself completely states the action, so no object is required. This chapter is concerned with the passages that contain the verb עשׂה and one or more of the elements. The expression עשׂה חֶסֶד also occurs three times without any preposition, because the patient is not specified. The elements אֱמוּנָה and אֱמֶת appear with עשׂה but no preposition; these passages are considered in Section 5 although they are not shown in Table 7.1.

B. עשׂה *Syntagms Containing Field Elements*

Passages using עשׂה with חֶסֶד and/or another field element are treated in an order that generally follows the arrangement of Table 7.1. Passages having the same agent and patient are grouped together, taking first those in which God is the agent, followed by the ones in which the agent is a leader, a man, and finally a woman. In each group, those with the same patient are also kept together and are taken in the order God, Leader, Man, Woman. There are, however, several occasions where more than one syntagm occurs in the same incident; all syntagms are treated together, when the first one is encountered. For example, in Josh. 2.12-14 the expression עשׂה חֶסֶד עם is used first with a woman as agent, then with man as agent, and עשׂה חֶסֶד וֶאֱמֶת עם also occurs; these are all discussed under the heading Man as agent and the passage is also listed under the other headings as appropriate, with a note referring to the discussion.

Prep.	Verb	Object	God	Leader	Man	Woman	Total
עִם	עשה	חֶסֶד	7	9	9	3	28
		חֶסֶד וֶאֱמֶת	1	1	1	–	3
		טוֹב	1	1	–	–	2
		טוֹבָה	–	1	1	–	2
	יטב	–	3	–	–	–	3
ל	עשה	חֶסֶד	5	1	–	–	6
		טוֹבָה	2	–	–	–	2
		טוֹב בְּעֵינֵי	–	1	3	1	5
		יְשׁוּעָה	1	–	–	–	1
		תְּשׁוּעָה	1	–	–	–	1
		מִשְׁפָּט וּצְדָקָה	–	1	–	–	1
		צְדָקָה וּמִשְׁפָּט	1	–	–	–	1
	יטב	–	14	2	4	–	20
אֵת	עשה	חֶסֶד וֶאֱמֶת	1	–	1	–	2
		חֶסֶד וְרַחֲמִים	–	–	1	–	1
		טוֹבָה	–	1	1	–	2
		צְדָקָה	1	–	–	–	1
	יטב	–	3	–	–	–	3

Table 7.1. *Syntagms: Number of Occurrences of Each Syntagm*
in Each Agent Category

2. עשׂה חֶסֶד עִם

The basic expression עשׂה חֶסֶד עִם is used with God as agent and also
with each type of human agent. Passages in which the expression
עשׂה חֶסֶד וֶאֱמֶת עִם occurs are also mentioned, giving a reference to the
relevant discussion.

A. God as Agent
1 Kgs 3.6 // 2 Chron. 1.8—This verse commences Solomon's prayer
for wisdom when Yahweh appears to him at Gibeon. The Chronicler
gives only a very brief account of this incident, but the essential
details are the same as those recorded in the book of Kings. Sakenfeld
(1978: 145) regards David's upright behaviour as a prior act that is a
basis for Yahweh's חֶסֶד. However, Solomon refers specifically only to
the culmination of Yahweh's חֶסֶד to David, whose son is now
succeeding him in fulfilment of the promise given through Nathan
(2 Sam. 7.12-16). This is evidence of Yahweh's faithfulness, and also
of his commitment to David as well as to his people Israel. David, too,

is committed to serve Yahweh and to walk uprightly before him, even though his record is not unblemished; but when he fails he returns in penitence to Yahweh who forgives and restores him. The repeated גָּדוֹל חֶסֶד[1] embraces the relationship between Yahweh and David throughout the establishment of the kingdom; but it also underlines Yahweh's persistence and patience in his commitment to David, while David's upright walk is evidence of his commitment to Yahweh and is not to be regarded as a factor which induces Yahweh to express his חֶסֶד גָּדוֹל to him. Glueck (1967: 78-79) emphasizes the mutual obligations that arise from a covenantal relationship and mentions the loyalty of David towards Yahweh as well as the loyalty of God towards David. His final comment deals with the attribute גָּדוֹל which Solomon applies to Yahweh's חֶסֶד; this, he says, does not change the obligatoriness which he found to be characteristic of חֶסֶד, but it emphasizes that it is the חֶסֶד of Yahweh which he promised to extend to David. There is, then, a personal and mutual commitment of Yahweh to David and of David to Yahweh which is deep and enduring, and provides the required setting for acts of חֶסֶד; in this instance, the commitment is formalised in a covenant relationship.

Gen. 19.18-20 records Lot's response to the angels who, having brought him and his family out of Sodom, urge them to take refuge in the hills before the city is destroyed. Glueck (1967: 43-44) treats this passage as an example of human חֶסֶד; he acknowledges that Lot's guests are represented as angels but does not regard them as messengers from Yahweh, nor does he mention any connection between this pericope and those which precede (Abraham's intercession with Yahweh on behalf of Sodom, 18.16-33)—and follow (where Yahweh is named as the one who destroys Sodom, 19.24-28). He claims that the reciprocation by Lot's guests of his conduct towards them is called 'great' because they are represented as angels, which means that their חֶסֶד 'is portrayed as grace or mercy'. Sakenfeld (1976: 97-101) argues cogently against Glueck's position and groups this passage with examples of God's חֶסֶד. She insists first that Yahweh is the agent and second that the act of חֶסֶד is the saving of Lot's life both from the attack by the men of Sodom on the previous night and also from the ensuing destruction of Sodom.

---

1. In its second occurrence, חֶסֶד is object of the verb שׁמר; this is noted in Section 1C of Chapter 8.

Sakenfeld finds many points of resemblance between this incident and the return of Jacob to Canaan which she has already discussed.[1] She groups these two passages, which centre on Jacob and on Lot, with others that are concerned with Yahweh's relationship with different individuals in a context of specific aid to the person (1976: 93), and she bases his חֶסֶד on his 'responsible care for that person' (p. 107). 'Yahweh's immediate responsibility for Lot' depends on two factors (p. 100): first, Lot's relationship with Abraham, to whom the promise was made; and second, Lot's righteousness. The city was destroyed because there were not even ten righteous men, but Lot proved himself to be righteous by protecting the messengers from the men of Sodom. In terms of the commitment proposed as the prerequisite for חֶסֶד, Yahweh's commitment to Lot stems from his commitment to Abraham and is a consequence of Abraham's intercession for Sodom; and Lot's commitment to Yahweh is evident in his insistence that the messengers accept his hospitality. It is immaterial whether, or when, Lot realizes that the messengers are from Yahweh, for his treatment of them is in accordance with the neighbourly conduct that is desired by Yahweh.

Gen. 24.12-14 records the prayer of the steward on his arrival at the well outside the city where Abraham's brother lived (v. 15). The agent of חֶסֶד is Yahweh and the patient is Abraham. Glueck (1967: 70-72) finds its basis in the covenant, since he understood Yahweh's חֶסֶד to be the covenantal relationship between him and Abraham. Sakenfeld (1978: 102-104) notes the steward's repeated address to Yahweh as 'God of my master Abraham', which focuses attention on the personal relationship between Yahweh and his covenant partner Abraham, and she asserts that Yahweh assumed responsibility for Abraham when he established that relationship. Thus both these writers allude to Yahweh's commitment to Abraham; and there is at the same time no doubt about Abraham's commitment to Yahweh—indeed, it is this very commitment which has prompted him to send the steward to his relatives. The content of the חֶסֶד is, first, the almost immediate answer to the steward's prayer and, consequently, the provision of a wife for Isaac from Abraham's family, thus maintaining the purity and the continuity of Abraham's line.

1.   See comments on Gen. 32.10-12 in Section 1 of Chapter 9.

Gen. 24.48-49 concludes the steward's account, to the members of
Rebecca's family, of the mission on which Abraham sent him. He tells
them of his prayer by the well, and thus reveals that Yahweh has
chosen Rebecca as Isaac's bride. Without mentioning his appeal for
Yahweh's חֶסֶד for his master, he now awaits their response, aware of
some of the factors that they must consider. That Abraham has moved
to a distant land and that Rebecca must journey there, however, does
not alter the fact that they are near kinsfolk with a continuing commitment to each other's welfare. He uses the expression חֶסֶד וֶאֱמֶת
because he desires that, just as Yahweh has caused him to succeed up
to this point, so his host's reply will enable him to return home with
his mission successfully completed. He has already recognized that
Yahweh's חֶסֶד proves his faithfulness to Abraham; he now requests his
hosts to be faithful to the responsibility placed on them as members of
his master's family, to recognise and accept their moral obligations to
him, and thus to secure the continuity of Abraham's line.

Job 10.12—While complaining about God's dealings with him, Job
remembers that he has received life as well as חֶסֶד from God's hands.
Evidence for Yahweh's commitment to Job and of Job's to Yahweh is
found in the prelude to the book; Yahweh declares that Job is upright,
fears God and shuns evil (Job 1.8; 2.3), and he affirms his confidence
in Job by allowing him to be put to the test. In the epilogue, Yahweh
demonstrates his commitment to Job by accepting his prayer on behalf
of his friends and restoring his fortunes (Job 42.9-10); by so doing he
confirms Job's commitment. The content of Yahweh's חֶסֶד is expressed,
at least in part, in the second colon of Job 10.12—his careful
oversight of Job's spirit.

Ruth 1.8—Naomi, commencing her journey back to Judah, prays for
Ruth and Orpah as she urges them to return to their mothers' homes.
This is one of the few occasions on which one person invokes חֶסֶד יהוה
on behalf of others;[1] moreover, the intended recipients are foreigners,
non-Israelites. It is also one of the very few passages in which there is
both an ostensive and also a functional occurrence of the element חֶסֶד,
indicated first by the particle כַּאֲשֶׁר following חֶסֶד and second by the

1. Other examples are found in Gen. 24.12, 2 Sam. 2.6 and possibly 2 Sam.
15.20.

repetition of עשׂה עם after the particle. The functional occurrence is an example of human חֶסֶד—the treatment accorded by Ruth and Orpah to Naomi and her husband and sons throughout their stay in Moab; it should not be restricted to the commencement of their journey with Naomi, which is, as Sakenfeld (1978: 109) rightly points out, the climax of their חֶסֶד. However, this is not the only time that Naomi is in need—she and her family were in desperate need when they arrived in Moab, and Ruth and Orpah 'freely met their responsibility for her' and for her family in the intervening period.

Naomi commends her daughters-in-law for their commitment to the whole family group that included their husbands while they were alive and now is concentrated on her, the sole surviving member of the migrant family. But what of the commitment that is needed for a favourable answer to Naomi's prayer? What is the commitment of Ruth and Orpah to Yahweh? Orpah turns back after Naomi's second urging (vv. 11-14), leading to the conclusion that she is not prepared to commit herself to Naomi's God. Ruth refuses to return and responds to Naomi's third urging by a clear statement of her commitment to Naomi and to Yahweh, the God of Naomi (vv. 15-18). The remaining chapters of the book detail the outworking to Ruth of Yahweh's חֶסֶד and show the extent of his commitment to the Moabitess; but, since nothing further is known about Orpah, it is idle to speculate on the way in which Yahweh responded to Naomi's prayer as it affected her.

B. *Leader as Agent*
2 Sam. 10.2 // 1 Chron. 19.2—These two passages have minor differences in wording that do not affect the meaning. David, learning of the death of Nahash, the Ammonite king, proposes to extend חֶסֶד to his successor, Hanun. Nahash is a foreigner—a non-Israelite; both writers mention the חֶסֶד he extended to David, although nothing is known about the nature of this חֶסֶד. If, as is highly probable, Nahash from Rabbah of the Ammonites (2 Sam. 17.27) is also this king of the Ammonites,[1] deductions may be made concerning the relationship

---

1. KB (1958: 610) regards them as two different people. However, Bright (1972: 205) and McCarter (1980: 270-74) both speak of Shobi and Hanun as brothers: their father Nahash is therefore 'from Rabbah of the Ammonites' and also 'king of the Ammonites'.

between David and Nahash from the desire of his son Shobi to help
David as he goes into exile at the beginning of Absalom's rebellion.
But such deductions can only be a matter of speculation and conjecture. Both Glueck and Sakenfeld profess complete ignorance of the
background to this incident, but they speculate on its nature and then
build their respective positions on their reconstructions. Glueck
(1967: 50) says that although there was no formal covenant between
David and Nahash their friendship was similar to an alliance, and he
describes them as friends and allies who were both under an obligation to show חֶסֶד to each other. Sakenfeld (1978: 75-77) bases her
extensive discussion largely on the assumption that David and Nahash
had concluded a treaty between equals, and she proceeds to speculate
about the origin of that treaty. It is true that 'the text certainly
suggests a positive relationship between David and Nahash', and this
provides a starting point that is free from conjecture and speculation.
The existence of a formalized agreement between the partners is a
secondary consideration; what is important is a commitment of the
partners to each other. In the context of such a commitment,
Nahash—at a time and in a manner that are both unknown—extends to
David what he recognizes as חֶסֶד; and now, on the death of Nahash,
David sees an opportunity to make an expression, which befits their
commitment to each other, to the son of Nahash. The nature of this
proposed act is also a matter for conjecture; for Hanun rejects David's
overtures to him and shows that he will not reciprocate David's
commitment to his father. And where there is no mutual commitment
there can be no חֶסֶד.

2 Chron. 24. 22—After Jehoiada's death, Joash turned away from
Yahweh (vv. 15-19) and responded to Zechariah's warning by com-
manding his execution (vv. 20-22). The nature of Jehoiada's חֶסֶד is not
specified. It doubtless commenced with the preservation of Joash's
life, when Athaliah destroyed the rest of Judah's royal family, and it
continued over his boyhood while he was being reared and trained in
the priest's home; it certainly includes Jehoiada's part in proclaiming
Joash king and the good influence he had on him (v. 2).[1] Jehoiada had

---

1. Glueck (1967: 51) uses this passage to illustrate the principle he has enunciated on p. 50: 'The loyalty that a subject showed his king had to be reciprocated with
loyalty'. He agrees that 'Jehoiada always had shown his king, Joash, חֶסֶד' and adds
that 'Joash...was also otherwise obligated to Jehoiada', citing the deliverance from

a persistent and enduring commitment to Joash, and the response of the king to the priest's influence shows that he too was committed to Jehoiada—at least during Jehoida's lifetime. חֶסֶד here refers to a wide range of conduct that is beneficial to the recipient; it is always performed in the context of a mutual commitment between the two parties involved.

Gen. 21.22-23—Abimelech's request to Abraham contains an ostensive as well as a functional occurrence of חֶסֶד. In the ostensive use, the agent is Abimelech, king of Gerar, who is here classified as a leader, whereas Abraham, the patient, is classified as a man. The same persons are involved in the functional use, but their roles are reversed so that the agent is a man and the patient a leader. From the earlier episode involving Sarah (Gen. 20), Abimelech learns that God is protecting Abraham and his entourage. Prior to this incident, Abimelech has allowed Abraham to settle in his territory, and afterwards (even though Abraham and Sarah have concealed from him the true nature of their relationship) he invites Abraham to dwell wherever he wishes. This treatment of Abraham is undoubtedly what Abimelech regards as his חֶסֶד. Glueck (1967: 45) treats this episode as an extension, from the personal to the political level, of the obligations of a host towards his guest who is here described as a גֵר. The hospitable reception and protection, as well as the return of Sarah to her husband, are all included in Abimelech's obligations and are therefore part of his חֶסֶד. However, this key passage enables Sakenfeld (1978: 70-75) to pinpoint weaknesses in Glueck's position[1] and to develop her own insights into the nature of חֶסֶד. Nevertheless, she agrees with Glueck that חֶסֶד is correctly applied to behaviour that is appropriate to a covenant relationship, and she sums up the content of the חֶסֶד of the two partners in the statement that Abimelech asks Abraham to refrain from causing him more trouble, just as Abimelech, previously, had not intentionally brought trouble upon Abraham. There is, therefore, general agreement concerning the type of conduct which is here called

---

Athaliah as the source of this obligation—which he appears to exclude from Jehoiada's חֶסֶד. Sakenfeld (1978: 159), on the other hand, seems to restrict Jehoiada's חֶסֶד to 'secretly preserving... and crowning' Joash.

[1] 1. See reference to this passage in Section 1C of Chapter 1.

חֶסֶד; but there is a difference of opinion about the basis for such conduct.

In several cases חֶסֶד has been seen as the conduct of parties committed deeply and personally to each other. Here, too, Abimelech's actions demonstrate a developing commitment to Abraham, seen initially as an awareness of his obligations towards the stranger in his territory but moving on to a deeper relationship that he seeks to perpetuate by inviting Abraham to enter into a similar commitment to his host. Hence, underlying all Abimelech's treatment of Abraham is his commitment to the guest whom he has allowed to reside under his protection—a commitment that is eventually mutual and is made formal and ratified in a בְּרִית in which each partner recognizes and accepts his obligation toward the other (Gen. 21.22-27, 32), a commitment that is mutual and is intended to endure, like that between David and Jonathan.

2 Sam. 9.1, 9.3, 9.7—David intends to fulfil his promise to Jonathan (1 Sam. 20.14-17).[1] In response to his enquiry about surviving descendants of Saul (v. 1), Ziba, one of Saul's household servants, is brought to him. Ziba tells David that Jonathan's son Mephibosheth is still alive (v. 3), and when he is brought to the king, David first allays his fears and then reveals his intentions (v. 7). The expression under consideration changes slightly each time it is put into the mouth of David, but Glueck and Sakenfeld have both allowed these subtle differences to pass almost unnoticed. Sakenfeld (1978: 88-90) says the suggestion that David does not know whether any of Saul's family are still alive is probably a dramatic device. However, it is not surprising that Saul's descendants were not immediately visible to the one who had succeeded Saul. David was, after all, only the second king of Israel, and it was not known whether he would deal with members of Saul's house in the same manner as the kings of the surrounding nations dealt with their rivals. There is no need to turn to secular history to discover what the custom was; there are records of what occurred later.[2] Jehoram put all his brothers to death when he was

1. And, at the same time, he will fulfil his former promise to Saul (1 Sam. 24.21-22).
2. Examples in the northern kingdom are recorded in 1 Kgs 15.27-29; 16.9-11; 2 Kgs 10.6-11. The cases noted in the text took place in the southern kingdom, among the descendants of David.

established on the throne of Judah (2 Chron. 21.1-4). Ahaziah, the son of Jehoram and Athaliah, succeeded his father but his short reign ended when Jehu put him to death. Athaliah then almost succeeded in destroying the whole royal family of the house of Judah and seized the throne (2 Chron. 22; cf. 2 Kgs 11.1-3). These two purges may be traced to the influence of Jezebel (a foreigner, the daughter of Ethbaal king of the Sidonians) upon Athaliah. David's advisors doubtless know of his relationship with and love for Jonathan, so the simple term חֶסֶד (v. 1) signifies clearly to them what his intentions are; but it is essential that he should set the mind of Ziba at rest, for if the servant has any suspicions, he could protect his master by refusing to disclose his whereabouts. David effectively allays Ziba's suspicions by using (v. 3) the modified term חֶסֶד אֱלֹהִים. Glueck (1967: 49) notes briefly and pertinently that this may signify the fact that David is 'ready to show the same inviolable חֶסֶד as does God to those who are near to him'. The king takes great care (v. 7) to allay the fears of Mephibosheth: no longer the simple term חֶסֶד, but again a meaningful and personal modification as he refers to Jonathan, and the immediate statement of what he intends to do for his friend's son, emphasized by the use of the infinitive absolute.

Sakenfeld adopts an ambivalent stance with respect to the content of David's חֶסֶד, referring to the two-fold significance of the phrase 'eating at the king's table'. On the one hand, David takes Mephibosheth under his own protection, thereby thwarting the plans of any who might wish to destroy Saul's descendants. On the other hand, David protects himself by placing Saul's grandson under surveillance. Even if the focus of the narrator is on the former aspect, that does not dispose of the latter alternative, which, containing a not inconsiderable element of the agent's self-interest, can hardly be described as an expression of חֶסֶד, for this is always seen to have as its primary concern the well-being of the patient. חֶסֶד is here expressed in a practical way in the context of a lasting commitment between two persons. The commitment in this case was originally that which stood between David and Jonathan; but now David transfers that commitment from the father to his son, and although Mephibosheth could not realistically do other than welcome David on his return from exile after the defeat of Absalom (2 Sam. 19.24-30), his answer (v. 26) to the king's question, together with his reference (v. 28) to David's gracious act in saving his life and his final comment (v. 30), stands as evidence of his continuing commitment to David.

C. *Man as Agent*

Gen. 21.23 has been included in the previous group of passages, and others—including Gen. 40.14, Judg. 8.35 and 2 Sam. 2.5—that also contain a syntagm with one of the additional lexemes will be considered in Chapter 9.

Josh. 2.12-14—Rahab shelters the two spies sent by Joshua to Jericho and diverts the men charged by the king to find them. She tells the spies that she knows Yahweh has given Jericho into their hands; these verses are the conclusion of this conversation before Rahab sends the men on their way. The three occurrences of the word חֶסֶד are considered together here, even though the first instance strictly belongs to the following subsection since Rahab herself is the agent.

Glueck (1967: 44) and Sakenfeld (1978: 64-70) both agree that the חֶסֶד extended by Rahab consists of all that she does to prevent the spies from falling into the hands of the king of Jericho; they have little to say about the content of the חֶסֶד requested by Rahab since she herself makes the details clear in her request: it is the preservation of the lives of herself and her family. Sakenfeld reconstructs 'a probably more original Hebrew text', omitting the portion of v. 14 that blatantly imposes a condition on one who makes a request for חֶסֶד—even though the spies repeat it in their final instructions to Rahab (vv. 17-20); indeed these are the last words ringing in her ears as the men depart. But are the words 'If you do not divulge this matter' necessarily a condition imposed on Rahab[1] or on her family? The fact that Rahab is a foreigner raises a question about her understanding of the peculiarly Hebrew concept of חֶסֶד: is she intended to be seen as conscious of the rich connotations of the word put into her mouth by the narrator, including the mutual commitment required of the parties involved?

1. The form of the verb is second person masculine plural, although the second feminine singular occurs in other Hebrew MSS. Rahab has just made a request on behalf of all the members of her family, and the plural verb indicates that all of them must keep silence. The singular, used by the spies in v. 20, forbids Rahab to tell even her own family about the mission of the spies; to ensure their preservation all she needs to do is to make sure that they are in the house at the appropriate time.

On another occasion, Syrians—also foreigners—use the word חֶסֶד with, apparently, only a vague idea of its meaning. The account of Ahab's decisive defeat of the Syrians is given in 1 Kgs 20.26-34. Ben-hadad, fearing for his life, takes refuge in the city where his servants convince him that Ahab may be persuaded to spare his life, reminding him that the kings of Israel have a reputation as מַלְכֵי חֶסֶד.[1] The narrator, who clearly disapproves of Ahab's subsequent actions (vv. 35-42), is not concerned with the Syrians' idea of חֶסֶד, but both Glueck (1967: 51-52) and Sakenfeld (1978: 51-54) find in this passage support for their respective treatments.[2] Even if there had been a previous covenant between Ahab and Ben-hadad, the interchanges between the two kings recorded in the earlier portion of 1 Kings 20 refute the idea that they have any commitment with respect to each other's welfare; nor is there such a commitment subsequent to their meeting. The Syrians who used the term were unaware of its true meaning, and it is unwise to interpret Ahab's treatment of Ben-hadad as an example of חֶסֶד—especially as there is no evidence to suggest he knows the basis of Ben-hadad's approach, which is the belief that Ahab may be a מֶלֶךְ חֶסֶד.

Similarly, it must not be assumed that Rahab is aware of the commitment that is the necessary prerequisite for חֶסֶד. She knows that her position is hopeless, and the 'chance' arrival[3] of the spies at her home provides an opportunity from which she has everything to gain and nothing to lose—and isn't this what is obvious to observers when one person extends חֶסֶד to another? So she makes her bargain with the spies: 'I've just saved your lives; you must save mine when you return'. The spies point out that חֶסֶד involves much more than 'one good turn demands another', and they outline the sort of commitment required from each party by the other. She expects them to keep faith with her, and they request her to keep faith with them by refusing to

1. Although חֶסֶד frequently precedes a noun, this is one of the rare occasions where it follows a noun in the construct state. Compare אַנְשֵׁי־חֶסֶד (Isa. 57.1).
2. Glueck (1967: 52; cf. KB 1958: 271) claims that the sackcloth and ropes 'were the signs of their unconditional surrender' but Sakenfeld (1978: 52 n. 55) cannot clearly determine the significance from the various explanations given.
3. It is interesting—but pointless—to speculate whether the spies would have been similarly treated if they had chanced to arrive at a different house; cf. 'all the inhabitants are disheartened/discouraged' (vv. 9, 11).

disclose[1] the arrangements they have made. They clinch the matter by assuring her that she can depend on them, emphasizing the faithfulness that is an essential component of every act of חֶסֶד by using the fuller expression חֶסֶד וֶאֱמֶת.

Judg. 1.24—The first chapter of Judges records some of the 'mopping-up' operations after the death of Joshua as various Israelite tribes captured territory still occupied by the original inhabitants. The brief account of the capture of Bethel by the house of Joseph (vv. 22-26) records the request made by the spies to one of the residents as he comes out of the city—'Show us how to enter the city, and we will extend חֶסֶד to you'. The scanty details do not throw any light on the nature of חֶסֶד, and the temptation to read into it the whole breadth of the concept must be resisted. חֶסֶד is offered as an inducement to render a service, and it is expressed by sparing the lives of the man and his family when the city is taken. The spies commit themselves, and all who attack the city, to the man and his family; they honour this commitment by sparing the lives of this small group of people.

1 Sam. 15.6—Saul was commanded to carry out the sentence of destruction pronounced by Yahweh on the Amalekites when they attacked the people of Israel after their exodus from Egypt (Exod. 17.8-16). The Kenites were living with the Amalekites, and Saul warned them to leave because they had shown חֶסֶד to all Israel during their journey from Egypt. The Kenites and the people of Israel enjoyed a friendly relationship; but the record does not identify the expression of חֶסֶד to which Saul here alludes. These friendly relationships led to a commitment between the two people and the Kenites grasped the opportunity to render helpful service to Israel. Clearly Saul, and apparently the Kenites also, are aware of some assistance given by the Kenites to Israel at some time after their departure from Egypt. Saul calls this assistance חֶסֶד and he now rewards the Kenites for this friendly action of their forefathers.

1 Sam. 20.8, 20.14-15—The first of these verses uses the preposition עַל instead of עִם, and properly belongs to Section 5, but this variant

1.   Glueck does not mention this request, and Sakenfeld deletes it. The necessity for the request is clearly the fact that all who knew what had been arranged would seek refuge in her house as the city faced destruction.

occurs only here. The subject matter of the three verses is not unrelated; they have been discussed earlier.[1] Various attempts have been made to resolve the difficulties involved in the fourfold repetition of וְלֹא in vv. 14-15.[2] Jonathan requests from David חֶסֶד for himself and for his family. He moves abruptly from David's present predicament to the future, implying (v. 13) that David will succeed Saul as king. His assumption of his death is followed almost immediately by his hope for continuing life; this is admittedly awkward, but the awkwardness may be linked to the stress and agitation which Jonathan undoubtedly experiences while talking with his friend. Possibly Jonathan moves the emphasis from himself as an individual in the earlier part of v. 14 to himself as the progenitor of his family at the end of the verse. The following translation takes account of these points, leaving the text unchanged: 'If I myself am not still alive so that you cannot act in חֶסֶד יהוה towards me personally—so that I may not die, do not ever cut off your חֶסֶד from my descendants'. Interchanging the last two clauses makes the change in emphasis more apparent.

2 Sam. 3.8—Abner, the commander of Saul's army, has secured the allegiance of all but the tribe of Judah for Ishbosheth, the son of Saul, and has established him as king in Mahanaim (2 Sam. 2.8-10). During the battles between Saul's followers and David's, Abner strengthens his own position and Ishbosheth accuses him concerning his relationship with Saul's concubine (3.6-7). Abner replies angrily, declaring his intention of establishing David on the throne of both Israel and Judah, and promptly transfers his allegiance to David and persuades the elders of Israel to do the same (vv. 9-21). Abner's angry outburst may indicate that he has no personal ambition to be king, and that his support for Ishbosheth arises from his genuine desire to promote the

---

1. See Subsection 5A a in Chapter 5.
2. Driver (1913: 164) says that the second וְלֹא in this 'difficult passage' 'must be treated as merely resumptive of the first'. His translation brings this out: 'And wilt thou not, if I am still alive..., wilt thou not show toward me the kindness of Yahweh, that I die not'. However, 'most moderns prefer וְלוּ for וְלֹא twice: "And *oh that*, if I am still alive, *oh that thou wouldest*..."' (Italics in original). He points out that resumption of either form 'would be most unusual'. The translations given by Hertzberg (1964: 169) and by McCarter (1980: 336) adopt both the substitution and the resumption.

welfare of Saul's family even though he does not include Ishbosheth among those who are recipients of his חֶסֶד. This, however, does not explain his sudden change of direction. The narrative does not clarify the matter; most likely Israel's defeat by David (2.17) convinces Abner that even with the support of all Israel he is no match for David,[1] so he decides to transfer his allegiance to him.

The deep and enduring commitment characteristic of Abner's service to Saul during his lifetime is not transferred to Saul's sole surviving son. Possibly there has been tension and friction between the new king and the king-maker; Ishbosheth's accusation does not ease the situation but instead brings it to flash-point. Such friction and distrust leaves no room for that commitment which is a prerequisite for an expression of חֶסֶד in many of the cases examined; hence Abner does not mention Ishbosheth among those to whom he is extending חֶסֶד.

D. *Woman as Agent*
Two passages in this category contain the same syntagm with another agent, and have already been considered: Josh. 2.12 with man as agent, and Ruth 1.8 with God as agent.

Gen. 20.13 concludes Abraham's explanation to Abimelech after he returns Sarah to her husband. Abraham and Sarah have collaborated in this deception, for Sarah says, 'He is my brother', and Abraham also says, 'She is my sister' (vv. 2, 5). All the relevant facts are given by Abraham (vv. 11-12): they are husband and wife who have the same father but not the same mother, and they made this arrangement because, as Glueck (1967: 39) points out, Abraham fears that the attractiveness of his wife will lead to his murder.[2] There can be no doubt about Sarah's commitment to Abraham for she complies with his request[3]—she is prepared to do whatever he thinks is necessary to preserve his life. Abraham's commitment to Sarah is more difficult to

---

1. Sakenfeld comes to a similar conclusion, saying (1978: 30), 'It could certainly be disadvantageous [for Abner] to be the most powerful man on the losing side'.

2. A similar incident occurred in Egypt; see Gen. 12.10-20, especially vv. 11-13, where the word חֶסֶד is appropriate but is not used. See also Section 2 of Chapter 9.

3. Although Glueck appears to regard this as a command, Sakenfeld (1978: 27) doubts that it is in fact a 'command or demand on Abraham's part'.

discern. However, Abraham has persisted in caring for his wife even though she is unable to bear the child they both desire; and this affords some evidence of his commitment to her. But they also know that Sarah will bear his son (17.15-21; 18.9-15). Why, then, does Abraham expect Sarah to risk again the treatment she had received in Egypt? Does he think that it cannot happen in Gerar even though he has found no evidence of the fear of God there? Or is he confident that because Yahweh has promised them a son he will protect Sarah? He does this, of course, though not in the way Abraham anticipated. However these questions are answered, Sarah's commitment to her husband is undisputed; his commitment to her is very real even though it is not so apparent.

E. עשׂה חֶסֶד וֶאֱמֶת עִם

Three passages use this syntagm. The expression חֶסֶד וֶאֱמֶת is also discussed in Chapter 10.

2 Sam. 2.5-6–God is the agent; the expression עשׂה טוֹב אֶת is also included in these verses, and both syntagms are considered in Section 3 of Chapter 9.

Gen. 47.29—A leader, Joseph, is the agent; another syntagm also occurs here, and the verse is examined in Section 5B of Chapter 8.

Josh. 2.14—The syntagm is used with a human agent and has already been noted in Section C since עשׂה חֶסֶד עִם also occurs twice.

F. *Summary*

When the expression עשׂה חֶסֶד עִם is used,

1. There is a commitment between the two parties involved. When there is no such commitment (2 Sam. 3.8), the word חֶסֶד is not appropriate.
2. The outcome is beneficial to the patient—preservation of life: Lot (Gen. 19.18-20), Abraham (Gen. 20.13), Rahab (Josh. 2.12-14), the man of Bethel (Judg. 1.24), Joash (2 Chron. 24. 22); perpetuity of Abraham's line (Gen. 24.12-14; 24.48-49).

3. עשׂה חֶסֶד לְ

In five of the six occurrences, including two pairs of parallel passages, God is the agent. The agent is a leader in the other occurrence.

A. *God as Agent*

Exod. 20.5-6 // Deut. 5.9-10—Yahweh forbids his people to make and worship idols. The wording of the closing portion is not identical in the parallel accounts of this commandment, but these minimal differences do not affect the sense. The punishment for those who disobey is stated before the reward; both punishment and reward are stated, without details, in very general terms. The syntagm under consideration is used for the reward; the nature of the חֶסֶד is not specified, but the agent is Yahweh and the preposition introduces the recipients—a large number of those who love and obey Yahweh. The verb form is pointed as a participle,[1] thus underlining the constant availability of Yahweh's חֶסֶד to those who qualify to receive it and suggesting that Yahweh will actively promote the welfare of his obedient people.

2 Sam. 22.50-51 // Ps. 18.50-51—David's song celebrates his deliverance from his enemies, and the passages have been noted earlier[2] where attention is focussed on the parallelism in the second line and on the different spelling and pointing of מגדיל. Another slight variation in the first line interchanges the words יהוה and בַּגּוֹיִם; this, however, does not affect the sense. Here, Yahweh is the agent while the patient includes both David and his descendants; and the participial pointing of the verb is again significant and also important. Its significance is in its emphasis on the continuing, enduring nature of Yahweh's חֶסֶד which has been evident during David's life and is expected to be extended also to his successors. It is important because it brings into sharper focus the growing impression that חֶסֶד is not merely an emotion or an attitude: it is an emotion that leads to an activity directed towards the welfare of the recipient.

Jer. 32.17-18—Jeremiah, at Yahweh's bidding, buys a field in Anathoth even though Jerusalem is at the time besieged by the army of Babylon. Then he prays to the Creator of the heavens and the earth, incorporating a direct quotation from Exod. 20.6, even though the order of rewarding and punishing is reversed so that the verse as a

---

1. See GKC (1966: 356, §116 *a*)—The verbal character of the participle is shown by its being 'in some way connected with an *action* or *activity*'. Further, the active participle (which is present here) 'indicates a person... conceived as being in the continual uninterrupted *exercise* of an activity'. (Italics in original).

2. See Section 2A in Chapter 6.

whole bears a greater resemblance to similar statements in Exod. 34.6-7 and Deut. 7.9-10. This syntagm, again used with God as agent, does not disclose the nature of the patients, although by inference they are those who are obedient to Yahweh. Although this passage does not provide any fresh insights, it confirms what has been stated above.

B. *Leader as Agent*

1 Kgs 2.7—Shortly before his death, David requests Solomon to provide for the sons of Barzillai at his own table. Barzillai's welcome, to which David alludes as an expression of חֶסֶד, is recorded in 2 Sam. 19.31-40, where David invites him to join his court.[1] Barzillai's commitment to David is evident in his provision of food for the king throughout his exile (v. 32); it is also apparent during the flight from Absalom, for Barzillai brings various necessities to David and his men (2 Sam. 17.27-29). David's commitment to Barzillai first finds expression when he seeks to maintain the welfare of his friend; since he will not be able to continue this commitment much longer, he urges Solomon to accept the responsibility.[2] The continuation of חֶסֶד, arising from a commitment to the father, to his son is not new; David himself seeks to do this to Mephibosheth for Jonathan's sake and also to Hanun for Nahash's sake. Now he introduces a new dimension by extending the role of the agent from the father to the son, asking Solomon to continue his (David's) commitment to Barzillai's family.

C. *Summary*

Here again the commitment between the parties involved, and the promotion of the welfare of the patient are evident.

4. עשׂה חֶסֶד . . . אֶת

This syntagm occurs on three occasions, and each time חֶסֶד is in a composite expression with another element. Gen. 32.11, where God is

---

1. See discussion of 2 Sam. 19.38 in Section 4A of Chapter 9.
2. Glueck (1967: 53) says that Barzillai's earlier actions placed David under an obligation, which he did not forget but passed on to Solomon; in fact, 'David ordered... commanded Solomon to act in accordance with חֶסֶד'. Sakenfeld (1978: 60-64) has difficulty in fitting this incident into her schema. She justifies the use of חֶסֶד to describe Solomon's action by the 'admittedly speculative' suggestion that 'there were factions opposed to the Barzillai family' who were exerting 'pressures on him [Solomon] to remove the sons of Barzillai from royal patronage'.

the agent, and Gen. 24.49, with a man as the agent, both have the compound expression חֶסֶד וֶאֱמֶת. In the former passage, considered in Section 1 of Chapter 9, the syntagm יטב עִם also appears. The latter verse is treated in Section 2A above with other syntagms appearing in the pericope. The third passage also has a man as the agent.

Zech. 7.9-10—Conduct towards one's fellows is closely linked with true worship of Yahweh.[1] The human agent and patient are specified only as אִישׁ אֶת־אָחִיו. This is one of the few occasions when the two elements חֶסֶד and רַחֲמִים are joined syndetically.[2] רַחֲמִים is not found elsewhere as the object of עשׂה and may be attracted into this syntagm by the conjunction of the two elements. The content of חֶסֶד or רַחֲמִים is not defined more precisely than in the following injunction not to oppress widows, orphans, aliens or the poor. The close linkage of the elements obscures the differences between them—whatever may be said of one may equally well be said of the other. Glueck frequently emphasizes the distinction between חֶסֶד and רַחֲמִים; his brief comment on this passage (1967: 62) draws attention to the closeness of חֶסֶד to רַחֲמִים, but he asserts that חֶסֶד 'embodies the idea of obligation' while רַחֲמִים does not. Bowen (1938: 133) disagrees with Glueck on this point, saying that רַחֲמִים sometimes expresses an obligation and that it is here, with חֶסֶד, also an expression of brotherliness.[3] Glueck also states (p. 102) in his summary of the chapter dealing with חֶסֶד as divine conduct: 'The characteristic of loyalty which belongs to the concept of חֶסֶד is alien to the concept of רַחֲמִים'. Although he often refers to loyalty in connection with חֶסֶד, he does not perceive that—in the form of commitment—it is not essential when רַחֲמִים is being expressed,[4] but it is indispensable to the expression of חֶסֶד. This loyalty may arise from a covenant, which figures largely in Glueck's study; it may give rise to a covenant, or it may be quite independent of any covenant relationship. But neither a personal loyalty nor, as Glueck rightly recognizes, a covenant relationship precludes a person from extending

---

1.   Compare Isa. 58.1-12.
2.   The other occurrences are in Jer. 16.5; Hos. 2.21; Ps. 103.4; Dan. 1.9. In both Isa. 63.7 and Ps. 25.6 a plural form of חֶסֶד occurs with רַחֲמִים.
3.   Bowen (1938: 110) makes the same statement in his discussion of Isa. 63.7, where he nevertheless agrees with Glueck's assertion that חֶסֶד and רַחֲמִים 'are closely related'.
4.   See also the discussion at the end of Section 1A of Chapter 6.

חֶסֶד to another and at the same time acting compassionately—in
רַחֲמִים—towards him or her.

5. *Sundry* עשׂה *Syntagms*

A few other passages use עשׂה with a field element, but in most cases
there is no preposition in the syntagm. 1 Sam. 20.8 contains the only
example of חֶסֶד with עשׂה and עַל; it has been considered in Section 2C
above. In 2 Chron. 31.20 the verb is followed by לִפְנֵי (replacing the
more usual בְּעֵינֵי) after a string of three substantives; one is the element
אֱמֶת while the others are additional lexemes.[1]

Three occurrences of עשׂה חֶסֶד without a preposition, and passages in
which another field element is used in a similar construction, will now
be investigated.

A. *God as Agent*

Jer. 9.22-23—Yahweh declares that he practises מִשְׁפָּט, חֶסֶד and צְדָקָה;
hence he is the agent and the patients are human. He contrasts those
who know him in this way with those who trust in wisdom, strength
and wealth, which do not bring security. Opinions differ about the
significance of the last clause, 'in these I delight', which may mean
that Yahweh not only acts, but he also delights in acting, in the
manner he has just described; that is, אֵלֶּה looks back to and encom-
passes חֶסֶד מִשְׁפָּט וּצְדָקָה. It may also mean that those who know him must
obey him by doing those things which delight him; in other words, אֵלֶּה
refers not to things but to persons: those who show they know
Yahweh as an ethical God (cf. Bowen 1938: 112). In its context,[2] both
interpretations are possible; for the God who desires his people to
return to him desires also to see them behaving in accordance with a
commitment to each other that results in the well-being of their
fellows.[3]

---

1. See Section 4C in Chapter 9.
2. Judah's stubborn rebellion (vv. 12-13), reflected in the conduct of the people
to each other, provides evidence that they do not know Yahweh (vv. 2-5) and precedes the threat of punishment designed to bring them in repentance back to Yahweh.
3. This view is adopted by both Bowen (1938: 112—'knowledge of God
involves not only an acquaintance with the ethical character of Yahweh but also
the practice of these qualities on the part of his followers... [These] are qualities
mutually expressed by Yahweh and his followers') and Glueck (1967: 88—'The

B. *Man as Agent*

Ps. 109.16—The psalmist reacts, in moral indignation, against one who attacked him unjustly and also neglected his moral obligation to show special concern for the weak and needy. His oppressor is withholding חֶסֶד from those around him. In this human interpersonal situation, the content of חֶסֶד includes actions that promote the well-being of one's neighbours. The psalmist also expresses (v. 12) the wish that none will extend—in the sense of draw out or prolong[1]—חֶסֶד to him.

Neh. 13.14—Nehemiah recounts his reforms involving purification and maintenance of the temple, sabbath observance and marriage to foreigners. He concludes each portion of his account with a petition for Yahweh to remember him for what he has done (vv. 14, 22, 31); the term חֶסֶד occurs in his first two requests, but it has a human agent—Nehemiah—only in this verse.[2] The consonantal text of v. 14 is ambiguous, but חסדי is pointed as a plural in the Masoretic text. Hence this is an example of חֲסָדִים applied to acts by which a person demonstrates zeal for Yahweh's temple. Two more examples occur in 2 Chronicles; the persons involved are kings and have therefore been classed as leaders—Hezekiah (2 Chron. 32.32) and Josiah (2 Chron. 35.26). While these passages do not contain the verb עשה, they should be considered alongside this passage—for they appear in a similar context that relates to the temple and its worship; and also the agent is clearly identified in each case, but there is some uncertainty about the identity of the patient, who has accordingly been classed as unspecified. Both Glueck and Sakenfeld assume, without discussion, that the patient is Yahweh.

The term חֶסֶד is never applied to the activities of those who built the tabernacle or the temple, nor to the ministrations of the priests in the services of the temple. Why, then, is it used for the activities of these two kings and this governor? It must first be decided who benefiit from the actions. Hezekiah, Josiah and Nehemiah all restored the

---

acceptance of Yahweh is to be understood here in a two-fold sense: one acknowledges Yahweh in his being and actions, and recognizes that the acceptance of Yahweh compels the exercise of חֶסֶד מִשְׁפָּט וּצְדָקָה by people toward one another and toward God').

1.   The verb is מָשַׁך, which is used with חֶסֶד as object also in Ps. 36.11 and Jer. 31.3; in both cases the agent is Yahweh.

2.   For comments on Neh. 13.22, see Section 5B of Chapter 5.

temple in response to Yahweh's desire that his people should be able
to worship him there—which they were unable to do before the
restoration occurred. But the temple, like the tabernacle before it,
came into existence in response to the command of Yahweh.[1] חֶסֶד,
however, is not used of such actions; and this may well be the reason
for its absence from the activities of the builders and the priests. The
temple restorations make it possible for the people to worship Yahweh
again in the place he had appointed and in the manner he had decreed;
the immediate beneficiaries are the people themselves. Only by
availing themselves of the restored facilities and services can they
please Yahweh—in obedience to his command, not as an act of חֶסֶד.
The חֶסֶד of each of these leaders, then, is not directed to Yahweh as
patient; since it is for the benefit of the people themselves, they are the
patients and these are examples of human חֶסֶד. A new dimension may
be discerned in this usage, since a large number of people benefit
from the action of a single individual—the חֶסֶד of the leader affects the
people at large rather than another individual. Further, the
commitment of the leader is primarily to Yahweh himself, as is also
the commitment of the people; but this does not preclude the mutual
commitment of leader and people to each other.

Only Nehemiah's first reform is described as חֲסָדִים (Neh. 13.14)—
possibly, but not necessarily, because his specific acts relate to the
temple and its use. This appears to be an exceptional use of חֶסֶד
because it is directed by a human to the temple—which is non-
personal. The preposition בְּ is, however, never used to introduce the
patient to whom חֶסֶד is directed, and there is no reason to assume that
this is its function here; rather it defines the sphere in which
Nehemiah's חֲסָדִים operate. Yahweh and his worship benefit from the
acts which Nehemiah describes as חֲסָדִים—ejecting Tobiah, cleansing
the chambers in the temple court, bringing the tithes into the store-
houses and arranging for the distribution to the Levites so that they
can resume the duties assigned to them; but the Levites and indeed the
people as a whole also benefit from these actions, since they are again
able to worship Yahweh as he desires. Nehemiah's actions may not be
directed towards any of those named as beneficiaries; they are,
nevertheless, the patients.

---

1.   See Deut. 12.5-7. The command is often prominent also in the following
chapters.

C. *Miscellanea*

In a few passages, another field element is closely associated with the verb עשׂה.

אֱמֶת occurs twice as the object of עשׂה.

Neh. 9.33 contains the expression אֱמֶת עָשִׂיתָ, where the agent is Yahweh, the subject of the verb. This passage has been discussed in Section 1 C of Chapter 6.

Ezek. 18.9 includes לַעֲשׂוֹת אֱמֶת among the regular practices of a man who is righteous. Such acts are directed towards his fellows, so both agent and patient are human.

אֱמוּנָה is the object of עשׂה in one passage.

Prov. 12.22 contrasts עֹשֵׂי אֱמוּנָה with lying lips, in a context of interpersonal conduct; the agent is human and so, presumably, is the patient who is not specifically mentioned. The contrast in v. 17 is again between אֱמוּנָה and שֶׁקֶר; truth and falsehood are juxtaposed in both verses.[1]

Each of these elements also occurs with a prefixed בְּ in association with עשׂה. The prefix is used instrumentally, giving the element an adverbial function; consequently these expressions differ radically from those already considered.

עשׂה בֶּאֱמֶת is used in Judg. 9.16, 19, where both agent and patient are human. An additional lexeme also occurs (v. 16) in one of the עשׂה syntagms; these verses are discussed in Section 1 of Chapter 9.

עשׂה בֶּאֱמוּנָה occurs twice in similar circumstances, in 2 Kgs 12.16 and 22.7. The subject of the verb each time is the workmen who are repairing the temple; the verb is used intransitively, so there is no patient.

These passages which use other field elements with the verb עשׂה have little in common with those in which חֶסֶד is closely associated with this verb. They do not afford any fresh insights into the relations between חֶסֶד and the other elements, nor do they elucidate the more common syntagm in which חֶסֶד is the object of עשׂה.

---

1. Compare also אֱמֶת // שֶׁקֶר in v. 19.

6. *Overview*

Passages which contain עשׂה חֶסֶד syntagms reveal:

The parties involved have, with very few exceptions, a commitment to each other; and this is true when both agent and patient are human as well as when Yahweh is the agent. Exceptions include Abner and Ishbosheth (2 Sam. 3.8), and Rahab and the spies (Josh. 2.12-14). Orpah's commitment to Yahweh is doubtful (Ruth 1.8), but nothing is known of her life in Moab after Naomi and Ruth return to Bethlehem. Yahweh's commitment to Lot depends on the fact that he is Abraham's relative rather than on his personal relationship with Yahweh (Gen. 19.18-20).

The content of חֶסֶד is frequently expressed clearly in the narrative and demonstrates that חֶסֶד is not just a sentiment or an emotional reaction to a set of circumstances; it is a practical activity which is beneficial to the patient. Often in interpersonal situations the action has the aim of preserving life—as in the cases of Sarah and Abraham (Gen. 20.13), the spies and Rahab's family (Josh. 2.12-14), the spies and the man of Bethel (Judg. 1.24), and Jehoiada and Joash (2 Chron. 24.22). It is expressed by caring for those in need (Zech. 7.9-10), or in making provision for others—as David did for Jonathan's son (2 Sam. 9.7) and for the sons of Barzillai (1 Kgs 2.7). For Abraham and Abimelech it involves promoting and preserving the welfare of each other (Gen. 21.12-13). When Yahweh is the agent, the outcome is also practical—the preservation of Lot's life (Gen. 19.18-20), the provision of a wife for Isaac (Gen. 24.12-14) and of a husband for Ruth (Ruth 1.8), and the fulfilment of his promise to establish David's son as king in succession to him (1 Kgs 3.6).

When other elements occur with חֶסֶד in these syntagms, it is rarely possible to draw lines of demarcation between them; but when elements, without חֶסֶד, appear with the verb עשׂה there is still an emphasis on the activity which, however, does not retain the characteristic features associated with חֶסֶד.

עשׂה חֶסֶד is the basis of a set of syntagms that are particularly appropriate, since they focus attention on the practical nature of חֶסֶד. To do, to show, to practise חֶסֶד are all suitable translations for these syntagms, as is also to express חֶסֶד—provided that the expression is not confined to mere words: it is the deed that is important.

Chapter 8

SYNTAGMS—ELEMENTS WITH OTHER VERBS

חֶסֶד is frequently the object of עשׂה. Verbs whose object is occasionally חֶסֶד are שׁמר, זכר, עזב and נתן. Passages containing the same verb are grouped together: שׁמר is discussed in Section 1, זכר in Section 2, עזב in Section 3 and נתן in Section 4. Section 5 examines another fairly common syntagm which contains חֵן but never חֶסֶד.

1. The שׁמר Syntagms

The verb שׁמר covers a wide semantic range, just like its frequent translation—the English verb 'keep'. It also takes a variety of subjects (those who keep...) and objects (that which is kept); the subject and object together frequently restrict the verb to a limited portion of its semantic range. Lexical items in the semantic area of 'commands', which are often found as the object of שׁמר—מִצְוָה (64 times), חֹק (35 times) and מִשְׁפָּט (13 times)[1]—also occur frequently as objects of the verb עשׂה. When שׁמר takes these and similar objects, its subject is *always* a human, and there is often an addendum that frequently uses the verb עשׂה and stresses the need for people to obey these 'commands'. The 'commands' are those of Yahweh, and it is significant that Yahweh is *never* the subject of שׁמר—or of עשׂה—in these collocations.

בְּרִית, an additional lexeme belonging to the 'commands' semantic area, occurs 16 times as the object of שׁמר; nine times it is alone, and another seven times it is closely linked in series with חֶסֶד. All occurrences of בְּרִית and/or חֶסֶד with שׁמר are examined in this section rather than deferring the בְּרִית passages to the next chapter. Section A

---

1. These figures have been obtained from the passages Even-Shoshan (1983) lists under collocations. However, these lists are not always complete; in the entry under מִשְׁפָּט (p. 723), שׁמר is shown as its collocate only three times, but in the entry under שׁמר (p. 1182) there are 13 passages in which מִשְׁפָּט or its plural collocates with the verb. These plural forms are not shown as collocates on p. 723.

investigates the passages where שׁמר בְּרִית is found. The longer expression שׁמר הַבְּרִית וְהַחֶסֶד is the subject of Section B, while the passages using שׁמר and חֶסֶד are examined in Section C where the use of נצר (a synonym of שׁמר) with חֶסֶד is also noted. Section D looks at other elements occurring as objects of שׁמר.

A. שׁמר בְּרִית

Nine passages contain שׁמר and בְּרִית but not חֶסֶד; only one refers to a human covenant: that which the king of Babylon made with a member of the royal family whom he had brought back to Babylon (Ezek. 17.12-13). In the other passages, the covenant is always Yahweh's. The subject of the verb is, in all nine passages, human—never God. Most of these passages contain an addendum that includes one of the 'command' words.

1. Gen. 17.9-10—God impresses on Abraham the necessity for him and his descendants to keep the covenant of which circumcision is the sign.
2. Exod. 19.5 expresses Yahweh's desire to make Israel his precious possession, on condition that they obey his voice and keep his covenant.
3. Ps. 103.18—Yahweh's חֶסֶד endures for those who keep his covenant and obey (עשׂה) his instructions.
4. Ps. 132.12—Yahweh promises to establish the dynasty, provided David's descendants keep his covenant and his statutes.

The next three passages differ slightly from the preceding ones; in the first two the negative particle precedes the verb.

1. 1 Kgs 11.11—Yahweh rebukes Solomon for not keeping his covenant and decrees; consequently the kingdom will be taken from his son.
2. Ps. 78.10—The people of Ephraim did not keep God's covenant and they refused to live in accordance with his law.
3. Deut. 29.8—The verb here takes as object the words of the covenant: the covenant stipulations[1] that Moses, at Yahweh's command, urges the people to keep and to obey (עשׂה).

---

1. See also Exod. 34.28, where the phrase applies specifically to the ten commandments.

B. שֹׁמֵר הַבְּרִית וְהַחֶסֶד לְ

Seven passages contain a form of the expression 'keeping the covenant
and חֶסֶד to', with Yahweh either the subject of the verb, or the antecedent to whom the participle relates. The covenant is Yahweh's, and
he is the agent of חֶסֶד. Those to whom, or for whose benefit, Yahweh
keeps his covenant are always—except in one passage where they are
not named—introduced by the preposition לְ, and they are also the
patients, the beneficiaries, of Yahweh's חֶסֶד. Five times an adaptation
of the expression in Deut. 7.9 is used in the invocation of a prayer
addressed to Yahweh—at the dedication of Solomon's temple (1 Kgs
8.23 // 2 Chron. 6.14) and in prayers of confession (Dan. 9.4; Neh.
1.5; 9.32). In the dedicatory prayer the patients are Yahweh's servants
who continue wholeheartedly before him, but Daniel 9 and Nehemiah
1 retain the original—those who love Yahweh and keep his commands. Three passages repeat the verb שׁמר, once with Yahweh as
subject and once with a human subject.

Deut. 7.12 repeats the statement of v. 7 with a different emphasis.
Keeping and obeying (עשׂה) Yahweh's laws is either a reason for or a
condition on the following assertion that Yahweh will keep his
covenant and חֶסֶד with them. NIV uniformly treats this latter phrase as
hendiadys,[1] translating it as 'covenant of love'. Yahweh's חֶסֶד is not
expressed in his destruction of those who hate him (v. 10), but rather
in the blessings (vv. 13-16) he desires to lavish on his faithful people.
Punishment has its rightful place, seen more clearly in Nehemiah 9,
where its purpose is to bring his rebellious people to their senses and
so to induce them to confess their sins (vv. 16-37) and return to him,
seeking his forgiveness. Neh. 9.17, Neh. 9.31 echo Exod. 34.6-7
emphasizing the brevity of the punishment in contrast to the lasting
blessing, the limitation of the anger in contrast to the abundance of the
חֶסֶד and the richness of the רַחֲמִים. A similar pattern emerges from the
prayer in Daniel 9—confession of sin (vv.5-6, 9b-11, 15) and seeking
forgiveness (vv. 9, 19) in order to avert the wrath of Yahweh (vv. 16,
19); again with emphasis on Yahweh's רַחֲמִים (vv. 9, 18). Far from
being a consequence, and the content, of a covenant (Glueck 1967:
73), חֶסֶד underlies and undergirds Yahweh's covenant; it endures,
though it is not expressed, even when the covenant is broken.

---

1.   This figure of speech is treated in Chapter 10.

Punishment, even destruction, is still there—for those who persist in
their rebellion against Yahweh; his commitment to his people is still
there also, strong and unwavering, and his abundant חֶסֶד with his rich
רַחֲמִים enable him to moderate the punishment and thus induce and
encourage his wayward people to return. He receives them when they
repent, renewing the covenant with them so that they again experience
his חֶסֶד.

C. נצר/שמר חֶסֶד

Three passages use שמר, and two use נצר, with חֶסֶד but without בְּרִית.

1 Kgs 3.6 has been discussed in Section 2A of Chapter 7. Sakenfeld
(1978: 145), noting the absence of the word בְּרִית, follows up her
earlier comment (p. 134, referring to Deut. 7.9-10) that the verb שמר
is less appropriate for חֶסֶד than it is for בְּרִית. On the contrary, the verb
is most appropriate in this context, where Yahweh is the subject of the
verb as well as the agent of the חֶסֶד whose patient is introduced by לְ.

First, שמר בְּרִית never occurs when Yahweh is the subject; it always
has a human subject who is keeping Yahweh's covenant, and it is
never followed by לְ since there is no patient involved. Hence the presence of בְּרִית is neither appropriate nor relevant.

Secondly, the appropriate verb is presumably עשה, which already
occurs here in the syntagm עשה חֶסֶד עִם, which relates to Yahweh's
dealings with David during his lifetime, that is, in the past.

Thirdly, the time-frame for שמר is the present—brought into sharp
focus by 'this day'—after the death of David (cf. 2.10), and the
speaker uses a different verb to draw attention to the fact that Yahweh
continues to treat David's son in the same way as he had treated David
while he was alive.

Thus the expression שמר חֶסֶד is far more appropriate than שמר בְּרִית
in this context, where the subject of the verb is Yahweh.

Ps. 89.29 refers to the establishment of the dynasty (vv. 30-31), and
uses the terms חֶסֶד and בְּרִית in parallel. Significantly, the verb שמר is
used with חֶסֶד (not with בְּרִית) supporting the conclusion of the previous
paragraph. Yahweh twice asserts that David can rely on his חֶסֶד
(vv. 25, 34) and between these assertions the present passage states
that this חֶסֶד is not simply for David himself (again לְ introduces the

patient), during his lifetime: it continues forever, being experienced
also by his successors.

In both 1 Kings 3 and Psalm 89, Yahweh remembers the חֶסֶד he has
extended to David and continues to direct it to those who succeed him.

Hos. 12.7—The prophet urges the wayward people to return to Yahweh.
The subject of the verb is the people whom he addresses; they, too,
are the agents of the חֶסֶד, and the unspecified patients are their
fellowmen. In the context of interpersonal relationships he exhorts
them to keep חֶסֶד וּמִשְׁפָּט, thus reminding them that their return to
Yahweh will also involve changing their attitudes to each other.

Two passages contain חֶסֶד in close association with נצר, which is almost
synonymous with שמר.[1] Exod. 34.7 is the only occasion on which חֶסֶד
is the object of this verb. Yahweh is the agent of the חֶסֶד, and the
particle לְ introduces the patient; in both these respects the construction in this passage agrees with the first two passages considered in
this section. There does not appear to be any reason why one verb is
chosen rather than the other. The subject of the verb in Ps. 61.8 is וֶאֱמֶת
חֶסֶד, which the psalmist invokes upon the king (v. 7).

D. שמר *with Other Elements*
Two elements, אֱמֻנִים (Isa. 26.2) and אֱמֶת (Ps. 146.6), occur as the object
of the verb שמר. The subject in Isaiah 26 is 'the righteous nation'; the
patient of אֱמֻנִים is not specified, but the context indicates that the
people's faithfulness, like their trust, is directed towards Yahweh.
Yahweh is the subject in Psalm 146, and again no patient is specified;
but the context (vv. 5-9) reveals that Yahweh remains faithful to his
people, especially to those who are in need.

The thought of faithfulness, loyalty, commitment is again evident in
both passages.

E. *Summary*

1. שמר בְּרִית always has a human subject, and the covenant is
   usually Yahweh's. This is similar to the pattern of שמר with

---

1. Even-Shoshan (1983: 1182) gives נצר as one of the synonyms for שמר and
(p. 778) the only synonym for נצר is שמר, appropriate for all its occurrences.

other words from the 'commands' semantic area, but it is quite different from the pattern when חֶסֶד and שׁמר are together in the syntagm.

2. שׁמר הַבְּרִית וְהַחֶסֶד is always used with Yahweh as both subject of the verb and agent of חֶסֶד; the covenant is Yahweh's, while the patient is always introduced by לְ.

3. שׁמר חֶסֶד is also used with Yahweh as both subject and agent, with לְ introducing the patient.

4. נצר is, in one passage, also used in identical circumstances.

חֶסֶד and בְּרִית occur, either separately or together, as objects of the verb שׁמר. The situational context when חֶסֶד appears, whether alone or with בְּרִית, is never found when שׁמר takes בְּרִית or other 'commands' words as its object. In this syntagm חֶסֶד is more remote than בְּרִית from the semantic area of 'commands'.

Yahweh's חֶסֶד undergirds his covenant.

Yahweh's acts of חֶסֶד underline his commitment to his people, even in their waywardness. This enables him to moderate the punishment meted out to the rebels, which encourages them to return to him, resulting in the covenant relationship being renewed.

There is a relationship between the terms חֶסֶד and בְּרִית. They both belong in the realm of interpersonal dealings; they both demand the commitment of the parties to each other. But there is a fundamental difference between the two concepts. A בְּרִית can be set out in writing on some form of material and therefore has a more tangible aspect, whereas חֶסֶד is less tangible: בְּרִית connotes a specific agreement reached at a fixed time and place, whereas חֶסֶד refers to an act, performed for the benefit of a person in need, in the context of a deep and enduring commitment between the parties involved.

2. *The* זכר *Syntagms*

This verb, like שׁמר, occurs more frequently with בְּרִית than with חֶסֶד. But, when used with זכר, these two lexical items never occur together. Each time זכר occurs with בְּרִית, Yahweh is the subject of the verb; eight passages assert that he either does or will remember his covenant,[1] while the remaining three passages assert that Yahweh has remembered his covenant.[2]

A form of the verb רחם follows זכר in Hab. 3.2, where the prophet beseeches Yahweh to be compassionate towards those who experience his wrath and judgment. חֶסֶד occurs six times with זכר, four times in a plural form. On three occasions it is accompanied by another element. The passages are conveniently grouped according to the subject of the verb זכר.

A. זכר: *Human Subject*

Twice the verb has a human subject in this syntagm.

In Isa. 63.7[3] the prophet feels a compulsion to remind Israel of Yahweh's חֲסָדִים, which they are no longer experiencing because of their rebellion against him (v. 10).

In Ps. 106.7 the psalmist confesses that he and his generation and their forefathers have all sinned (v. 6). In Egypt their fathers rebelled against Yahweh and did not remember his רֹב חֲסָדִים towards them. Yet Yahweh delivered them, saving them from their enemies (ישׁע, vv. 8, 10; גאל, v. 10). חֶסֶד is here also parallel to נִפְלָאוֹת, an additional lexeme.

B. זכר: *God as Subject*

In the four remaining occurrences of this syntagm, Yahweh is the subject of the verb זכר. Two passages state that Yahweh remembers.

Jer. 2.2—Two persons are involved: Yahweh is the speaker, and he addresses Israel. חֶסֶד and אַהֲבָה are both in the construct state; each precedes a substantive with pronominal suffix referring to Israel in her youth and her bridal state, and applies also to the preceding noun. For many commentators this passage refers to the חֶסֶד and the אַהֲבָה of Israel for Yahweh; that is, the agent for both nouns is Woman and the patient is God. For example, Bright (1965: 9) translates portion of this verse as 'I remember your youthful devotion, your bridal love', making Israel the agent but leaving the patient unspecified. An alternative view, which can be traced back at least to the early eighteenth

---

1. Gen. 9.15, 16; Lev. 26.42, 45; Ezek. 16.60; Ps. 105.8; 111.5; 1 Chron. 16.15. In Lev. 26.42, זכר occurs twice and בְּרִית three times.

2. Exod. 2.24; 6.5; Ps. 106.45.

3. This passage is discussed in Section 5B of Chapter 5 and in Section 1A of Chapter 6.

century, reverses the roles, making the agent God and the patient Israel. The Excursus in Section C below notes that

1. all other passages with patient Unspecified are in fact examples of חֶסֶד to a human; in all except one both agent and patient are human;
2. Israel's fickleness and apostasy is evident in the 'betrothal' period—much earlier than the 'honeymoon' period of the 'wilderness wandering';
3. Fox (1973) advances cogent arguments in favour of Yahweh's חֶסֶד and אַהֲבָה towards Israel; that is, in Jer. 2.2 the agent is God and the patient is Woman.

A paraphrase of this passage is: 'I remember in your favour my חֶסֶד extended to you in your youth and my אַהֲבָה for you in your bridal state'. This interpretation adds to the dimension of Yahweh's חֶסֶד, enhancing and enriching its meaning, showing that Yahweh resolutely and unyieldingly holds on to his people even when they are guilty of apostasy. This is in contrast to the dilution of the content of חֶסֶד required by the alternative view: the חֶסֶד of Israel towards Yahweh, which he remembers, is a dim and blurred reflection of the חֶסֶד that people extend to each other.

Ps. 98.2-3a—Yahweh remembers his חֶסֶד and his faithfulness. He is the agent, and the house of Israel is the patient to whom he directs his חֶסֶד.[1] Although the subject of זכר is the same in this and the previous passage, the connotation of the verb is quite different; here, Yahweh's remembering implies that he has continued to express his beneficence to his people.

The remaining two passages contain a prayer that Yahweh will remember his חֶסֶד.

Ps. 25.6—The close association of רַחֲמִים with חֶסֶד has been noted previously. חֶסֶד, in the plural, follows רַחֲמִים, and the psalmist links them together again, asserting that they have endured.

2 Chron. 6.42—The conclusion of the Chronicler's version of Solomon's dedicatory prayer has no counterpart in 1 Kings 8. Solomon beseeches Yahweh to remember 'the חֲסָדִים of your servant David', but it is not clear whether David is the agent of these acts or

---

1. For comment on the lexical items in this passage, see Sections 2A and 2B in Chapter 6.

whether the construct is to be regarded as a dative, in which case Yahweh is the agent—'your חֲסָדִים for/to David your servant'. In the original analysis, Yahweh is specified as agent and David as patient. Whichever alternative is adopted, the context suggests that the expected outcome will be for Solomon's benefit as well as for the benefit of the people of Israel.

C. *Excursus*—חֶסֶד *Patient Unspecified*

Jer. 2.2 is one of 11 passages in which it is difficult to decide whether the patient of חֶסֶד is human or divine. Three of these (2 Chron. 32.32; 35.26; Neh. 13.14) have been discussed in Section 5B of Chapter 7 and another (Jon. 2.9) is examined in Section 3A below; in each case, the patient has been reclassified as Man. Two passages in Isaiah and four in Hosea have an unspecified patient; each requires only that חֶסֶד refers to conduct between human parties. חֶסֶד is often closely associated with בְּרִית, so that when one term is used the other comes to mind also. The covenant spells out the relationship between Yahweh and his people and it is often assumed that חֶסֶד applies to the way the covenant partners relate to Yahweh, being frequently directed by the people to their God. However, the covenant has another function: it also spells out in detail Yahweh's expectations for his people's conduct towards one another.

Isa. 40.6—The usage of חֶסֶד here has been the subject of protracted discussion. Some accept the need to emend the text; others find a new meaning for חֶסֶד[1] and accordingly retain the text as it stands. North (1964: 75-77) asserts that this passage contrasts human transcience with divine permanence, since 'all flesh' means humankind as distinct from God; he states unequivocally that the focus is on human חֶסֶד as practised between human partners. Andersen (1986: 66-68), succinctly and effectively demolishing arguments based on emending the text and on introducing different meanings, agrees with North saying that 'human חֶסֶד is unsubstantial, transitory, ephemeral. It contrasts with the חֶסֶד of Yahweh, which endures for ever, like his word.'

Isa. 57.1—אַנְשֵׁי־חֶסֶד is parallel with הַצַּדִּיק, pointing to human conduct, in a human-to-human relationship. In Hos. 6.4 it is again human חֶסֶד that is transitory.

---

1. For example, Kuyper (1964: 13) and Whitley (1981: 520) advocate a much earlier suggestion that חֶסֶד here means 'strength'.

Hos. 6.6—The prophet attempts to persuade the people to express
חֶסֶד and knowledge of God practically in their dealings with one
another; Yahweh's pleasure is greater when he sees his people extending חֶסֶד to each other than when they present offerings to him and
ignore their responsibilities to and for each other. Andersen (1980:
430) associates the practice of חֶסֶד with the observance of the
Decalogue, which 'does not include rules for the offering of
sacrifices'.[1]

חֶסֶד parallels צְדָקָה (Hos. 10.12), and is linked closely with מִשְׁפָּט (Hos.
12.7). Each verse in its context points to right human conduct as the
prerequisite for acceptance with God.

All these passages (except Jon. 2.9, where the agent is Yahweh and the
patient is human) are examples of חֶסֶד expressed by one human party
to another, so that both agent and patient are human. There is also the
recurring thought that such conduct is not only acceptable to Yahweh
but that it is an essential component of their relationship with him.
חֶסֶד, however, cannot be seen as a response to, nor as prescribed by,
the commands of Yahweh; it is

> the spontaneous reaction of one person to another who is in need
> performed in the context of a commitment of each person to the other.

Jer. 2.2—Yahweh and Israel are the two persons involved here, and
commentators generally accept that faithless Israel (represented as a
woman) is the agent and God is the patient towards whom Israel
directs her חֶסֶד and her אַהֲבָה. Bright notes (1965: 14) that חֶסֶד 'has a
wide range of connotations' but it 'does not properly describe a
quality that men exhibit towards God'; yet he concludes: 'In the days
of wilderness-wandering Israel was Yahweh's bride, devotedly loyal
to him'. Hence, for Bright, Israel is the agent and Yahweh the patient
of חֶסֶד.

Glueck (1967: 59-60) discusses the verse under the heading 'חֶסֶד as
human conduct—its religious meaning' and speaks of the חֶסֶד 'which
Israel showed Yahweh'. Sakenfeld (1978: 169-81) describes Hos. 4.1,

---

1.   Compare Andersen (1986: 75): 'it does not follow that nothing is involved in
חֶסֶד here [Hos. 6.4, 6] but relationship with God. This lack of חֶסֶד is associated with
covenant violation, with treachery against God (6.7); but when the specifics are
itemized, they repeat the catalogue of 4. 2—murder, violence, robbery, adultery'.

Jer. 2.2 and Hos. 6.6 as three salient texts dealing with the 'religious' usage of human חֶסֶד; and she claims that the word is 'stretched' as it is transferred to the religious sphere from the secular realm. She finds (p. 173) that 'religious חֶסֶד is directed both to God (almost necessarily in Jer. 2.2, probably in all three examples) and also to fellowmen...' McKane (1986: 26) also adopts this interpretation; his translation reads, 'I remember the loyalty of your youth, your love for me as a bride'.

It is a reasonable inference from the text that the patient is God; but in this case Jer. 2.2 is unique, the only passage in which human חֶסֶד is directed to Yahweh. חֶסֶד does indeed cover a wide range of meanings, and it is always possible that there may be exceptions—or even a single exception—in the ways in which a word is used. But such singular cases should first be subjected to a careful investigation to determine whether they are in fact exceptions.

Jeremiah 2, headed 'Israel indicted for her sins' (Thompson 1980: 125), emphasizes the dire consequences of Israel's unfaithfulness to Yahweh. Both Thompson and McKane (1986: 26, 30) note that later verses contrast with the first three verses, using headings like 'Recollection of a lost love and loyalty' (vv. 1-3), and 'A history of apostasy: the case against Israel' (vv. 4-13). However, Bright (1965: 17) asserts that Israel was 'devotedly loyal' to Yahweh during the wilderness wanderings, and traces the commencement of her apostasy to 'the beginning of Israel's life in the Promised Land' (vv. 6-7) and finds (vv. 11-13) a description of 'an apostasy so complete as to amount to a change of gods'. But to readers of the final form of the corpus the seeds of apostasy were planted much earlier than this: on their way to the Promised Land, the people complained because they longed for meat instead of manna (Num. 11.1-6). Shortly afterwards, they rebelled against Yahweh when they heard the report of the spies who returned from the Promised Land (Num. 13.25–14.4). This was in the 'honeymoon' period. Yet even in the 'betrothal' period the incident of the golden calf (Exod. 32.1-10) is evidence of Israel's fickleness and her readiness to rebel. Is this the חֶסֶד of Israel's youth that Yahweh remembers? If so, it is only a pale reflection of the חֶסֶד that humans extend to one another.

Sakenfeld (1978: 171-72) suggests that in Jer. 2.2 לְךָ probably means 'on your behalf' and supplies a thread of hope to the statement of fact. This is how lexicologists and grammarians understand this type of construction.[1] But if the content of Israel's חֶסֶד is what has just been suggested, Yahweh's words constitute a threat rather than 'a thread of hope'; what is there in Israel's fickleness and apostasy that he can remember to her favour?

Fox (1973) examines this verse carefully and in detail, arguing that it does not support 'the theory of the "desert ideal"', as so many commentators believe. He makes the following points (pp. 442-46) about the various components of the verse.

1. חֶסֶד נְעוּרַיִךְ is structurally equivalent to חַסְדֵי דָוִד which refers to the חֶסֶד Yahweh gives to David;
2. זָכַרְתִּי לָךְ חֶסֶד is equivalent to שמר חֶסֶד with לָךְ as the dative of advantage; the meaning is: 'I have maintained for you the kindness (of the time of your youth)';
3. the fact that Israel went after Yahweh (לֶכְתֵּךְ אַחֲרַי) implies that Yahweh 'led her in the desert. This shows kindness in the guide, not necessarily loyalty in the guided'.

That is, the חֶסֶד—and also the אַהֲבָה—is not Israel's but Yahweh's. Added to these points is the possibility that the pronominal suffixes function as datives[2] when transferred to חֶסֶד and אַהֲבָה which, in the construct state, cannot carry suffixes; the reference, then, is to Yahweh's חֶסֶד 'for you in your youth' and Yahweh's אַהֲבָה 'for you as a bride'.

McKane (1986: 27) acknowledges that an early reference to Yahweh's loyalty and love in Jer. 2.2 is found in W. Lowth's commentary (published in London in 1718), and he mentions Fox's article but immediately dismisses it because Fox is particularly interested to show that v. 2 refers only to Yahweh's grace. On the other hand Zobel (1986: 62), who regularly substitutes 'kindness' for חֶסֶד throughout his article, argues in favour of this interpretation, claiming that 'in

---

1. KB (1958: 256) proposes for this verse the meaning 'I remember חֶסֶד to your favour'. Compare also GKC (1966: 381, §119*u*)—after verbs of saying and the like, the preposition לְ has 'the sense of *in reference to, with regard to...*'

2. Dahood (1970: 376-78) lists many passages in the Psalms where pronominal suffixes function as datives, either with substantives or with verbs. He frequently refers to this use of the suffix in his comments; see for example his remarks on Ps. 20.3 (1965: 127) and on Ps. 57.11 (1968: 55). See also the treatment of this passage by Andersen (1986: 71).

view of the frequency with which our term [חֶסֶד] occurs in the OT, a single passage cannot bear the burden of proof. Human beings can receive the kindness of Yahweh, but they cannot do him acts of kindness'.

Summing up, the passage may be paraphrased as: 'I remember in your favour my חֶסֶד extended to you in your youth and my אַהֲבָה for you in your bridal state'. Here there is hope that is no mere thread; it is a reality and it replaces the threat. This hope is based in Yahweh's faithfulness, his commitment to his chosen people that endures in the face of Israel's fickleness and blatant rebellion. Once again Yahweh's חֶסֶד persists and underlies the punishment that is designed to persuade Israel to return to him. This passage, so interpreted, adds to the dimension of Yahweh's חֶסֶד, enhancing and enriching its meaning, showing that Yahweh resolutely and unyieldingly holds on to his people although they are guilty of 'flagrant, inexcusable and incomprehensible apostasy'.[1]

D. *Summary*

When people are reminded of Yahweh's חֶסֶד (Isa. 63.7; Ps. 106.7), there are overtones of rebuke for their rebellion against him. When Yahweh remembers his חֶסֶד, it is either because he is no longer able to extend it to his faithless people (Jer. 2.2) or because he is continuing to express it to those who are serving him faithfully (Ps. 98.2-3). This is also the thrust of the prayers (Ps. 25.6; 2 Chron. 6.42) that Yahweh will remember and continue to show his חֶסֶד.

3. *The* עזב *Syntagms*

עזב occurs more frequently with חֶסֶד than with בְּרִית. The three occurrences[2] of עזב with בְּרִית all assert that the people of Israel have forsaken their covenant with Yahweh. The verb עזב seems twice to have a human subject and חֶסֶד as object; but there are alternative interpretations. עזב collocates with חֶסֶד twice and twice with חֶסֶד וֶאֱמֶת; three times Yahweh is the agent of חֶסֶד.

---

1. Compare Thompson (1980: 160).
2. 1 Kgs 19.10, 14; Jer. 22.9.

A. עזב *with* חֶסֶד

In two passages these words are closely associated.

Jon. 2. 9—The subject of the verb is 'those who worship vain idols', balancing חַסְדָּם in the second half of the verse. The verbs have different forms, and they are opposed semantically. Treating the pronominal suffix as a dative completes the opposition between the two cola to give the translation 'Those who revere vain idols forsake the one who extends חֶסֶד to them'.[1] The one whom they forsake is Yahweh; he is the agent, and the patient is human.

Ruth 2.20—Glueck (1967: 41-42) includes this in חֶסֶד as human conduct, making Boaz the agent of חֶסֶד as well as the subject of the verb. Sakenfeld (1978: 104-107) argues that Yahweh is both subject and agent. Both RSV and NIV present ambiguous translations, possibly in order to preserve the ambiguity that is evident when the apparently simple text is subjected to a careful examination. Several matters need to be resolved in the sentence

בָּרוּךְ הוּא לַיהוה אֲשֶׁר לֹא־עָזַב חַסְדּוֹ אֶת־הַחַיִּים וְאֶת־הַמֵּתִים

Prepositional אֵת is sometimes found with the word חֶסֶד, but the verb is always עשׂה, not עזב. אֵת is also frequently used with עזב—not as a preposition but as the sign of the object. If this is the case here, then חַסְדּוֹ is the subject of עזב, even though this is very rare in narrative passages.[2] It is then probable that יהוה standing immediately before אֲשֶׁר is the antecedent of this relative particle, rather than the more remote הוּא (i.e. Boaz), and also the antecedent of the pronominal suffix. Glueck rejects this possibility because the Hebrew Bible usually describes the dead as 'having absolutely no relationship with God', and hence it is most unlikely that the writer intends to represent the dead as receiving חֶסֶד from God.[3] He then cites Ruth 1.8 to support his

1. Compare Andersen 1986: 76.
2. חֶסֶד is often found in poetic passages as the object of the verb, and these cases are frequently seen as examples of personification. 2 Sam. 7.15 provides another example in narrative, although a few manuscripts have a first person singular verb here and thus make חֶסֶד the object. However, the text on which this study is based retains the third person singular verb, with חֶסֶד as subject.
3. Glueck bases his assertion on Isa. 38.18; Pss. 6.6; 16.10; 88.12. These passages, however, do not justify the confidence with which he claims 'absolutely no relationship'.

claim that Boaz 'had shown חֶסֶד to the living and the dead'. Do
Naomi's words necessarily mean that her daughters-in-law had shown
חֶסֶד to the men after they had died? Rather, these actions occurred
during their lifetime.[1] Naomi remembers these actions, and expresses
her gratitude to Ruth and to Yahweh who is the ultimate source of the
חֶסֶד shown by her daughters-in-law. Perhaps the narrator, seeing the
end from the beginning, reminds his readers that he is recording the
answer—for Ruth—of Naomi's prayer for her daughters-in-law. חֶסֶד
יהוה is the central concept; it is being experienced by the living, but it
is an expression of Yahweh's commitment to the whole family—to the
living and, while they were still living, to those who are now dead. An
adequate translation is 'May Yahweh, whose חֶסֶד has not forsaken the
living and the dead, bless him'.

B. עזב *with* חֶסֶד וֶאֱמֶת

Gen. 24. 27—The object of the verb is חֶסֶד וֶאֱמֶת. Abraham's steward
gives thanks to Yahweh because he has not forsaken חַסְדּוֹ וַאֲמִתּוֹ towards
his master.[2] Here Yahweh is both the agent of חֶסֶד and also the subject
of the verb.

Prov. 3.3—The writer urges his reader not to allow חֶסֶד וֶאֱמֶת to
forsake him. Neither the agent nor the patient is specified; but its
context is fatherly advice to a young man, so both agent and patient
are human[3]—the agent being the young man himself. The practice of
extending חֶסֶד וֶאֱמֶת to one's fellows is commended in v. 4 as conduct
that wins the favour of both God and human beings.

C. *Summary*

Gen. 24.27—Only here does the negative particle accompany the verb

1. See discussion of Ruth 1.8 in Section 2A of Chapter 7.
2. This incident is discussed also in Section 2A of Chapter 7. Other verbs
express the deprivation of חֶסֶד, and in each case a compound of מִן designates the one
deprived. Note מֵעִם after כרת (1 Sam. 20.15), after פּוּר (Ps. 89.34), and after סוּר
(1 Chron. 17.13); מֵאֵת after אסף (Jer. 16.5), and after סוּר (Ps. 66.20); and מִן itself
after סוּר (2 Sam. 7.15). Moreover, in this last instance חֶסֶד is the subject of the verb,
as mentioned in the discussion of Ruth 2.20 above. Also, it is the חֶסֶד of Yahweh in
all cases except the first; in 1 Samuel 20 it is David's חֶסֶד for Jonathan.
3. Glueck (1967: 62) includes this passage among those which treat חֶסֶד as the
conduct of people towards each other. Compare Andersen (1986: 80)—'The Proverbs
extol חֶסֶד as a superlative human virtue'; he cites 3.3 as the first example of this.

עזב when חֶסֶד is object. The sense of עזב לא ...מֵעֵם and of שמר...לְ are almost identical with that of עשׂה...עִם.

4. *The* נתן *Syntagms*

This verb does not appear with בְּרִית and it appears less frequently with חֶסֶד than with two other elements, רַחֲמִים and חֵן. In all except one passage, Yahweh is the subject of the verb, but he is rarely associated with the keyword as agent, since in most cases the application occurs in a human situation.

A. נתן *with* חֶסֶד
When חֶסֶד occurs with נתן it is accompanied by another field element.

Mic. 7.20—חֶסֶד is linked with אֱמֶת, both as objects of the verb. Yahweh is the subject of the verb and also the agent; the patient in each case is introduced by the particle לְ—Jacob receives אֱמֶת while Abraham receives חֶסֶד from Yahweh. Yahweh is willing to forgive the sins of his people (vv. 18, 19); their penitence, although not mentioned, is implied. The חֶסֶד in which Yahweh delights (v. 18) is that which he manifests to his people by toning down his wrath;[1] there is also the assurance that he will have compassion—רחם—on them. רחם, חֶסֶד and אֱמֶת are thus all closely related with pardon and forgiveness.

Dan. 1.9—Yahweh is again the subject of the verb, the instigator of the חֶסֶד but not its agent; his part is the 'softening up' of the official who mediates Yahweh's חֶסֶד וְרַחֲמִים to Daniel and his companions by permitting them to test their proposed diet. The immediate outcome of this 'divinely inspired' human חֶסֶד is that the Jewish youths do not defile themselves by eating the food provided by the king of Babylon. There is not even a remote possibility of a covenant relationship between the official and Daniel,[2] nor is there any reason to suspect

1. This thought, as both Sakenfeld (1978: 212) and Bowen (1938: 100) note, recalls that of Exod. 34.6-7.
2. Glueck (1967: 101-102) places this incident in a section dealing with חֶסֶד יהוה as 'divinely ordered conduct of others toward His faithful'. In one such passage Glueck describes חֶסֶד as treating another 'as if there were a covenantal relationship between them'; in another, Yahweh induces 'the Persians to deal with them in the spirit of covenantal loyalty'. For Sakenfeld (1978: 164-65) this 'case is borderline

that they are committed to each other; yet the commitment of Daniel to Yahweh is made patently clear in the narrative while the final outcome is evidence of Yahweh's commitment to Daniel.

B. נתן *with* רַחֲמִים

רַחֲמִים occurs in six more passages with the verb נתן. Each time Yahweh is the source, but in all except one passage the רַחֲמִים is again mediated by a human agent. The mediating human agent is introduced in four passages by לִפְנֵי—Joseph as the responsible authority in Egypt (Gen. 43.14), the captors of the people of Israel (1 Kgs 8.50; Ps. 106.46), and the king of Persia (Neh. 1.11). The human agent is the king of Babylon (Jer. 42.12), who is the subject of the verb רחם, which occurs alongside רַחֲמִים.

In the exceptional case (Deut. 13.18) Yahweh is the subject of all three verbs, two of which indicate that he is also the agent of this רַחֲמִים to his penitent people. The context (vv. 12-17) makes it clear that the people must be diligent in obeying Yahweh if they are to experience his רַחֲמִים.

The existence of a relationship or a commitment between the human participants is purely fortuitous. It exists only in the Genesis 43 incident, but this is not known to Jacob when he makes his petition before allowing Benjamin to accompany his brothers to Egypt, nor is it known to the brothers when they again come into Joseph's presence. Essential features in these instances of giving and receiving רַחֲמִים are:

1. a party in a situation of need, but powerless to do anything about it; and
2. a person in a position of authority who perceives the need of the other party, is affected by the situation and decides to act in such a way as to mitigate the circumstances, even though there is no obligation or compulsion to do anything.

רַחֲמִים is a deep-seated emotion, but it does not remain simply a feeling of goodwill.[1] It is an emotion expressed in practical assistance, which may take place after a seemingly chance encounter between two parties even though one has not been previously aware of the existence

---

between divine and human חֶסֶד, falling off on the human side' and she concludes that since 'חֶסֶד has fallen together with רַחֲמִים... it was important for the narrator to comment on God's role in the matter'.
1. See also Section 1A in Chapter 6.

of the other. The outcome in each example underlines the practical
nature of the expression of רַחֲמִים. Joseph's acts extend far beyond
supplying food for his brothers; the ultimate outcome is the reunion
of the whole family with him in Egypt. The king of Persia gives
Nehemiah permission to go to Jerusalem with the necessary letters of
safe-conduct and more importantly provides resources for rebuilding
Jerusalem. The king of Babylon's response is also practical—he will
allow those who are obedient to Yahweh to remain in their own land.
The outcome in the remaining two cases is presumably the deliverance
of Yahweh's people from captivity, following which the captors allow
them to return to their homeland (cf. Ps. 106.47).

C. נתן *with* חֵן
נתן is used seven times with חֵן as object.

Gen. 39.21—The jailer, who has no commitment to the prisoner,
looks favourably on Joseph and elevates him to a responsible position
in the prison. This is in consequence of the חֶסֶד Yahweh extends to
Joseph. The expression נטה חֶסֶד אֶל occurs only here, although the
preposition עַל replaces אֶל twice, in Ezra 7.28 and Ezra 9.9. Yahweh
is the subject of the verb and the agent of the חֶסֶד; the preposition
introduces the patient, but the חֶסֶד is mediated by the king. The king,
favourably disposed towards those returning to Jerusalem with Ezra,
makes adequate provision for their needs; this, however, does not
comprise the content of the חֶסֶד, but it can be seen as the outworking
of חֶסֶד יהוה. These two passages exhibit many features in common with
those where the expression נתן רַחֲמִים לִפְנֵי occurs: a party in need but
unable to do anything about it, and a person in authority who gives
practical help. The intervention of Yahweh, who is committed to his
people whether in captivity or in Jerusalem, emphasizes that the benefactor is not in any way committed to the beneficiaries. Similarly,
Yahweh's commitment to Joseph, which is prominent throughout the
Joseph story, underlies the חֶסֶד that he—not the jailer—extends to him
in Genesis 39.

Exod. 3.21; 11.3; 12.36—In the first two passages, Yahweh prescribes
the outcome, the fulfilment of which is described in the third passage:
the Egyptians give gold and silver jewellery, as well as clothing, to the

people of Israel before their departure. Here, too, the intervention of Yahweh is necessary in view of the lack of commitment between the Egyptians and the people of Israel.

Three other passages (Ps. 84.12; Prov. 3.34; 13.15) refer to the granting of חֵן to humans. They do not throw any light on the nature of חֵן; nor do they enable any conclusions to be drawn concerning the relationship between חֵן and חֶסֶד.

D. *Summary*

No uniform pattern emerges when נתן is used with the elements חֶסֶד (twice), רַחֲמִים (six times) and חֵן (six times); but on most occasions Yahweh is the subject of the verb. The following features are common to several passages in which Yahweh is the subject of the verb but not the agent of the activity described by the element:

1. the patient is a person in need but unable to do anything about it;
2. the agent is in a position of authority who gives practical assistance;
3. the existence of a commitment between agent and patient, if it exists, is not essential.

The passages, and the elements involved are:

1. Dan. 1. 9—חֶסֶד;
2. Gen. 43.14; 1 Kgs 8.50; Ps. 106.46 and Neh. 1.11—רַחֲמִים;
3. Gen. 39.21; Exod. 3.21; 11.3 and 12.36—חֵן; and also Gen. 39.21; Ezra 7.28 and 9.9—נטה חֶסֶד אֶל/עַל.

5. *A Common Syntagm with* חֵן

The syntagm מצא חֵן בְּעֵינֵי occurs approximately 40 times; and yet חֵן is never replaced in it by חֶסֶד. Here is a contrast between חֶסֶד and חֵן—just as חֶסֶד is never used as the object of מצא, so חֵן is never the object of עשׂה. Also, investigating this syntagm provides answers to two questions raised previously—whether חֵן is, like other derivatives of the root חנן, restricted with respect to Yahweh as patient; and what is the relative status of the agent and patient of חֵן. The syntagm always occurs in a situation in which both agent and patient are persons; it has been analysed in accordance with its transformation, 'A FAVOUR P', where A, the agent from whom the חֵן emanates, is introduced by בְּעֵינֵי, and P, the patient or recipient of חֵן, is the subject of מצא. Section A examines the basic syntagm מצא חֵן בְּעֵינֵי. Section B considers the extended statement אִם־(נָא) מצא חֵן בְּעֵינֵי. Finally, the relative status of agent and patient in these syntagms, and with other derivatives of the root חנן, is discussed in Section C.

A. מצא חֵן בְּעֵינֵי

This basic expression—'to look favourably on'—is used 24 times; in 19 passages the patient stands in deference before the agent. The passages in which this expression occurs are classified according to the nature of the statement—whether it asserts, or requests, or anticipates, or queries the favourable disposition of one party towards another; brief comments follow on each passage. However, passages containing the syntagm more than once are treated together—for example, Genesis 32–33, with Esau as agent and Jacob as patient; Exodus 33–34, and also Numbers 11, where Yahweh is the agent and Moses the patient; and Ruth 2, where Boaz is agent and Ruth is patient. All occurrences of the expression in each pericope are discussed together when the first one is encountered, and, where the extended statement occurs in these groups, its treatment is also included in this section and not in the following one. The passage reference is also included in the appropriate place.

a. *Assertion*
Eleven passages make an assertion that someone looks with favour on another person.

Gen. 6.8—Yahweh looks favourably on Noah, doubtless because Noah is righteous, blameless, and walks with God. Yahweh, the agent, is clearly superior in status.

Gen. 19.19—The situational context is the destruction of Sodom.[1] Lot affirms that the messengers of Yahweh have looked with favour on him—his concern for their safety may be regarded as Lot's prerequisite 'good conduct'. Lot requests permission to take refuge in the

---

1. See also Section 2A of Chapter 7.

small town nearby rather than escaping to the hills. His deference to the messengers is clearly shown in his manner of addressing them.

Gen. 39.4—Potiphar looks with favour on his slave Joseph, and entrusts to him the management of his household. The superior–inferior status of the master and the slave is beyond dispute. Potiphar's favourable disposition can be attributed to Joseph's 'good conduct'.

Exod. 33.12-17 contains the basic expression four times and the extended expression once. The narrator does not record Yahweh's assertion that Moses has found favour in his sight. Moses (v. 12) quotes the words of Yahweh, and Yahweh affirms (v. 17) the statement that Moses has just made. Although Moses is the leader of the people, he leads them in obedience to Yahweh; and this accounts for both the difference in status and also the 'good conduct' on which Yahweh's favourable disposition to Moses is based. The outcome is Yahweh's deeper revelation of himself to his servant.

Moses uses the extended statement (v. 13) in his request for Yahweh to reveal himself. The very use of the expression emphasizes the difference of status between agent and patient, and the importance of the request is apparent from the immediate context. The conversation occurs shortly after the affair of the golden calf. Yahweh has told Moses to lead the people to the land he has promised them; he will send an angel before Moses, but he will not accompany them lest he destroy them. Moses also uses the basic statement after requesting a fuller disclosure of Yahweh's person and his ways; such a revelation will assure him that Yahweh is continuing to look on him with favour. Moses asks Yahweh to show him his glory (v. 18), but his underlying request is for Yahweh's presence with him (vv. 13-16). Moses again uses the basic statement (v. 16), but he is no longer concerned about himself as the recipient of Yahweh's favour, for he now includes the people of Israel also, and wonders how the surrounding nations will know that Israel is any different from themselves. He insists it is only the presence of Yahweh with them that distinguishes them from other nations.

Exod. 34.9 fits naturally in this group of passages. After the renewal of the covenant and of the stone tablets, Yahweh proclaims his name as he passes before Moses. Prostrating himself and addressing Yahweh as 'my Lord', Moses repeats his former request—that Yahweh will accompany his people—and adds to it two others: that he will forgive their sin, and that he will reinstate them as his inheritance, that is, as his precious possession. Moses prefaces this threefold request with the extended expression. The difference of status and the importance of the request are both evident here also.

Ruth 2.2-13—Ruth acknowledges to Naomi that her status is inferior to that of the as yet unknown land-owner (Ruth 2.2), and later she twice emphasizes the difference in status between Boaz and herself, a stranger and a foreigner (Ruth 2.10, 2.13).

These passages use the basic expression in an assertion that someone looks with favour on someone else, as do another six[1] that have not been discussed in detail. Each portrays the patient in a deferential attitude before the agent, whose status is superior to that of the patient. Several passages provide evidence that the favourable disposition of the agent is a consequence of the previous 'good conduct' of the patient.

b. *Request*

The basic statement occurs six times in a request for favourable treatment. The parties involved, with the situationally superior mentioned last, are Jacob and Esau (Gen. 33.15), Shechem and Jacob's sons (Gen. 34.11); the famine-stricken Egyptians and Joseph (Gen. 47.25), Hannah and Eli (1 Sam. 1.18), David and Nabal (1 Sam. 25.8), and Ziba and David (2 Sam. 16.4). These passages are in harmony with those which assert that there is such a disposition, but only insofar as attention is drawn to the agent's superior status; however, this fact is not emphasized in Genesis 34. On two occasions, in Gen. 34.11 and 1 Sam. 25.8, the request is not granted; and there is no uniformity with respect to the role of the 'good conduct' of the party making the request.

c. *Anticipation*

Four instances of the basic expression occur in passages that use the expression more than once. Two of these, Exod. 33.15 and Ruth 2.2,

---

1.   1 Sam. 16.22; 20.3, 29; 2 Sam. 14.22; 1 Kgs 11.19; Prov. 3.4.

have been noted above. In each case the speaker anticipates that a favourable disposition will be forthcoming.

Genesis 32–33 records the return of Jacob to his homeland and his meeting with his brother Esau. As he nears the end of his journey, Jacob sends messengers ahead of him to greet Esau. Jacob (Gen. 32.6) anticipates that Esau will be favourably disposed towards him; indeed, this is the reason why he has sent his message to Esau, so that 'you may look favourably on me'. Being informed that Esau is coming to meet him with a considerable number of men, Jacob decides to placate Esau before they meet. He selects from his livestock a gift that he sends ahead to express his homage to Esau. Their reunion is very cordial, and Esau is unable to understand why Jacob has offered this present. Esau's question is recorded (Gen. 33.8), as is Jacob's answer: he simply repeats the message he had sent by his servants—that 'my lord may look on me with favour'. With the extended statement (Gen. 33.10) Jacob urges Esau to accept the gift that has already been delivered to him,[1] and thus brushes aside his brother's protestation that he doesn't really need it. Esau's acceptance is important for Jacob, since his gift is designed to make amends for his previous maltreatment of Esau. Jacob is aware that his status is subordinate to Esau's.

After accepting the gift, Esau persistently offers to see him safely on his way. Jacob has given (Gen. 33.13-14)—with suitable deference to his brother, referring to himself as 'servant' and to his brother as 'my lord' twice—a valid reason why he should not accept Esau's offer to lead the way (33.12). When Esau suggests leaving some of his men to help Jacob and his party, Jacob points out that there is really no need and uses the basic statement (Gen. 33.15) as a polite refusal of Esau's offers, asking him to look on him favourably. So Esau departs and leaves Jacob to go his own way. The difference in status between agent and patient is again evident; but the request is not related to the previous 'good conduct' of the patient, nor is it based on the actions of the agent.

Each passage confirms the difference in status between the agent and the patient. The matter of 'good conduct' does not appear to be relevant to the anticipated favourable disposition; but there is one new feature found in Jacob's large gift selected from his livestock, by

1. This is the only occasion on which the extended statement is not used to introduce a further request.

means of which he attempts to make sure of Esau's favour. Possibly this is his endeavour either to make amends for or to cover up the deception that precipitated his departure.

d. *Question*

Two of the three questions about the favourable disposition occur in passages considered previously (Exod. 33.16; Ruth 2.10).

Num. 11.11, 15—Moses is frustrated because he cannot provide meat for the people. He infers (v. 11) that Yahweh is no longer favourably disposed towards him. However, he remembers his subordinate status for he is Yahweh's servant. The extended expression (v. 15) follows the basic statement (v. 11). As Moses faces the complaining people without any prospect of being able to provide for them himself, his distress is so great that he implores Yahweh to take his life immediately. This request is followed by the statement that usually occurs first; but it clearly is intended to emphasize the request and its importance to the suppliant.

Passages in which the favourable attitude is questioned provide further evidence that the basic statement is normally used in a situation where the agent is of superior status compared with the patient.

e. *Condition*

The basic statement, preceded by the particle אִם, is twice the protasis of a conditional sentence.

Deut. 24.1 commences the statement of a law that regulates what may happen after a marriage has been terminated. A husband may divorce his wife 'if she displeases him' for a reason specified in the law, but he may not then take her back again.

2 Sam. 15.25—David, leaving Jerusalem at the beginning of Absalom's insurrection, instructs Zadok to take the ark of God back into the city, expressing the hope that he will return 'if Yahweh looks favourably on me', and thus commits his future into Yahweh's hands.

B. אִם־(נָא) מָצָאתִי חֵן בְּעֵינֶיךָ

The extended expression—'If I have found favour in your sight'—is always used with the patient, as the subject of the verb (in the first person), making the request directly to the agent (in the second person); there is never any intermediary between the two parties. It is, on all occasions except one, followed by a further request—for something that is of special significance for the suppliant who recognizes his or her subordinate status with respect to the agent. Here it is a rather elaborate and beseeching 'please' that prefaces a request.[1] Five of these occurrences have already been noted.[2]

Gen. 18.3—When Yahweh appears to him at Mamre, Abraham urges the visitors to accept his hospitality. He emphasizes his deference, which he has also demonstrated by prostrating himself before them.

Gen. 30.27—The expression does not share the characteristic features noted in its other occurrences. After the birth of Joseph, Jacob requests Laban to allow him to return with his family to his own country. Laban uses the extended expression, and he does not attempt to subordinate himself to Jacob, nor does he make a request of Jacob; he simply states that he has discovered that Jacob's presence with him has resulted in his (Laban's) being blessed by Yahweh.

Gen. 47.29—Jacob makes known his desire to be buried with his fathers in the land of Canaan. The extended statement introduces his request for Joseph to act in חֶסֶד וֶאֱמֶת towards him; and this further emphasizes the importance Jacob attaches to the place of his burial. Jacob, as the father of Joseph, may (from the family viewpoint) be of superior status to his son, who in fact occupies a pre-eminent position under the pharaoh; but the reality is the situation that will exist after Jacob's death. Joseph's status is then superior; being alive, he is able to make arrangements for his father's burial in accordance with his request; due to his pre-eminence, he is able to carry out those arrangements.

Gen. 50.4—After Jacob's death, Joseph asks members of the pharoah's household to request, on his behalf, permission to carry out his father's instruction to bury him in Canaan. Joseph uses the extended expression to introduce his request, and thus emphasizes its importance. No stress

---

1. Compare Lofthouse (1933: 30)—'When the word [חֵן] is used in making a request, it seems no more than an elaborate way of saying "please"'.
2. Gen. 33.10 is the only occasion on which the extended statement does not precede a further request; see Subsection A c above. Other passages are Exod. 33.13; 34.9; 1 Sam. 20.29 (all in Subsection A a), and Num. 11.15 (Subsection A d).

is laid on the status of the agents relative to the patient, but this is the only occasion when the expression is addressed to a group of people.

Num. 32.5—Members of the tribes of Reuben and Gad see the advantages of settling with their flocks and herds in the suitable pasture lands east of Jordan—a matter of no small importance to them—so they introduce their petition to Moses with the extended expression. They recognize their subordinate status, and they emphasize the importance of their request by proposing that their armed men accompany the other tribes and help them to establish themselves on the other side of the Jordan (vv. 16-19). In accepting the obligation that Moses proposes, they again affirm their submission (vv. 25, 27; cf. v. 31).

Judg. 6.17—Gideon draws attention to his own insignificance (v. 15), and twice addresses the speaker as 'my lord' (vv. 13, 15), tacitly acknowledging the superior status of the visitor. The importance of a sign is underlined by his attitude throughout the incident: he acknowledges his insignificance, and he asserts that Yahweh has abandoned his people to the Midianites (v. 13).

1 Sam. 27.5—David seeks permission to settle in one of the remote towns of Achish's domain. The difference of status between the king and his servant is apparent. David does not disclose to Achish the special significance of his request, but the narrator reveals how David keeps his men occupied while living in Ziklag (vv. 8-12).

Esther 5, 7—Esther's request (Est. 5.8), that the king and Haman dine with her on the following day, does not appear to be of any special significance; nor does the narrator explicitly mention the difference in status between Esther and the king. This incident can only be understood in the complete context in which it occurs, especially Est. 3.8-11 and 4.8-14. Esther approaches the king, accutely aware of her subordinate status, and adding emphasis to this by appending to the extended statement the words 'if it please the king'. At the banquet, Esther requests the king to spare the lives of her people (Est. 7.3). She introduces her request by slightly modifying the extended expression, emphasizing her even greater awareness of her subordinate status and her utter dependence upon the king's favourable disposition, thus underlining the urgency of her request both for herself and for her people. The immediate outcome is the execution of Haman and the promotion of Mordecai. Esther makes a further plea (Est. 8.5) prefaced by another modified expression[1] and augmented again by 'if it please the king'. The king instructs Mordecai to draw up another decree, which permits the Jews to protect themselves from those who attack them (Est. 8.7-13). It is this final request, supplementing the earlier one, that is of vital importance to Esther and to the Jews.

C. *Status of Agent and Patient*
The syntagms considered in this section are regularly used in a situation where there is a disparity between the status of the persons involved. The extended expression is almost always the preface to a request; this is sometimes directed to Yahweh, but more frequently it occurs in an interpersonal situation involving two human parties. The request is always made by one party directly to the other, without any intermediary, and the one making the request invariably adopts a deferential attitude towards the other who is represented as being superior either in position or in status. The relative status of agent and patient with certain of the חנן derivatives has been noted previously. Table 8.1 lists these derivatives and the two expressions that have been considered in this section, showing the number of times each is used with various agents and patients.

AGENT	GOD		LEADER				MAN				WOMAN
Patient	L	M	G	L	M	W	G	L	M	W	L
חנן	2	42	3	–	1	–	10	1	17	–	2
התחנן	–	–	3	–	1	–	10	1	2	–	2
תְּחִנָּה	–	1	7	2	–	–	13	1	1	–	–
תַּחֲנוּן*	–	–	1	–	–	–	15	–	1	–	–
חֵן	10	8	–	2	8	6	–	1	18	5	–
מָצָא חֵן	5	3	–	1	6	1	–	–	5	3	–
אִם מָצָא חֵן	3	2	–	1	2	2	–	1	3	–	–

Table 8.1. *Agent–Patient with* חנן *Derivatives*

All entries in the second row (התחנן) are also included in the first row (חנן); they show that when התחנן is used, the patient is usually of superior status to the agent. Agent and patient are both classified as

---

1.   The usual בְּעֵינָיו is replaced by לְפָנָיו.

Man in two cases. Joseph's brothers (Gen. 42.21) chide themselves for not heeding his pleas when he was in their power before they sold him as a slave. Similarly, Job's complaint that his servant ignores his master's pleas (Job 19.16) indicates a reversal of status if not of roles. Thus התחנן is only used when a person implores the favour of one whose status is superior to that of the suppliant, and this accounts for all occasions when the verb חנן is used with an agent of subordinate status to the patient. This restriction does not apply to other forms of the verb חנן.

תְּחִנָּה and *תַּחֲנוּן, which both mean 'a supplication for favour', are also normally used with an agent whose status is superior to that of the patient. Twice תְּחִנָּה is used with both agent and patient classified as Leader referring to the same incident, in which King Zedekiah is in a position and status superior to that of the imprisoned Jeremiah, who implores the king not to send him back to his death (Jer. 37.20; 38.26). תְּחִנָּה is also used with agent and patient both classified as Man in Josh. 11.20. The setting is the wars of extermination waged by Israel against the inhabitants of Canaan; with God on their side, Israel is superior to the Canaanites whose supplications will be rejected. An exceptional use occurs in Ezra 9.8, where God is agent and man is patient; here it is best regarded as a near synonym for חֵן. Again, both agent and patient of תַּחֲנוּנִים are classified as Man (Prov. 18.23). There is, however, a difference in status between them, since one is rich and the other is poor.

Entries in the last two rows of Table 8.1 are also included in the fifth row which gives the figures for all uses of חֵן in interpersonal situations. When חֵן occurs in a situation where the agent's status is superior to the patient's, the expression מָצָא חֵן בְּעֵינֵי is most frequently used. Preceding subsections have noted the relative status of agent and patient. In this syntagm the supplicant uses the expression, is the subject of the verb and is also the patient who seeks the favour of one of superior status. Thus, in these cases, also, the supplication is made by a subordinate to the one of superior status. This investigation has confirmed observations made by Lofthouse (1933) that

1. with the verb חנן 'the action passes from the superior to the inferior;...and that, whatever its character, it cannot be enforced or claimed' (p. 30), and

2. that the noun חֵן is used 'chiefly of men between whom there is or can be no specific bond or covenant' (p. 31), 'where there is no tie or claim' (p. 33).

D. *Summary*

1. מצא frequently takes חֵן, but never חֶסֶד, as its object; whereas עשׂה frequently takes חֶסֶד, but never חֵן, as its object.
2. The question of commitment is irrelevant when מצא and חֵן occur together.
3. There is a difference of status between the two parties involved when the expression מצא חֵן בְּעֵינֵי is used. In this expression, חֵן resembles other derivatives of the root חנן— תְּחִנָּה, התחנן and *תַּחֲנוּן—normally used by a suppliant of lower status.
4. חֶסֶד and חֵן contrast with each other in several ways, including:
    a. their usage with the verbs מצא and עשׂה;
    b. the notion of commitment—essential for חֶסֶד, but irrelevant for חֵן;
    c. the relative status of agent and patient—irrelevant for חֶסֶד, but essential for חֵן.

6. *Overview*

Syntagms investigated comprise the verbs שׁמר, זכר, עזב and נתן with either חֶסֶד or another field element. Various forms of the expression מצא חֵן are also examined.

עשׂה is the verb most commonly found in close association with חֶסֶד; it draws attention to the practical nature of the deeds that are called חֶסֶד.[1]

שׁמר is used with חֶסֶד and בְּרִית and has different connotations, depending on whether חֶסֶד is present or not; the presence of חֶסֶד also affects the usage of the syntagm:

1. When used with חֶסֶד, with or without בְּרִית, Yahweh is always both subject and agent, and the patient is introduced by לְ;
2. When used with בְּרִית alone, the subject is always human, and a patient is never mentioned;
3. the covenant is always Yahweh's.

---

1. Further details are found in the overview in Section 6 of Chapter 7.

נצר is also used once with חֶסֶד when Yahweh is both subject and agent and the patient is introduced by לְ.

זכר is used with חֶסֶד sometimes accompanied by other elements:

1. when Yahweh is subject, זכר usually implies that he is continuing to act in חֶסֶד;
2. when the subject is human, זכר involves remembering Yahweh's past acts of חֶסֶד.

עזב is used with חֶסֶד but displays no uniform pattern; twice, with negative particle, it refers to the continuing experience of חֶסֶד יהוה.

נתן is used with חֶסֶד accompanied by other field elements:

1. Yahweh is always the subject, and initiates חֶסֶד, usually extended by a human agent;
2. also used with רַחֲמִים and חֵן, Yahweh is again the initiator but the agent is human.

מצא is frequently used with חֵן but never with חֶסֶד:

1. commitment is not relevant;
2. the parties involved differ in status.

Examining verbs used with חֶסֶד reveals points of resemblance and difference between חֶסֶד and the other lexical items occurring with the verbs.

1. When used with the verb שׁמר
    a. בְּרִית is closer than חֶסֶד to the semantic area of 'commands';
    b. Yahweh's חֶסֶד undergirds his בְּרִית, reveals his commitment to his people, enables him to moderate punishment which is intended to result in renewing the covenant relationship with those who repent and return to him.
2. The verb נתן is used only twice with חֶסֶד, but it occurs six times with each of רַחֲמִים and חֵן. Several times Yahweh is the subject of the verb, but not the agent of the activity described by the element. These passages exhibit the following features:
    a. the patient is a person in need but unable to do anything about it;
    b. the agent, in a position of authority, gives practical assistance;

c. a commitment between agent and patient, if it exists, is not essential.

3. The usage of the verb מצא reveals contrasts between חֶסֶד and חֵן:

a. חֶסֶד is never used with מצא, and חֵן is never used with עשׂה;

b. with חֵן, but not with חֶסֶד, relative status of agent and patient is important;

c. with חֶסֶד, but not with חֵן, commitment between agent and patient is important.

Chapter 9

SYNTAGMS—LEXEMES WITH עשׂה

Statistics in Table 7.1 relate to various עשׂה syntagms, many of which contain the element חֶסֶד. The vast amount of material involved has been distributed between three chapters. Chapter 7 considered field elements used with the verb עשׂה, while Chapter 8 discussed elements used with other verbs. This chapter examines עשׂה syntagms incorporating additional lexemes, as listed in Table 7.1, seeking meaning relationships between the elements and the lexemes that replace them. The most frequently occurring lexemes are members of the טוב family; those which are not followed by בְּעֵינֵי are discussed in Sections 1 to 3, while those which are followed by בְּעֵינֵי, as well as similar expressions using יָשָׁר in the place of טוֹב, are grouped together in Section 4. Expressions containing other lexemes listed in the table are considered in Section 5. The order of treatment generally follows the arrangement of the table.

Sakenfeld (1978: 24; cf. pp. 44, 234), investigating acts of חֶסֶד between human partners, finds the following features are 'normally present in situations in which the word חֶסֶד is appropriate'.

1. Does this act make provision for an essential need?
2. Is this act directed by a powerful party towards one who is weaker?
3. Is the agent free not to perform this act?
4. Is the agent the sole available source of assistance?
5. Does the agent recognize his or her responsibility based on some relationship with the other party?

This relationship, Sakenfeld says (p. 233), might be an intimate personal one, either between members of a family or between a king and his advisors, or it might be a voluntary and non-intimate one, as between individuals or parties who are political rivals.

1. *The Preposition* עִם—*The* טוב *Family, without* בְּעֵינֵי

Gen. 26.28-29—Abimelech requests Isaac to enter into a treaty of peaceful coexistence with him. Abimelech treated Isaac well while he was under his protection in Gerar. He forbade his subjects to touch Isaac and Rebecca (v. 11), under penalty of death; and, realizing that Yahweh was blessing Isaac, Abimelech requested him to move away (v. 16). Isaac's greeting to Abimelech (v. 27) shows that he did not regard this request as a peaceful approach—the two parties involved did not see eye to eye in this incident. There is, therefore, an element of subjectivity, or relativity, in the determination of what is, or is not, טוב.

Abimelech recognizes his responsibility to secure the safety of Isaac, his guest; he accepts that responsibility willingly and freely, and persists in fulfilling his obligation even after he knows that Isaac has deceived him regarding his relationship with Rebecca. By ensuring Isaac's safety, Abimelech performs an essential service that Isaac is unable to provide for himself. Moreover, Abimelech is the more powerful party, the only one who is able to act in this way, yet he is free not to perform this service to his guest. Thus, the expression עשׂה טוב עִם satisfies all the criteria that Sakenfeld has laid down for the expression עשׂה חֶסֶד עִם, and consequently the criteria are inadequate, since they do not afford a means of distinguishing between חֶסֶד and טוב.

This incident concerning Isaac and Abimelech is similar to incidents between Abraham and Abimelech (Gen. 20–21), but there are also several striking contrasts. There, Abimelech calls his beneficial treatment of Abraham חֶסֶד; but here his beneficial treatment of Isaac is טוב. In the earlier incident, Abimelech was aware of Yahweh's presence with and protection of Abraham but he nevertheless invited him to remain in his territory;[1] his treatment of Abraham is based on his commitment[2] to the guest whom he has allowed to reside under his protection. Here, however, Abimelech urges Isaac to move away (Gen. 26.16-17). Knowing that Isaac's prosperity is evidence of Yahweh's presence with him, Abimelech nevertheless envies Isaac and fears that he may lose some of his possessions and his power to Isaac.

---

1. Gen. 20, noting especially v. 15.
2. See discussion of Gen. 21.22-23 in Section 2B of Chapter 7.

His actions are motivated by his own self-interest; he does not make
any commitment to Isaac—indeed, envy, fear and self-interest do not
provide any foundation for such a relationship, which must be firmly
based on mutual trust. The treaty virtually draws boundaries between
the two parties, to keep Isaac and Abimelech apart; it is a treaty of
mutual exclusion rather than one of peaceful coexistence. In the
absence of a deep personal commitment to each other, the writer
refrains from attributing to Abimelech the term חֶסֶד and substitutes
טוב.

Gen. 32.10-13—Jacob returns to his homeland after his long sojourn
with Laban and learns that Esau is coming with four hundred men to
meet him. He makes appropriate peparations and then prays to
Yahweh, the God of his fathers Abraham and Isaac, asking to be
delivered from Esau. The writer puts into Jacob's mouth (vv. 10, 13)
the words יטב עם referring to what Yahweh has promised to do in the
future, and (v. 11) the expression עשׂה חֶסֶד וֶאֱמֶת which refers to what
Yahweh has done in enabling Jacob to rear his large family and to
increase his possessions. The former expression (v. 13) relates to the
promise Yahweh made to Jacob when he departed from Canaan (Gen.
28.10-15), and looks back to the original promises made to Abraham.[1]
The succession from Abraham through Isaac to Jacob is about to be
confirmed, and both terms refer to the promised blessing of their
progeny. But can these two expressions be interchanged?

Sakenfeld (1978: 93-97) makes pertinent comments on vv. 10-13;
but since her focus is on the word חֶסֶד, the use of the verb יטב does not
come within the purview of her study. She finds in this and other
passages a close correspondence between the חֶסֶד which Yahweh shows
to individuals and that which is found in human personal relationships;
so she applies her criteria also to passages in which Yahweh is agent.
Features present here include Jacob's essential need, which is the
preservation of life, for himself and members of his family and his
retinue; since there is no human to assist Jacob, the sole source of
deliverance is obviously Yahweh; and the human request for divine
help suggests the presence of other features of חֶסֶד—such as
circumstantial dominance in a situation of need, and freedom not to
fulfil the need. Yahweh has caused Jacob to prosper and gain in

1. See, for example, Gen. 12.2; 13.14-17; 22.17.

wealth, although these are not usually components of חֶסֶד acts, and he has overcome obstacles that Jacob was unable to handle. The writer uses חֶסֶד in Jacob's prayer, she presumes, because of the personal relationship which God himself established when he appeared to Jacob and promised to assume responsibility for Jacob's welfare. Two other facts emphasize Jacob's faithfulness within the relationship: Yahweh's command that Jacob return to the land where he will meet Esau, and Jacob's obedience to this command.

Such perspicacious insights are a feature of Sakenfeld's examination of the texts; but an investigation of the question of commitments in this passage leads to different conclusions. The word אֱמֶת—which, with אֱמוּנָה, has been found as an essential component of חֶסֶד[1]—is used alongside חֶסֶד (v. 11). The occurrence of אֱמֶת here focuses attention on the faithfulness of Yahweh in his acts of חֶסֶד to which Jacob refers. Moreover, this faithfulness is not primarily to Yahweh's nature or to his promises, nor is it to Abraham and Isaac, to whom he made those original promises; it is to Jacob himself, and to the promises which Yahweh made to him as he departed from Canaan. The writer uses the compound expression to acknowledge Yahweh's commitment to Jacob which has been evident throughout his absence from his homeland. There is a commitment to the person who is the beneficiary, and the word חֶסֶד is applied to the benefits that Jacob has already received. But Jacob's future is still uncertain, for he has yet to confront the brother who threatened to kill him and who is approaching with a force large enough to accomplish this purpose. Jacob's prayer is, as Sakenfeld (p. 94) correctly notes, virtually 'a request for an additional act of חֶסֶד. However, Jacob has already admitted that he is not worthy to receive the benefits that Yahweh has bestowed on him, and he doubts whether Yahweh's loyal commitment will continue; in these circumstances the writer uses the word יטב. In this passage, then, each expression is used in the most suitable context.

Judg. 8.34-35; 9.16-19—These two passages refer to the treatment of Gideon's family after his death. Sakenfeld (1978: 54-58) refers to 9.16 when she discusses 8.35, which she classifies as 'חֶסֶד based on a prior act not called חֶסֶד'. She examines various explanations for the

---

1.   See Chapter 6—Section 1B for אֱמוּנָה, and Section 1C for אֱמֶת.

alternation between חֶסֶד (v. 35) and טוֹבָה (v. 16) referring to the same
action. The widespread contrasting usage of טוֹבָה and רָעָה leads her to
conclude that the use of טוֹבָה instead of חֶסֶד (9.16b) possibly heightens
the sarcastic emphasis on the wicked deed of the men of Shechem. The
agents are different: the Israelites did not do חֶסֶד to Gideon's family
and the Shechemites failed to do טוֹבָה; and she considers that, in the
respective contexts, the word חֶסֶד is more appropriate in v. 35 than in
v. 16 where, however, it is 'not wholly inappropriate'. Finally,
recalling that the word חֶסֶד usually refers to positive action of deliverance or protection, she states that in Judg. 8.35 it highlights the specific
failure of Israel to rescue the sons of Gideon from Abimelech's
treachery. However, did the Israelites have prior notice of
Abimelech's intentions? The plot, laid in Abimelech's home town
among his own kinsfolk, was not broadcast from the housetops; nor
did the gang of 'reckless adventurers'[1] send messengers ahead of them
to announce the purpose of their sudden swoop upon Ophrah. Israel
failed to rise up to rescue them because they did not know about the
mass murder until after the event. Perhaps the חֶסֶד they omitted was
their failure to bring the murderers to justice, rather than their
inability to rescue Gideon's sons from Abimelech.

There is still the question of loyalty to consider. When he used the
compound adverbial expression[2] 'in good faith and honourably' in
vv. 16 and 19, Jotham could have been thinking of loyalty—"Were
you acting loyally...?" Gideon was the leader through whom Yahweh
had rescued the people of Israel from the Midianites; those who had
benefitted from his leadership could be expected to show their appreciation by committing themselves in loyalty to him. Had this been the
case, Israel's treatment of Gideon's family after his death might have
been in accordance with their commitment to him; in such circumstances חֶסֶד is used appropriately in 8.35 for the expression of that
commitment. But the men of Shechem have refused to entertain even
the thought of a committed loyalty to Gideon—as they have
adequately demonstrated in the murder of Gideon's sons. Hence the

1. This NIV translation of the two adjectives linked in 9.4 is most appropriate,
and fits in well with the secrecy surrounding the plotting and the urgency of its
execution.

2. This expression occurs only here and in Josh. 24.14, where the words, in
reverse order, modify the verb עבד as Joshua urges the people of Israel to fear
Yahweh and to serve him in loyal commitment.

word חֶסֶד is not appropriate in Jotham's explanation of his parable, and
the writer thus uses the alternative expression in Judg. 9.16.

חֶסֶד and טוב syntagms are juxtaposed in Gen. 32.10-11 (עשׂה חֶסֶד וֶאֱמֶת
with עם (יטב עם אֵת) and Judg. 8.35 (עם עשׂה חֶסֶד) alongside עשׂה טוֹבָה עם);
they confirm the conclusion reached in the discussion of Gen. 26.28-
29, that Sakenfeld's criteria are inadequate to distinguish between חֶסֶד
and טוב. Moreover, they support the proposal made there, that a
commitment between the parties involved is an essential feature of the
situations in which חֶסֶד appears but is not essential for the use of טוב.

This is also apparent in Num. 10.29-32, where Moses uses the
expression יטב עם with Yahweh as subject and agent and Israel as
patient (v. 32) and also יטב לְ with Israel as subject and agent and
Hobab as patient (vv. 29, 32). The record does not elaborate on the
nature of the benefits that Yahweh promised, but they undoubtedly
include establishing his people in the land. יטב satisfies most of
Sakenfeld's criteria for חֶסֶד. However, Yahweh is not free to withhold
this benefit, but this does not depend on any mutual commitment
between Yahweh and Israel; it arises from Yahweh's faithfulness to
himself and to his promise. Sakenfeld's features are again present in
the human situation. However, Hobab is reluctant to leave his home
(v. 30). He is unwilling to make a commitment to Moses and the
people of Israel; consequently יטב, not חֶסֶד, is used.

This syntagm occurs also in Ps. 119.65, where affirmative answers
can be given to some of the questions posed above; but there is
insufficient evidence to determine whether the act provides for an
essential need. The alliterative structure of the psalm accounts for the
use of the lexeme טוב that commences four verses, while another has
טוב as its initial word.

2. *The Preposition* לְ—*The* טוב *Family, without* בְּעֵינֵי

1 Sam. 25.30-31—This passage contains the noun טוֹבָה as the object of
עשׂה and also a form of the verb יטב, both referring to David's
appointment as king. The agent is Yahweh and the patient is David,
both times introduced by the preposition לְ. Sakenfeld's criteria apply
to secular uses of חֶסֶד, where both parties are human, and not to those
in which Yahweh is the agent; but her justification for their applica-

tion to such cases has been noted.[1] Yahweh had commanded that David be anointed as Saul's successor (1 Sam. 16.11-13), so Abigail's use of the terms refers to the provision of an essential need, which involves the fulfilment of Yahweh's promise and intention. Yahweh is undoubtedly the superior party, but it is doubtful whether he is free not to perform this act; not on account of his commitment to David but rather on account of his own faithfulness to himself and to his word. He is the only available source of assistance, since David has repeatedly refused to take the initiative against Saul—most recently in the incident (1 Sam. 24) to be discussed in Section 3 below. That Yahweh recognizes his responsibility to act is evident in the sequel, when David becomes king. חֶסֶד is therefore not appropriate in this context because, on Sakenfeld's criteria, the agent is not free but is bound to perform the act.

1 Kgs 8. 66 // 2 Chron. 7.10—At the end of the account of Solomon's dedication of the temple,[2] the expression עָשָׂה הַטּוֹבָה לְ occurs with Yahweh as agent, David and also Israel as patient. Applying Sakenfeld's criteria confirms the results just noted: the establishment of the kingdom under David and the building of the temple by Solomon—which are included in these benefits that caused the people to rejoice—fulfilled Yahweh's promises and depended upon Yahweh's faithfulness to himself and to his promises rather than his commitment to his people.

Other passages which use a form of the expression יטב לְ with reference to Yahweh's goodness lead to the same conclusion.

Exod. 1.20—The beneficiaries are the Hebrew midwives in Egypt; Yahweh is faithful to his own people, but the primary consideration is his purpose for Israel and therefore his faithfulness to himself and his promises rather than his commitment to his people. Examples abound in Deuteronomy[3] where Moses frequently uses the expression יטב לְ as he exhorts the people to obey Yahweh's commandments in order that they may enjoy the benefits he has promised to their forefathers; and

---

1.   See discussion of Gen. 32 in Section 1 above.
2.   The chronicler's version is almost identical with that of the historian; he replaces עָבְדוּ by וְלִשְׁלֹמֹה.
3.   See Deut. 4.40; 5.16, 29; 6.3, 18; 12.25, 28; 22.7. Compare also Jer. 7.23; 38.20; 42.6.

it occurs when Joshua warns the people that disobedience will deprive them of these benefits (Josh. 24.20). Yahweh is, however, under no obligation to provide the promised blessings, as is apparent when he withdraws his benefits from his disobedient people.

Gen. 12.13-16—In this account of Abram and Sarai's stratagem to preserve Abram's life during their stay in Egypt, the expression יטב ל occurs twice. On both occasions, Abram is the patient, introduced by ל; the agents are the Egyptian people (v. 13) and the pharaoh (v. 16). Abram does not call Sarai's act חֶסֶד here, as he does in the later incident with Abimelech.[1] The יטב expressions are not substitutes for חֶסֶד. There is no mutual commitment between Abram and the pharaoh or the Egyptians; consequently members of the טוב family are used here since חֶסֶד is not apposite.

Gen. 40.14 records Joseph's request, וְעָשִׂיתָ־נָּא עִמָּדִי חֶסֶד, during his imprisonment, after he has given a favourable interpretation of the butler's dream. He also uses יִיטַב לְךָ impersonally, but the agent is the pharaoh who will restore the butler to his former position. Sakenfeld (1978: 46-48) describes this as a request for 'חֶסֶד based on a prior act not called חֶסֶד'; she admits that there are difficulties in the understanding of חֶסֶד itself, which she handles by seeking for a relationship or a bond between the two men. These difficulties, however, may be resolved by considering whether there is any commitment between the parties involved. The pharaoh's commitment to his butler—and to his other servants—simply does not exist; he is a despot, and the lives of his servants (even his most trusted ones, like his butler and his baker) are in his hands—he can dispose of them at will. In this relationship between the pharaoh and his servants, יטב but not חֶסֶד is applied to the pharaoh's act. Joseph, with Yahweh's help, is able to render service to the butler; all he asks in return is a tangible expression of the butler's appreciation, an appreciation based on the commitment he expects, and which he considers he deserves, because of his good turn to the butler. This incident introduces a deviation from the predominant usage of חֶסֶד in the context of a commitment that already exists; here the commitment is expected but does not yet exist. Thus, once again, the matter of commitment not only distinguishes between the

---

1.   See discussion of Gen. 20.13 in Section 2D of Chapter 7.

expressions but it also removes the difficulty created by seeking another basis for the act of חֶסֶד.

3. *The Preposition* אֶת—*The* טוב *Family, without* בְּעֵינֵי

2 Sam. 2.5-6—This passage contains עשׂה syntagms with חֶסֶד and also with a member of the טוב family, each with a different agent. David has been accepted as king by the people of Judah, and he is aware of the activities of Abner and Ish-bosheth in Gilead (vv. 8-11). He sends messengers to compliment the men of Jabesh-gilead on their חֶסֶד extended to Saul when they recovered his body, which they buried in Jabesh (1 Sam. 31.11-13). Sakenfeld (1978: 40-42) finds it difficult to fit this incident into her patterns, especially in connection with the relationship between the persons involved, but she concludes that the important feature is 'the personal character of the ongoing political relationship'. The term חֶסֶד, she says, makes it clear that Saul's proper burial was a matter of great importance, and it is appropriate because stealing the bodies was clearly a difficult and risky task. She overlooks the fact that the men of Jabesh performed this task, at great risk to their lives, as an expression of their loyal commitment to Saul. Their allegiance to him commenced at the beginning of his reign, when Saul delivered Jabesh-gilead from the besieging Ammonites (1 Sam. 11.1-11). This victory ensured to him the esteem and loyalty of the people of Jabesh. David recognizes their loyalty, and he sends messengers to encourage them to transfer their loyalty to him, since he has been anointed as king by the men of Judah. Sakenfeld implies (pp. 110-11) that this is the whole tenor of David's message, for she translates the טוב syntagm as 'I will make a treaty of friendship with you', and she has valid reasons for adopting it.[1] David wishes to extend חֶסֶד to the men of Jabesh, but he is not in a proper position to do so since he is formally in the camp of the enemy (1 Sam. 27.1-7; 29.1-11). The narrator neatly solves this problem, she says, by having David invoke Yahweh's חֶסֶד on them. There is, however, an alternative solution—in terms of the loyalties of the men of Jabesh-gilead. Their past commitment was to Saul, and their חֶסֶד reflects their commitment to Yahweh as well as to their divinely appointed ruler—hence David uses an apposite expression as he invokes Yahweh's

---

1. She quotes in support articles by Moran (1963: 173-76) and Hillers (1964: 46-47).

blessing on them. Their present commitment is also to Saul and his descendants and, until they commit themselves in loyalty to David, טוֹבָה but not חֶסֶד may be applied to any beneficent acts between him and them.

1 Sam. 24.19—The word טוֹבָה occurs in a situation where חֶסֶד is equally appropriate, according to Sakenfeld's criteria. The historian may put this word into Saul's mouth because he has already used the antonyms טוֹבָה and רָעָה (v. 18). However, the relationship between the king and his subject provides a more compelling reason for the use of the word. Saul's animosity towards David, rooted in his jealousy which drives him to seek the destruction of his anointed successor, dominates this relationship. In these circumstances there is no commitment, on Saul's part, to take care of the welfare and safety of David; quite the opposite, for the king's sole purpose is to destroy David. Knowing this, David refrains from taking the king's life, simply because Saul is Yahweh's anointed; he is committed to the preservation of the king's life, but this is not a commitment to Saul—it is a commitment to Yahweh. This is demonstrated by David's contrition (vv. 6-7), which is grounded in his relationship with Yahweh and is centered not on Saul as a person but on Saul as Yahweh's anointed. Likewise, his commitment to Saul's son Jonathan—not to Saul himself—prompts David to swear the oath at Saul's request (vv. 22-23); and this, too, can be traced to David's commitment to Yahweh. Hence, the word חֶסֶד is inappropriate because there is no bond or commitment binding the benefactor and the beneficiary, and consequently the use of the word טוֹבָה is appropriate here.

Jer. 32.40-41—It is strange that יטב, not חֶסֶד, occurs here in connection with Yahweh's new covenant. Yet the context (vv. 36-44) places great emphasis on the unilateral nature of this covenant: it is an expression of Yahweh's commitment to his people, but its existence does not depend on their commitment to him. In the absence of mutual commitment, normally present when חֶסֶד is used, a member of the טוב family is appropriate. Thus יטב in this situation plays down the necessity for Israel's commitment to Yahweh, which he nevertheless desires. Moreover, Yahweh's commitment to his people is such that the renewal[1] he offers them ensures that they will not turn from him again.

Other passages containing 'יטב + preposition' syntagms[2] confirm the conclusions formulated above.

4. *The* טוב *Family, with* בְּעֵינֵי

The expressions יָשָׁר בְּעֵינֵי ,טוֹב בְּעֵינֵי and יטב בְּעֵינֵי occur reasonably frequently. Attention is confined to passages in which the verb עשׂה is used with טוב (Section A) and also with ישׁר (Section C), while those which contain יטב בְּעֵינֵי are considered in Section B. The syntagm עשׂה חֶסֶד בְּעֵינֵי is not found in the Hebrew Bible, and the significance of this fact will be noted in Section 6 below.

A. עשׂה טוב בְּעֵינֵי
This syntagm appears in a variety of situations, frequently as an expression of assent to a proposed action—as in 1 Sam. 14.36, 40,[3] where the people agree with the suggestions made by Saul; it seems here to have some such meaning as, 'Do what you think is best'. It has a similar meaning in 1 Sam. 1.23 as Elkanah agrees with Hannah's proposal not to accompany him to the annual sacrifice; and also in Gen. 16.6 where Abram allows Sarai to decide how to deal with Hagar. With these words Eli (1 Sam. 3.18) accepts the judgment revealed by Yahweh to Samuel. Lot uses the same expression (Gen. 19.8) when he offers his virgin daughters to the men of Sodom in order that they may satiate their lust; and it is used in similar circumstances with regard to the Levite's concubine (Judg. 19.24).

The expression occurs five times, in different circumstances, in the course of Absalom's rebellion. David (2 Sam. 15.26) willingly leaves his future in Yahweh's hands. Shimei and Ziba hasten to ingratiate themselves with the king as he returns after Absalom's death, and place themselves at David's disposal (2 Sam. 19.19). Shortly after, Mephibosheth also comes to greet the returning king; aware of Ziba's

---

1. Compare also Jer. 31.31-34; Ezek. 11.19; 36.26-28.
2. Many of these are listed in footnote 3 on p. 224; see also Josh. 24.20; Jer. 40.9; Ruth 3.1.
3. See also 2 Kgs 10.5; 1 Chron. 21.23.

slander, he expresses his readiness to accept whatever treatment David
metes out to him (2 Sam. 19.28). Finally David, desiring to reward
Barzillai's faithfulness, invites him to come with him to Jerusalem
where David will provide for him. Barzillai graciously declines the
invitation but suggests that Kimham[1] accompany the king who could
'do for him (Kimham) whatever pleases him (David)' (2 Sam. 19.38).
In the following verse David expresses his agreement, echoing
Barzillai's words: 'I will do for him whatever pleases you'.

This syntagm is used in a wide variety of situations, and a variety of
persons is given the responsibility of deciding what is the appropriate
interpretation of טוב. This decision is left to

1. Yahweh in 1 Sam. 3.18 and in 2 Sam. 15.26;
2. the king—Saul in 1 Sam. 14.36, 14.40 and David in 2 Sam.
    19.19, 19.28 and 19.38;
3. a man—Barzillai in 2 Sam. 19.39;
4. a woman—Sarai in Gen. 16.6 and Hannah in 1 Sam. 1.23;
5. men—the Sodomites in Gen. 19.8 and the men of Gibeah in
    Judg. 19.24.

No doubt each of these persons has a norm by which to decide what
טוב means in a given situation; but it is most unlikely that all would
have the same norm in the same situation. The same norm would not
be used by the Sodomites and by Yahweh to determine what is טוב in
Gen. 19.8. Nor would the norm used by Sarai in Gen. 16.6 necessarily
be the same as that which Abram would use in the same situation.
Indeed, the norm applied by Sarai when she is upset and emotionally
disturbed—distraught and incensed is a more realistic description of
her emotional condition—by Hagar's insolence would in all prob-
ability be very different from the one she would use in her calmer
moments. All this indicates that the syntagm under consideration
emphasizes that there is a subjectivity, a relativity, involved in determining the content of טוב.

---

1. There is no evidence in the Masoretic text that Kimham is the son of Barzillai,
although this is stated in certain English versions that take notice of the addition
occurring in some manuscripts of LXX and also in the Syriac. Moreover, this name
appears with different spelling in v. 41.

B. יטב בְּעֵינָי

יטב frequently has the same sense as עשׂה טוב; but this does not apply to this syntagm, which is used impersonally in all except two cases. It occurs, often as a comment by the narrator, to indicate that something is a source of pleasure or of satisfaction to someone. The narrator (2 Sam. 3.36) adds an expression of the form discussed in the previous subsection to indicate that the people were pleased not merely by the specific act to which he has referred, but by everything which David did. These passages do not contribute to the present discussion.

C. עשׂה יָשָׁר בְּעֵינָי

This expression is used only five times with a human referent. A variant of 'everyone did as he saw fit' appears in Deut. 12.8; Judg. 17.6; Judg. 21.25. On both occasions in the book of Judges the writer disapproves of the occurrence he has just recounted, and implies that Yahweh also does not approve of people's conduct in Israel in the period immediately preceding the establishment of the monarchy. There is a slight variation in the words attributed to Moses, where he advises the people not to continue pleasing themselves but to obey Yahweh after they enter the promised land.

After their deception, the men of Gibeon accept Joshua's decision and submit themselves to him (Josh. 9.25), saying, 'Do to us whatever you think is good and right'. With similar words, Jeremiah submits to the princes of Israel (Jer. 26.14) who think he deserves to die because he has prophesied the destruction of Jerusalem. From the foregoing it appears that there may be a certain amount of latitude in determining what is יָשָׁר. However, the presence of טוב alongside יָשָׁר may be responsible for the subjectivity in these two examples, while the apparent disapproval in the passages in Judges and the explicit statements of Moses both indicate that יָשָׁר does not depend upon the whim of people but is in fact determined by Yahweh.

The most common form of this expression, 'to do what is right in Yahweh's sight', supports this conclusion. This occurs most frequently in a standard formula adopted by the writers, in both Kings and Chronicles, to epitomize the nature of the reign of many of the kings. Asa is highly commended in 2 Chron. 14.2, where the usual formula has the supplement טוב added, while the highest commendation is given to Hezekiah (2 Chron. 31.20) in the amended and supplemented form:

'He did what was good and right and faithful before Yahweh his God'.
For a large number of kings—especially but not exclusively those of
the northern kingdom—יָשָׁר is replaced by רָעָה in this formula.

5. *Other Lexemes*

A few passages substitute an additional lexeme for חֶסֶד in a syntagm
with עשה and a preposition that is either ל or אֵת. Each passage has been
checked to see whether Sakenfeld's criteria apply. The details of this
portion of the investigation are not recorded here, but attention is
drawn to those criteria, if any, which do not apply to the situation.

A. עשה...ל

עשה חֶסֶד ל occurs five times with Yahweh as agent[1] and once in a
human situation where the agent is a leader.[2] In each passage the
preposition introduces the patient, who is always both the recipient of
and the beneficiary from the act of חֶסֶד: the person who experiences
חֶסֶד also benefits from it. However, when חֶסֶד is replaced by another
lexeme or, in three cases, by a pair of lexemes joined by *waw* con-
junctive, the patient benefits from an act directed towards another
person or party in all except one incident, which is recorded in two
parallel passages.

Exod. 14.13—At the crossing of the Reed Sea, Israel benefits from
Yahweh's act, יְשׁוּעָה, directed towards the Egyptian army which
certainly did not benefit from this act.

1 Sam. 19.5—Jonathan, appealing to Saul on David's behalf, reminds
him that it was by David's hand that Yahweh won a great victory over
the Philistines. This act from which all Israel benefits was not directed
towards them but towards Goliath—and neither he nor the Philistines
were beneficiaries of the act.

Ps. 103.6—The compound term 'righteousness and justice' refers to
acts of Yahweh from which those who are oppressed benefit without

---

1. This syntagm is found in Exod. 20.6; Deut. 5.10; Jer. 32.18 and in the
parallel passages 2 Sam. 22.51 and Ps. 18.51.
2. 1 Kgs 2.7, where King Solomon is the agent.

being the direct recipients. The oppressors experience these acts of Yahweh.

2 Sam. 8.15 // 1 Chron. 18.14—A similar compound term occurs here. David's victories extended his dominion considerably, and the historian adds: 'David did what was just and right for all his people'. The people of Israel are both the recipients and the beneficiaries of David's just rule; but David is not free to disregard his responsibility to administer justice to the people of Yahweh—for this purpose Yahweh chose and appointed him. Yet this freedom must be distinguished from that which Sakenfeld sees as a characteristic feature of חֶסֶד; she says (1978: 234)[1] that the one to whom חֶסֶד has not been shown has no opportunity to 'get even' in the future, and the one who has neglected to show חֶסֶד has no fear of interference or recrimination. The kings of Israel, including David, always had (on the human level) the possibility of freedom not to administer justice; and there is ample evidence that the kings often failed in this respect. In the Bathsheba–Uriah episode (2 Sam. 11.1–12.23), David violates two fundamental laws and deservedly receives Yahweh's stern rebuke. David's freedom to disobey Yahweh but not to escape the consequences is illustrated also in 2 Samuel 24 (// 1 Chron. 21.1-27), where, despite Joab's protestations, the king insists on taking a census. In this sense David is free to disregard his responsibility; although the one in need cannot personally compel the response he desires, the king is answerable to Yahweh who has entrusted to him the task of administering justice to his subjects.

B. עשׂה...אֶת

עשׂה חֶסֶד אֶת occurs only three times,[2] and each contains a composite expression with another element.

1 Sam. 12.7 contains the only example of this syntagm with the additional lexeme צְדָקָה replacing the element חֶסֶד. Samuel reminds the

---

1.   Sakenfeld makes similar statements on pp. 24 and 44; and she often speaks of a person having no recourse if the appropriate expression of חֶסֶד does not eventuate.

2.   Zech. 7.9-10 uses the expression חֶסֶד וְרַחֲמִים and is discussed in Section 4 of Chapter 7. Two other passages (Gen. 24.49; 32.11) both contain the expression חֶסֶד וֶאֱמֶת; they are considered in Section 4B of Chapter 10.

people of all the 'righteous acts', or 'saving deeds', that Yahweh had performed. He then (vv. 8-11) refers to the exploits of leaders whom Yahweh used to deliver his people from their enemies and oppressors, and thus expands on the צִדְקוֹת יהוה. Israel is the beneficiary of these acts that are directed towards others who do not benefit from them. This serves to distinguish between חֶסֶד and צְדָקָה when they occur in this syntagm.

6. *Overview*

Several important points emerge from the examination of lexemes used in the עשה syntagms. They are drawn together and summarized here.

First, a weakness has been exposed in Sakenfeld's method. Her inductive study, analyzing passages using the word חֶסֶד, has revealed characteristic features of that word; but she has not considered whether these features are also characteristic of other words besides חֶסֶד. To adapt a mathematical term, Sakenfeld discovered features of חֶסֶד that are necessary, but she has not attempted to investigate whether these features are sufficient. Necessary features are essential to the object under discussion. A lexical item that does not possess the necessary features of חֶסֶד cannot be a synonym of חֶסֶד, but it does not follow that an item that does possess those features is in fact חֶסֶד. This can only be determined by considering sufficient features, for an item that possesses the necessary features but does not possess the sufficient features cannot be a synonym of חֶסֶד. Investigating words replacing חֶסֶד in certain syntagms has revealed that Sakenfeld's necessary conditions apply at least to members of the טוב family.

Secondly, a feature has been proposed which is sufficient—sufficient at least to distinguish between חֶסֶד and טוב. This feature has developed as the study proceeded, for חֶסֶד refers to an act which one person/ party performs for the benefit of another person/party, an act based in the mutual commitment between them. It is precisely this basic characteristic of personal commitment that has provided a means of distinguishing between טוב and חֶסֶד. Incidentally, the concept of personal commitment has also resolved satisfactorily, and more economically, some problems that Sakenfeld encounters.

Thirdly, another feature distinguishing between חֶסֶד and טוב has emerged from the consideration of the בְּעֵינֵי syntagms. For טוב, there may be different standards for different people in the same situations and also for the same people in different situations; in other words, a degree of latitude and relativity is inherent in the word טוֹב when it is accompanied by the word בְּעֵינַי. The fact that בְּעֵינַי is never used with חֶסֶד confirms the general impression that חֶסֶד is in the Hebrew culture an absolute in which there is no room for relativity or latitude. This, however, does not imply that a person in a given situation in which חֶסֶד is appropriate can consult a book of rules that sets out the appropriate course of action. The person in the situation will know what to do, and what he or she does is the same as any other person will do in the same situation.

The few examples of the עשׂה יָשָׁר בְּעֵינַי syntagms have shown that יָשָׁר is distinguished from טוֹב in that it is not subject to latitude or relativity. יָשָׁר is determined by Yahweh and not by any human being; it, too, is an absolute. This is not claimed to be a general distinguishing feature between the two lexemes, but it is apparent in the small sample that has been examined. Whether it is of more general application can only be determined by a careful inspection of all the occurrences of both lexemes. טוֹב and יָשָׁר each occurs approximately 30 times with בְּעֵינַי, but טוֹב appears at least 400 times and יָשָׁר over 100 times in the whole corpus.

Chapter 10

THE EXPRESSION חֶסֶד וֶאֱמֶת

The elements חֶסֶד and אֱמֶת collocate 51 times with each other. In 23 of
these collocations, a variant of the series חֶסֶד וֶאֱמֶת occurs. The most
radical departures are in Gen. 32.11, 'I am not worthy of all the חֲסָדִים
and of all the faithfulness...', and in Hos. 4.1, the only example where
אֱמֶת precedes חֶסֶד—'There is neither faithfulness nor חֶסֶד...' This is
indeed a collocation of the two elements, but because the terms appear
in reversed order it is not further considered. However, the former
expression is a variant of the series collocation and will be examined
in this chapter.

In the compilation of the statistics in Chapter 4 the series expression
was treated as two separate elements; but it is frequently asserted that
this is an example of hendiadys, a complex semantic unit. Kaddari
(1973: 169-70) claims that the phrase is a single semantic unit when it
is parallel to a simple semantic unit, as in Ps. 40. 11, and that it should
not be decomposed but should be translated as 'true kindness'. This
chapter examines the phrase and its two constituent elements, using the
methods adopted in earlier chapters. The distributions and the collocations of חֶסֶד, חֶסֶד וֶאֱמֶת and אֱמֶת are compared in Sections 1 and 2
respectively. Section 3 examines the use in parallel expressions of
חֶסֶד וֶאֱמֶת. Section 4 directs attention to the nature of hendiadys, and
especially to חֶסֶד וֶאֱמֶת as an example of this literary device.

1. *Distribution of* חֶסֶד וֶאֱמֶת

The statistics prepared in Chapter 4 have been revised, treating the
phrase and its constituent elements as three separate lexical items. The
figures for these items in the three main interpersonal categories,
which require both agent and patient to be personal, are set out in
Table 10.1 below. The first line for each item gives the actual number

of occurrences of that item. On 12 occasions אֱמֶת is used adjectivally or adverbially; these occurrences have been omitted because they do not fit into the agent–patient categories. The figures in the second line have been standardized by dividing each figure by the number of times the item occurs in a situation involving two human parties. חֶסֶד occurs 3.21 times with God as agent for each time it occurs in a human situation.

Item	God–Human	Human–God	Human–Human
חֶסֶד	170	0	53
	3.21	0	1
חֶסֶד וֶאֱמֶת	15	0	7
	2.14	0	1
אֱמֶת	17	6	13
	1.31	0.46	1

Table 10.1. *Distribution of Three Lexical Items* (Source: SRTKAP)

Differences between the distributions of חֶסֶד and אֱמֶת have been noted in Chapter 3. First, almost half the occurrences of אֱמֶת are in non-personal situations, but neither חֶסֶד nor חֶסֶד וֶאֱמֶת is ever used in such situations. Secondly, אֱמֶת occasionally occurs with God as patient, but חֶסֶד and also חֶסֶד וֶאֱמֶת are never used with God as patient. Table 10.1 shows that חֶסֶד and חֶסֶד וֶאֱמֶת are both used more frequently with God as agent than with a human agent—חֶסֶד more than three times as frequently and חֶסֶד וֶאֱמֶת more than twice as frequently. On the other hand, אֱמֶת occurs slightly less frequently with God as agent (17 times) than with a human agent (19 times). Thus there is a closer correspondence between the distributions of חֶסֶד and חֶסֶד וֶאֱמֶת than between those of אֱמֶת and חֶסֶד וֶאֱמֶת. Hence, in situations that involve a human patient when the agent is either God or human, the distribution pattern of חֶסֶד וֶאֱמֶת resembles that of חֶסֶד more closely than that of אֱמֶת.

Inspecting passages in which חֶסֶד וֶאֱמֶת is used reveals that
When God is agent:

1. Yahweh applies the term to himself once only—in his self-revelation to Moses (Exod. 34.6-7);
2. the patient is a man in all cases except one, when the psalmist requests God to direct חֶסֶד וֶאֱמֶת to a leader—the king who is, however, not named (Ps. 61.7-8);

3.   the phrase is frequently used during remarks that are addressed to God—often in the Psalms, but also by Abraham's servant (Gen. 24.27), by Jacob as he prepares for his first meeting with Esau (Gen. 32.11), and by David in his request for Yahweh's blessing on the men of Jabesh-gilead (2 Sam. 2.5-6).

When the agent is human:

1.   leaders are involved only on one occasion—when Jacob makes his last request to Joseph (Gen. 47.29);
2.   a woman is the patient only once—when the spies give Rahab their solemn undertaking that they will extend חֶסֶד וֶאֱמֶת to her when Yahweh fulfils his promise to give them the land (Josh. 2.14).

To summarize the distribution trends of these three items:

1.   Neither חֶסֶד nor חֶסֶד וֶאֱמֶת occurs in situations where God is the patient.
2.   When the patient is human with God as agent, there are more than three occurrences of חֶסֶד, and more than two occurrences of חֶסֶד וֶאֱמֶת, for each occurrence of the same item with a human agent.
3.   With a human patient, אֱמֶת is distributed more evenly between the two agents—God and human.

Hence the distribution patterns of חֶסֶד וֶאֱמֶת resemble those of חֶסֶד much more closely than those of אֱמֶת.

2. Collocations with חֶסֶד וֶאֱמֶת

Element	חֶסֶד	חֶסֶד וֶאֱמֶת	אֱמֶת	Lexeme	חֶסֶד	חֶסֶד וֶאֱמֶת	אֱמֶת
רַחֲמִים	18	3	3	טוֹב	24	4	11
אֱמוּנָה	18	2	–	בְּרִית	17	1	5
חַנּוּן	6	3	–	צְדָקָה	13	2	9
רְחוּם	6	3	–	יֹשַׁע	7	2	–
חֵן	5	2	1	נצל	6	2	5
חנן	3	1	–	טוּב	5	1	1
				יָשַׁע	4	1	1
				תְּשׁוּעָה	2	2	–

Table 10.2. *Lexical Items Collocating with* חֶסֶד וֶאֱמֶת
and More Frequently with חֶסֶד *than with* אֱמֶת

The collocation statistics have also been revised to determine the
figures presented in Tables 10.2–10.4. These tables set out the number
of times various lexical items (members of the field as well as
additional lexemes) collocate with חֶסֶד, חֶסֶד וֶאֱמֶת and אֱמֶת; the items are
arranged in the order of the frequency of their collocations with חֶסֶד,
and the elements are shown on the left hand side while the lexemes are
on the right. Several lexical items, mostly lexemes, are not included in
the tables because the total number of their collocations with חֶסֶד,
וֶאֱמֶת and אֱמֶת is less than 4. All items included in the first two tables
collocate with חֶסֶד וֶאֱמֶת; in Table 10.4 the items collocate with חֶסֶד
and/or אֱמֶת but not with חֶסֶד וֶאֱמֶת.

Direct quantitative comparisons cannot be made between the collocations of the various lexical items. Nevertheless, Table 10.2 indicates
that there are significant differences between the collocation trends of
חֶסֶד and אֱמֶת. For example, חֶסֶד and חֶסֶד וֶאֱמֶת both collocate with all
the items in the table, but אֱמֶת does not collocate with four of the
elements and two of the lexemes. The presence of חֶסֶד in the phrase
חֶסֶד וֶאֱמֶת may be largely responsible for the collocation of the compound expression with the elements רחום, חַנּוּן, אֱמוּנָה and חנן and also
with the lexemes ישע and תְּשׁוּעָה. There is, however, no occasion on
which the opposite attraction occurs, for whenever אֱמֶת and חֶסֶד וֶאֱמֶת
both collocate with a lexical item חֶסֶד is also found in collocation with
that item. Thus, חֶסֶד וֶאֱמֶת collocates with six items that are found in
collocation with חֶסֶד but not with אֱמֶת, and hence the collocations of
חֶסֶד וֶאֱמֶת resemble those of חֶסֶד more closely than those of אֱמֶת.

LEXEMES	חֶסֶד	חֶסֶד וֶאֱמֶת	אֱמֶת
מִשְׁפָּט	16	2	22
צֶדֶק	4	3	7
יטב	3	3	5

Table 10.3. *Lexemes Collocating with* חֶסֶד וֶאֱמֶת
and More Frequently with אֱמֶת *than with* חֶסֶד

The only lexical items collocating with the composite phrase and also
more frequently with אֱמֶת than with חֶסֶד are three additional lexemes
shown in Table 10.3. Another lexeme marks the point of transition
between the preceding tables—יָשָׁר collocates once with חֶסֶד וֶאֱמֶת and
eight times with each of the component elements. These facts do not
alter the situation noted at the end of the previous paragraph—that
חֶסֶד וֶאֱמֶת collocates with six items that are found in collocation with
חֶסֶד but not with אֱמֶת.

Table 10.4 completes the collocation figures for these three items. In no case is the number of collocations as great as 10, which was the figure set in Chapter 4 as the cut-off point for frequent collocations. Two of the elements and two of the lexemes collocate with חֶסֶד but not with אֱמֶת, while only one element collocates with אֱמֶת but not with חֶסֶד. The last four elements also collocate more frequently with אֱמֶת than with חֶסֶד. These facts, however, are not as significant as the one noted above—that אֱמֶת alone never collocates with four elements and two lexemes that are found in collocation with חֶסֶד וֶאֱמֶת.

Element	חֶסֶד	חֶסֶד וֶאֱמֶת	אֱמֶת	Lexeme	חֶסֶד	חֶסֶד וֶאֱמֶת	אֱמֶת
רחם	7	–	1	צַדִּיק	6	–	3
אַהֲבָה	6	–	–	נִפְלָאוֹת	6	–	–
שׂונֵא	5	–	1	גאל	4	–	–
אוֹהֵב	5	–	–	ידע	3	–	1
אהב	4	–	6				
אמן	3	–	6				
שפט	2	–	6				
שׂנא	–	–	4				

Table 10.4. *Lexical Items Collocating with* חֶסֶד *and* אֱמֶת *but not with* חֶסֶד וֶאֱמֶת

To summarize the collocation trends of these three items:

1. The presence of the element חֶסֶד in the phrase חֶסֶד וֶאֱמֶת may be responsible for the collocations of four elements and two additional lexemes with the compound expression.
2. Overall, the collocations of the phrase חֶסֶד וֶאֱמֶת are more compatible with those of חֶסֶד than with those of אֱמֶת.

Hence the collocation trends of חֶסֶד וֶאֱמֶת, like its distribution patterns, indicate that the compound expression has a greater affinity with חֶסֶד than with אֱמֶת.

3. *Parallels Involving* חֶסֶד וֶאֱמֶת

Passages containing חֶסֶד in parallel with other elements and with additional lexemes have been discussed in Chapter 6. The phrase חֶסֶד וֶאֱמֶת also occurs occasionally in parallel with some of the lexical items. Ps. 40.11-12 and 85.11-12 comply with Kaddari's criteria for semantic parallels. The context shows that the pronominal suffixes attached to each element of the complex expression in both verses of Psalm 40 refer to Yahweh. In v. 12 חֶסֶד and אֱמֶת are attendants sent by Yahweh

to protect the psalmist from danger—an example of personification.[1]
The parallelism between the first and third cola of v. 11 as they are
displayed in *BHK* is obscured in *BHS*. The features of this parallelism
show that these two lines have identical syntactic structure, but this is
not true of v. 12. Yet Kaddari (1973: 170 n. 15) points to the parallelism between חֶסֶד וֶאֱמֶת, 'righteousness' and 'faithfulness and salvation'
in v. 11, and between חֶסֶד וֶאֱמֶת and רַחֲמִים in v. 12. He thus indicates that
a compound term, חֶסֶד וֶאֱמֶת, is a single semantic unit here since it
parallels a simple semantic unit; but he does not apply this principle to
the other compound expression in v. 11—possibly because this is the
only place where אֱמוּנָה and תְּשׁוּעָה are closely contiguous. חֶסֶד is parallel
four times with רַחֲמִים and also twice with צְדָקָה; but only here do these
terms parallel חֶסֶד וֶאֱמֶת. Since אֱמֶת is frequently found as an essential
component of חֶסֶד, and since the compound expression resembles חֶסֶד
more closely than אֱמֶת in both its distribution trends and its collocation
patterns, there is no significant difference between חֶסֶד and the single
semantic unit חֶסֶד וֶאֱמֶת.

The three stanzas of Psalm 85 form a closely-woven unity.[2]
Previously (vv. 2-4), Yahweh turned aside from his anger and for-
gave his people. At present (vv. 5-10) they are straying again, and the
psalmist beseeches Yahweh to alleviate his anger and to express his חֶסֶד
by granting salvation to his people. When the psalmist's prayer is
answered, the four divine attributes, which are personified as attendants of Yahweh,[3] are in complete harmony (vv. 11-14). Yahweh's חֶסֶד
to those who have sinned is not inconsistent with his אֱמֶת to his own
holy nature; his gift of peace to human beings issues from and is
consistent with his characteristic צֶדֶק (v. 11). Their salvation also
produces harmony between God and human beings: those who fear
Yahweh (v. 10) lead lives of אֱמֶת under the watchful eye of their God
who is צֶדֶק (v. 12). Thus צֶדֶק is an attribute of Yahweh in both verses,
whereas אֱמֶת is divine in v. 11 but human in v. 12. The composite
expression חֶסֶד וֶאֱמֶת (v. 11) does not satisfy Kaddari's criteria for a
single semantic unit, since the word-pair in each colon is the subject of
a plural verb, the sense of which requires that the words in the pair
apply to two separate entities, one of which is the subject, and the other

1. Dahood 1965: 247.
2. Note the early emphasis on Yahweh's anger (אַף, עֶבְרָה, v. 4; אָנַף, אַף, v. 6),
which merges with and is replaced by the thought of his salvation (יֶשַׁע, vv. 5, 8, 10).
3. Dahood 1968: 289; compare also Weiser 1962: 574.

the object, of the singular form of the corresponding transitive verb. Yet, because אֱמֶת is an essential component of חֶסֶד, the composite expression may still be regarded as a single semantic unit.

The parallel constructions in two other passages—Ps. 57.4 and Ps. 89.15—do not satisfy Kaddari's criteria. The close relationship between חֶסֶד and 'salvation' in Psalm 85 is also found in Psalm 57, where חֶסֶד is replaced by חֶסֶד וֶאֱמֶת. This verse may be paraphrased as 'God will send his חֶסֶד וֶאֱמֶת from heaven to save me'; the word-pair is a personification, with חֶסֶד and אֱמֶת as the personal agents whom God sends to deliver the psalmist.[1]

The phrase חֶסֶד וֶאֱמֶת is parallel to another compound expression, 'righteousness and justice', in Ps. 89.15. This is the only occurrence of אֱמֶת in the psalm; and the phrase should again be regarded as a personification, since חֶסֶד and אֱמֶת, and perhaps also 'righteousness' and 'justice', are represented as attendants of Yahweh. The frequent repetition of אֱמוּנָה[2] throughout the psalm is an interesting feature that serves as further confirmation that אֱמוּנָה is an essential component of חֶסֶד when Yahweh is the agent and also that the two elements חֶסֶד and אֱמוּנָה cover areas in the semantic field that are in close proximity.

Consideration of these passages does not enable a distinction to be made between the semantic regions covered by חֶסֶד and אֱמֶת. However, the discussion in this and the two preceding sections indicates that the semantic area of חֶסֶד וֶאֱמֶת is much closer to that of חֶסֶד than to that of אֱמֶת.

To summarize: the expression חֶסֶד וֶאֱמֶת occurs five times;

1. twice it is a single semantic unit according to Kaddari's criteria;
2. three times it is the subject of a plural verb;
3. in each of the four passages it refers to qualities or attributes of Yahweh and
4. it is always an example of personification.

Do the personifications point to separate entities rather than to a complex unity? This is most unlikely, since one of the units—אֱמֶת—is

---

1. Compare Dahood 1968: 51.
2. אֱמוּנָה occurs in vv. 2, 3, 6, 9, 25, 34, 50.

frequently an essential component of the other—חֶסֶד. Two closely related characteristics of Yahweh are personified, and the repeated pronominal suffix focuses attention on Yahweh whose qualities are closely related. Moreover, the plural verb functions largely as an indicator of the personification which in its turn creates an atmosphere of elevation, dignity, and remoteness from ordinary experience. In such situations the writer often makes a deliberate stylistic choice to use a single complex expression instead of two separate but related lexical items.

4. חֶסֶד וֶאֱמֶת *as Hendiadys*

The expression חֶסֶד וֶאֱמֶת has greater affinity with חֶסֶד than with אֱמֶת, with respect to their situational distributions, and also with respect to their collocations. Because of the paucity of passages in which חֶסֶד וֶאֱמֶת occurs in parallelisms, it has not been possible to make comparisons with חֶסֶד, nor with אֱמֶת. The compound phrase is in parallelism with a single semantic item in each of its occurrences in Ps. 40.11-12; hence the phrase is itself a simple semantic item, and for other reasons it can be so regarded also in Ps. 85.11. Several times Glueck applies the term hendidadys[1] to the combination חֶסֶד וֶאֱמֶת, adding sometimes that אֱמֶת is a descriptive or an explanatory adjective.[2] Yet there are occasions when he is hesitantly ambivalent.[3]

A. *What is Hendiadys?*

Speiser (1964: lxx) describes hendiadys as 'a method whereby two formally co-ordinate terms—verbs, nouns or adjectives—joined by "and" express a single concept in which one of the components defines the other'. A similar definition in *The Oxford English Dictionary* (1933, *V*: 222) provides as an example 'two substantives with "and" instead of an adjective and a substantive'. The phrase חֶסֶד וֶאֱמֶת fits both the description and the example, at least when it is a single semantic item.

Very few articles have been written about hendiadys in Biblical

---

1.   Others besides Glueck and Kaddari who assert that חֶסֶד וֶאֱמֶת is an example of hendiadys include Dentan (1963: 43 n. 3), Kuyper (1964: 6-7), Speiser (1964: lxx, 180-81) and Weinfeld (1970: 188).

2.   See, for example, Glueck 1967: 55, 79, 102.

3.   Glueck 1967: 39, 54, 71-72.

Hebrew; those which exist usually discuss hendiadys in its relationship with other figures of speech. Two such articles, by Honeyman (1952) and Brongers (1965), associate it with merismus, a device used by writers as a substitute for generic terms to express general ideas, since such abstractions are not commonly lexicalized in Hebrew.

Brongers (1965: 110) deplores the tendency of modern translators to handle hendiadys incorrectly; using two nouns immediately after each other gives the reader the impression that there are two separate and distinct concepts. He says that some word-pairs have the form but not the content of hendiadys, since the components retain their independence although they are synonymous, as in hendiadys. He gives examples of such word-pairs, but he does not mention any criteria by which to decide whether such an expression is, or is not, hendiadys. However, he suggests (p. 112) that חֶסֶד וֶאֱמֶת and a few other similar expressions are used by the author to express the single idea for which an exhaustive, completely descriptive word does not exist.

Two other articles, by Avishur and van der Westhuizen, consider examples of hendiadys in association with parallelism; their aim is to determine the order of development of these and other constructions in the literature of the Hebrew Bible. Avishur (1971) does not consider the expression חֶסֶד וֶאֱמֶת because the separate terms do not appear together in the type of constructions he investigates. He says (pp. 74-75) that the combination of two words that are close to each other semantically expresses the common idea as a type of superlative, describing it in a very intensified and impressive manner.

Both Avishur and van der Westhuizen mention the rhetorical or literary effects of the constructions they examine. Another view of hendiadys—in English literature, to be sure—that considers the effects it produces is given by Wright (1981); this has been described by Loesch (1982: 99) as 'thorough and illuminating' and 'highly distinguished'. Wright concentrates on Shakespeare's *Hamlet*, and many of his insights on hendiadys are especially relevant to that play. However, some of his observations are also applicable to biblical Hebrew, particularly when he discusses the nature of hendiadys using illustrations from Latin and English literature, and when he looks at the use of the figure in several of Shakespeare's plays. Words like 'elevation', 'dignity', 'complexity' and 'grandeur' occur here more than once to describe the effects produced by examples of hendiadys.

Wright notes (1981: 168) that very little attention has been given to

the way Shakespeare uses hendiadys. Describing the device as 'the use
of two substantives, joined by a conjunction..., to express a single but
complex idea', he points out that the usual method of interpreting such
phrases 'does not account for the poet's deliberate stylistic choice' to
use two parallel nouns instead of a noun and adjective or a noun and
dependent noun. The author, he says, intends his readers 'to grasp two
ideas, not one', and the conjunction 'precisely registers the separate-
ness and successiveness of the two distinct segments of the event. The
perception may even be a triple one—of each idea in turn and then of
their combination or fusion.' Examples he gives (pp. 171-72) suggest
that

> hendiadys is often characterized by its elevation above the ordinary tone of
> conventional English and by a kind of syntactical complexity that seems
> fathomable only by an intuitional understanding of the way words inter-
> weave their meanings, rather than by painstaking lexical analysis.

As Shakespeare uses it, he says (p. 173), hendiadys almost always has
an 'elevating, dignifying, and even...estranging effect', and in it
'there is something more at work—not merely amplification or inten-
sification but an interweaving...of meanings'. Generally, 'the device is
appropriate to a "high style"' and occurs regularly 'in passages of a
certain elevation, dignity, or remoteness from ordinary experience'.

These articles illustrate two different approaches to hendiadys, and
the nature of the approach has some influence on the conclusions
drawn. On the one hand, Honeyman and Brongers treat merismus and
hendiadys as figures of speech that result in enrichment of the
vocabulary. On the other hand, Avishur and van der Westhuizen link
hendiadys with parallelism and the construct state—each of which is a
collocation of two or more words—and they draw attention to the
rhetorical effect of the constructions. This leads to the approach
adopted by Wright, who sees hendiadys as a device deliberately introduced by Shakespeare to produce an effect of complexity, dignity,
elevation, grandeur and remoteness from ordinary experience. To
what extent do such effects as these accompany the use of חֶסֶד וָאֱמֶת in
the Hebrew Bible?

B. חֶסֶד וָאֱמֶת *Used with God as Agent*

חֶסֶד וָאֱמֶת occurs twice in the account of the quest of Abraham's steward
to find a bride for Isaac (Gen. 24). On his arrival at the city of Nahor,
the steward prays that Yahweh the God of his master will extend חֶסֶד

to Abraham. He outlines the scenario by which Yahweh will reveal Isaac's wife and at the same time express חֶסֶד to Abraham. Almost immediately the daughter of Abraham's nephew arrives and does exactly what the steward has requested, as if she has overheard his prayer! She reveals that she is indeed a close relative of Abraham. The steward realizes that Yahweh has led him exactly to the place that Abraham specified and has brought to him the one person who satisfies the requirements prescribed by Abraham for his son's wife. The immediacy and the precision of Yahweh's answer to his prayer overwhelms him, and he bows in awesome wonder to praise and worship the God of his master Abraham. The narrator underlines the complexity and grandeur of the incident as the steward acknowledges that his master has received not the requested חֶסֶד but חֶסֶד וֶאֱמֶת (Gen. 24.27). The whole situation has a remoteness from the steward's ordinary experiences, which the narrator emphasizes by deliberately choosing the two nouns to underline the faithfulness of Yahweh—even though this is always an essential component of his חֶסֶד—in this expression of his חֶסֶד to Abraham. The hendiadys highlights the commitment of Yahweh to Abraham, and at the same time Abraham's commitment to Yahweh, which prompted him to send his steward on this quest.

Before accepting the hospitality offered to him, the steward acquaints his hosts with the details of his mission. He tells them of Abraham's instructions, his prayer at the well and its sequel, emphasizing the immediacy of the answer—'Before I finished praying'—and the willingness of Rebecca—'She quickly lowered her jar'—to attend to his needs. He stresses his dependence upon Yahweh, the God of his master, but does not mention the חֶסֶד that Yahweh is extending to Abraham. He knows that Rebecca is the one Yahweh has chosen; he is anxious to know the reaction of Bethuel and Laban, and he is aware of some of the factors upon which their decision depends. This also is no ordinary everyday experience for his hosts, and is sufficient reason for the narrator to place in the steward's mouth again the compound expression as he urges them (Gen. 24.49): 'Tell me whether or not you will extend חֶסֶד וֶאֱמֶת to my master'. The dignity and elevation of the situation is made plain as the steward voices his desire that his hosts will be faithful to their kinsman, just as Yahweh has already been.

Gen. 32.11—Jacob's future is uncertain as he returns to his homeland.
Esau's approach with four hundred men fills him with apprehension.
During his long absence he has become adept at looking after himself
and his own interests, a characteristic that his mother had actively
encouraged (Gen. 27.5-17, 42-45). In fear and distress, the self-suffi-
cient Jacob makes his plans and prays to the God of his fathers
Abraham and Isaac, seeking deliverance from Esau. The narrator
knows, however, that Jacob is approaching the turning-point in his
life, and he spares no effort to impress this upon the reader in his
description of Jacob's fear, his penitence, his nocturnal encounter, and
the climax in his peaceable reunion with Esau (Gen. 34.4-11). The
elements of complexity, grandeur, dignity and remoteness from
ordinary experience provide a natural setting for Jacob's use of the
complicated form of the hendiadys. Here, too, is the beginning of a
new relationship between Jacob and Yahweh, who is no longer merely
the God of his fathers but Jacob's own God (Gen. 33.20).

2 Sam. 2.6—This is a critical incident in David's progress towards
uniting the kingdom of Israel. He is the anointed king over his own
people, Judah. He knows the long-established loyalty of Jabesh-gilead
to Saul that prompted the men of Jabesh to risk their lives in order to
remove the bodies of Saul and his sons from the Philistines (1 Sam.
31.8-13). He knows, too, of the activity of Abner and Ish-bosheth in
the region of Gilead. A false move now could swing the men of
Jabesh-gilead away from David to align themselves solidly behind
Saul's son. David's approach is characterized by a diplomacy and
dignity that is intended to elevate the incident above the normal expectations of the people of Jabesh. The words of his messengers are
conciliatory, acknowledging and commending the Jabeshites' loyalty
to Saul; they form a context in which the hendiadys occurs quite
naturally and highlights the faithfulness that is inherent in Yahweh's
חֶסֶד. Although David's purpose is to transfer their allegiance from
Saul's family to himself, there is no open invitation for them to do so.
It is vaguely suggested (v. 7), and the hendiadys implicitly assures the
Jabesh-gileadites that David also will be faithful to those who commit
themselves to him.

2 Sam. 15.20—As David leaves Jerusalem when Absalom's rebellion
commences, he tries to dissuade Ittai of Gath from accompanying him,
concluding his appeal with the words חֶסֶד וֶאֱמֶת. There is some doubt

about the text here,[1] but as it stands, David's concluding words may be
a petition addressed to Yahweh on Ittai's behalf. After all, David or
any of his loyal followers cannot possibly extend חֶסֶד וֶאֱמֶת to Ittai if he
remains in Jerusalem while the others all seek refuge elsewhere; nor
will Absalom be likely to fulfil David's wish. Yahweh is the only one
from whom the faithful Ittai can receive the special treatment desired
by David during the king's enforced absence from Jerusalem. The
setting in which David uses the phrase is remote from ordinary
experience—especially for a king who has been chosen and appointed
by Yahweh. In this unusual situation, David conducts himself with
dignity, courtesy and consideration towards one who has only recently
joined his service and who is also a foreigner. Nothing is known of
Ittai's previous position in David's army, but this incident makes clear
his unswerving loyalty to the king as well as David's high regard for
him, which is confirmed in the sequel. All these features provide a
context in which hendiadys is most appropriate, and it again emphasizes the faithfulness that is an essential component of חֶסֶד.

חֶסֶד וֶאֱמֶת is used on three more occasions, in Ps. 61.8; Ps. 115.1 and
Ps. 138.2. Each time, the worshipful and reverent approach of the
psalmist to Yahweh underlines the solemnity, dignity and elevation of
the occasion and renders the setting appropriate for the use of the
hendiadys. Even though אֱמֶת is an essential component of חֶסֶד, the
expression emphasizes that Yahweh demonstrates his faithfulness to
his people when he extends חֶסֶד to them.

Exod. 34.6-7—חֶסֶד וֶאֱמֶת occurs in another setting that can only be
described as a sublime pinnacle, far beyond ordinary everyday
experience. In passages so far considered, the term has been applied
by people to Yahweh; but here, as he reveals himself, his name and his
character to Moses, Yahweh states among his attributes that he is
רַב־חֶסֶד וֶאֱמֶת. Yahweh's self-revelation (Exod. 34.6-9) is set in the after-
math of the episode of the golden calf (Exod. 32),[2] and precedes the

---

1.   Driver (1913: 314) finds the solution to this difficulty in the LXX, which
supplies וַיהוה יַעֲשֶׂה עִמָּךְ before חֶסֶד וֶאֱמֶת, claiming that these words have 'simply
dropped out of MT by homoioteleuton'. Many modern commentators and translators
adopt this amendment, including Hertzberg (1964: 339), Morris (1981: 79),
McCarter (1984: 360) and Gordon (1986: 273).
2.   Childs (1974: 610-11) says that the narrative which began with the story of

renewal of the covenant. The expression occurs in a particularly solemn context, coming from the mouth of Yahweh himself in the course of the theophany, and the prefixed רַב־ emphasizes both the solemnity of the occasion and the abundance of the חֶסֶד וָאֱמֶת that Yahweh is lavishing on his wayward people. While אֱמֶת is always an essential component of Yahweh's חֶסֶד, the hendiadys draws attention to his intention to commit himself again to the fickle people whom he has chosen. The profound impression of this solemnity and dignity is reflected in the number of times Yahweh's statement is echoed in the Hebrew Bible. Some of these echoes are indicated in Table 10.5.

	A	B	C	D	E	F	G	H	I	J	K	L
Exod. 20.5-6			+			+			+	+	+	
Exod. 34.6-7	+	+	+	+	+	+	+	+	+			
Num. 14.17-19		+	+	+			+	+	+			
Deut. 5.9-10			+			+			+	+	+	
Deut. 7.9-13			+							+	+	
Joel 2.12-14	+	+	+	+								+
Jon. 3.10-4.3	+	+	+	+								+
Nah. 1.2-3			+					+			+	
Ps. 86.5, 15	+	+	+	+	+	+						
Ps. 103.8-12, 17-18	+	+	+	+		+				+		
Ps. 145.8-9	+	+	+	+								
Neh. 9.17-19	+	+	+	+		+						
Neh. 9.31-32	+		+									

A	אֵל רַחוּם וְחַנּוּן	G	נֹשֵׂא עָוֹן
B	אֶרֶךְ אַפַּיִם	H	נַקֵּה לֹא יְנַקֶּה
C	חֶסֶד	I	פֹּקֵד עָוֹן אָבוֹת...רִבֵּעִים
D	רַב־	J	אֹהֵב
E	אֱמֶת	K	שֹׂנֵא
F	נֹצֵר חֶסֶד לַאֲלָפִים	L	נִחָם עַל־הָרָעָה

Table 10.5. *Exodus 34.6-7 and its Echoes*

The key in the lower half of the table sets out the words and phrases represented by each of the letters; A to I are taken from Exodus 34, J and K from Exodus 20, and L from Joel 2. Each passage included in the table contains at least two of the key items[1] from Exodus 34, and

the golden calf reaches its climax in ch. 34, with the restoration of the covenant that was broken in ch. 32. Similarly, Durham (1987: 450-55) refers several times to Exod. 32–34 as a unit.

1. Item A also occurs in Ps. 111.4 and in 2 Chron. 30.9, with יהוה replacing אֵל,

the items present in the various passages are indicated by the +
symbol. Frequently the allusion is a verbatim quotation, but sometimes synonymous expressions are used; e.g., סלח for נֹשֵׂא עָוֹן in Num.
14.19; Ps. 86.5; Neh. 9.17; and אֹיֵב for שֹׂנֵא in Nah. 1.2.

The hendiadys of Exod. 34.6 occurs only in Ps. 86.15, where it is
again preceded by רַב־. The psalmist commences with supplication and
ends with petition while in the central section he offers his adoration
and thanks to Yahweh. His attitude reflects that found in Psalms 115
and 138: he exalts Yahweh and expresses heartfelt thanks to him,
being very conscious of Yahweh's abundant faithfulness towards him.
He acknowledges that when Yahweh forgives (סלח) he is רַב־חֶסֶד; he
associates Yahweh's חֶסֶד גָּדוֹל with his deliverance (נצל); and because
Yahweh is אֵל־רַחוּם וְחַנּוּן אֶרֶךְ אַפַּיִם וְרַב־חֶסֶד וֶאֱמֶת he confidently requests
him to be merciful (חנן) and to assist him (ישע) in the danger he faces.
In such a situation, the hendiadys is no mechanical repetition of a
stereotyped formula; it comes naturally from the lips of the psalmist
and imparts the depth of its meaning to his earlier references to the
abundance of Yahweh's חֶסֶד.

Discussion of the passages from Exodus frequently centres around
the twin topics of punishment and forgiveness of sin and involves the
assignment of various portions of the text to later redactors. Bowen
(1938: 29-31) makes the following statements among others—

a. There is no suggestion of forgiveness in Exod. 20.5-6.
b. There is strong emphasis on God's intention to punish sin in
    Exod. 20.5 and also in Exod. 34.7. He refers to item I of
    Table 10.5.
c. Forgiveness (item G) becomes meaningless in the context of
    item I.
d. The expectation of many who use item A is not forgiveness
    but only Yahweh's faithfulness.
e. There is no suggestion of a forgiving spirit in item B; it
    simply means that Yahweh is not quick tempered: he will
    punish but not rashly.

He attributes to a later hand the passages that are closely related to
forgiveness, such as items F and G; yet he resists the temptation to do

and partially in Ps. 112.4. On the latter passage, see n. 1 on p. 66. Jer. 30.11 =
46.28 contains item H, while items F and I are echoed (the latter weakly) in
Jer. 32.18.

the same with items A and B, since he accounts for them in statements d. and e. above.

Dentan (1963), however, adopts a different approach. He acknowledges that in Exod. 34.6-7 the initial emphasis on forgiveness contrasts starkly with the concluding stress on punishment. He resolves this incongruity by reducing the emphasis on punishment, and concludes (p. 48) that the 'literary affinities with the Wisdom literature are so definite that one can assert with confidence that the entire formula is a product of the School of the Wise Men'. He notes (pp. 35-36) the quotation of the first part of the formula without the stern conclusion,[1] and continues,

> it is hardly conceivable that the shorter form, minus any reference to God's moral demands, can be original. As it stands in Exodus, the passage is a beautifully balanced statement with regard to the two most basic aspects of the character of God—His love and His justice. It is significant that love holds the primary place.

Unlike Bowen's dissertation and Dentan's article, the present study is not concerned with the various stages in the development of the text. In the theophany,[2] Yahweh presents a composite picture of divergent and seemingly irreconcilable aspects of his character and nature.[3] From the wider context (Exod. 32–34) it is clear that Israel has sinned and there is the very real possibility that Yahweh may annul the covenant and destroy the people he has chosen (Exod. 32.10). Yet the punishment is limited, restricted to the fourth generation, in striking contrast to the abundance of grace that extends to thousands of generations;[4] its

1. Items H and I in Table 10.5 are omitted from Joel 2.13; Jon. 4.2; Pss. 86.15; 103.8; 145.8 and Neh. 9.17.

2. This paragraph has benefitted greatly from Eichrodt's insights expressed in his discussion of 'Affirmations about the divine activity' (1961: 228-88) and 'Sin and forgiveness' (1967: 380-495). Also, the succint and penetrating treatment of this and related passages by Andersen (1986: 44-52) expresses admirably many of the ideas formulated during the current study.

3. The variety in this and related passages 'is due partly to the floundering of human thought when it reaches its limits—it is out of its depth. In these words there are paradoxes, contradictions, mysteries.' (Andersen 1986: 45).

4. The word דּוֹר occurs in this phrase only in Deut. 7.9, where it expresses the abundance of Yahweh's חֶסֶד which is implicit there but explicit in Exod. 34.6; Eichrodt (1967: 430) and Andersen (1986: 49) both accept that the writer's intention

purpose is to restore the disrupted fellowship (Exod. 33.5-11; 34.10-27). For Yahweh is a personal God with a personal interest in the entire chosen community and in each individual member of that community; he has the ability, and the willingness, to forgive and thus to maintain the relationship he has established with them. His forgiveness may be requested, but not demanded; it may be expected, but it is not an obligation that Yahweh accepted when he established his covenant. Reconciliation is always the gift of Yahweh's sovereign freedom; it can never be earned or merited. Eichrodt (1967: 475) rightly observes that to חֶסֶד יהוה—aptly described as his 'readiness to succour'—'it belongs also to forgive transgressions' and at the same time to ensure that the sins of the people do not destroy their relationship with him. The apparently irreconcilable aspects of Yahweh's character—his kindness and his severity, which are reserved for his friends and his enemies respectively—may also be seen as complementary; and, as Andersen (1986: 46) points out, no attempt is made to reconcile the contradictions that are left standing alongside each other.

Table 10.5 shows that most of the echoes of Exod. 34.6-7 include רַב- (item D) with חֶסֶד; and, indeed, the actual phrase רַב-חֶסֶד appears in both verses of Psalm 86 and in all of the passages indicated except two—Neh. 9.17 and Ps. 145.8—in which there are slight variations. Moreover, these are the only passages in which the phrase occurs, so it is always—and only—used as an attribute of Yahweh. In addition, רֹב is used at least three times with חֶסֶד[1] and twice with חֲסָדִים;[2] and on each occasion it is again an attribute of Yahweh. Further, whenever רַחֲמִים is qualified by either רַב[3] or רֹב[4] it is again an attribute of Yahweh; it is never a human attribute. In the light of the restrictions on these occurrences of רַב and רֹב, the reference is not so much to the quantity as to the quality[5] of the חֶסֶד (or the רַחֲמִים) of Yahweh.

---

is to refer here to generations, not to people. Compare also the contrast in Isa. 54 between vv. 7-8 and 9-10.

1. In Pss. 5.8; 69.14 (רַב-חֶסֶד) and Neh. 13.22; and possibly also in Ps. 106.45 and Lam. 3.32, where the singular form חסדו is punctuated as a plural.

2. In Isa. 63. 7 and Ps. 106.7.

3. The plural רַבִּים precedes רַחֲמִים in 2 Sam. 24.14 // 1 Chron. 21.13, and follows it in Ps. 119.156; Dan. 9.18; Neh. 9.19, 27, 31. Neh. 9.28 has רַבּוֹת רַחֲמִים.

4. In Pss. 51.3; 69.17.

5. Dahood notes that רַב has the connotation 'rich, wealthy' several times when it is used in a human context, as in Pss. 17.14; 37.16. He suggests (1968: 293) that in Ps. 86.5 it refers to the richness of Yahweh's חֶסֶד. See also comments on

Yahweh's חֶסֶד is so vastly superior to human חֶסֶד that the latter can only be a very pale reflection of the former. Sakenfeld's conclusion (1978: 211) to her discussion of some passages mentioned above is pertinent: Yahweh's חֶסֶד 'is far greater than that experienced in human relationships'.

Nah. 1.2-3 is the only echo of the theophany in which there is no mention of Yahweh's חֶסֶד or any of his other attributes of kindness. There is a striking contrast between this and all the other passages: the emphasis is on the severity of the 'jealous and avenging God' towards his enemies, and even the phrase 'slow to anger' acquires a more threatening tone because of its proximity to 'by no means leave unpunished' rather than to 'the compassionate and gracious God' as in the other passages. Here is further support for the close association of Yahweh's חֶסֶד with his readiness to forgive and his willingness to limit the punishment of those who return to him. His commitment to his people, which persists even when they rebel, provides a situational context in which he is able to manifest himself over and over again to them as 'the God who is rich in חֶסֶד and faithfulness'.

Although the word אֱמֶת does not appear explicitly in most of the passages that echo Yahweh's self-revelation, it cannot be assumed that the omission is deliberate. The writers have used an abbreviated form that will serve to recall the fuller and more solemn expression in Exod. 34.6-7 to the minds of their readers, since אֱמֶת is an essential component of חֶסֶד.

C. חֶסֶד וֶאֱמֶת *used with Human Partners*
All passages considered previously have applied the phrase in situations where God is the agent and the patient is human. There are only six passages where both agent and patient are human. The unusual circumstances surrounding its use in Gen. 24.49 as well as the dignity and elevation of the situation have already been noted.

Gen. 47.29—Jacob's dying wish is to be buried with his ancestors in the land of Canaan. As the direct descendant of Abraham and Isaac, Jacob is now the inheritor of the land promised to his ancestors (Gen.

Neh. 9.17, 31 with Exod. 34.6-7 in Section 1B of Chapter 8.

35.12). For him, it is of paramount importance that death shall not
sever his connection with the land, and Joseph is in the best position to
comply with his wish which, in the nature of the case, he is himself
unable to carry out personally or to ensure that it is carried out. All
these features—as well as the oath which, at his father's insistence,
Joseph swears—highlight the solemnity of the occasion, and
accordingly provide a setting in which the hendiadys is appropriate.

Josh. 2.14 is the only recorded case of חֶסֶד וֶאֱמֶת with a woman as
patient; it is promised by the spies to Rahab and, implicitly, to her
family. Rahab, a resident in Jericho and a foreigner, shelters and
protects the spies and thereby commits an act of treason. On the other
hand, the חֶסֶד promised by the spies—to save the lives of Rahab and
her family when Jericho is destroyed—can only be attained by making
an exception to Yahweh's law of the ban (Josh. 6.17, 22-25). The
irregularity of this incident removes it far from ordinary everyday
experience; this complexity renders it an appropriate setting for the
use of hendiadys. At the same time, the spies use the phrase partly to
assure Rahab of their genuineness and partly to emphasize that they
are acting not merely as humans but on behalf of Yahweh.

The three remaining passages are Prov. 14.22, 16.6 and 20.28, where
the situational context is usually that of normal human experience with
very little, if any, evidence of grandeur, dignity and elevation; so the
criteria suggested by Wright can rarely be applied. This is certainly
true for the first two passages, but Kaddari's criteria indicate that חֶסֶד
וֶאֱמֶת may be an example of hendiadys since it is parallel to a simple
semantic unit on each occasion.

D. *Summary*
This section has examined passages in which חֶסֶד וֶאֱמֶת occurs either
with God as agent or with a human agent. The context of each passage
in the first group exhibits one or more of Wright's features that
provide characteristic settings for the use of hendiadys: complexity,
dignity, elevation, grandeur, remoteness from everyday experience,
solemnity, sublimity. This is also true of the three narrative passages
in which חֶסֶד וֶאֱמֶת occurs with a human agent. These features have not
been found in the remaining passages with human חֶסֶד וֶאֱמֶת in a poetical
setting; but other reasons have been advanced to support the claim that

here too חֶסֶד וֶאֱמֶת may be regarded as an example of hendiadys.

Other poetical passages that refer to divine חֶסֶד וֶאֱמֶת have been investigated, but from another point of view, in Section 3. Wright's features are present in some at least of these psalms. Adequate evidence has already been provided to support the assertion that Wright's insights on hendiadys are relevant not only to Shakespeare's *Hamlet* but also to the expression חֶסֶד וֶאֱמֶת in biblical literature. Moreover, the occurrence of חֶסֶד וֶאֱמֶת in situations where there is 'a certain elevation, dignity, or remoteness from ordinary experience' serves to enhance the complexity and richness of this expression.

How, then, should a translator translate—or a commentator comment on—a complex expression that he or she has decided is both a single semantic unit and also an example of hendiadys? Neither the translator nor the commentator can make use of the devices available to the actor on the stage—intonation, facial expression, gesture—for conveying to the audience the complexity of the situation and of the phrase. It is, of course, more difficult for the translator than for the commentator to elaborate on the nuances of the expression and the complexity of the situation. A word-for-word translation will usually be quite unsuitable, but possibly something of the complexity can be expressed using dynamic equivalence. In the expression חֶסֶד וֶאֱמֶת the central word is חֶסֶד and the function of אֱמֶת is to modify this main word. When אֱמֶת is used as an attribute of a noun that refers to an inanimate object it can have the meaning 'reliable, genuine, lasting'. Modern translators frequently use similar adjectives to bring out the rich connotation of חֶסֶד itself[1]—'constant love' in NEB and GNB, 'steadfast love' in RSV, and 'unfailing love' in NIV. Koehler (1958: 60) includes חֶסֶד וֶאֱמֶת under the meaning *Beständigkeit* for אֱמֶת, where he gives the translations 'durable, perpetual'; under חֶסֶד (p. 318) he suggests the meaning 'lasting solidarity' for the only passage (Gen. 24.27) cited. The discussion above has shown that חֶסֶד וֶאֱמֶת means much more than 'true, genuine' חֶסֶד; it is rather the faithfulness, the trustworthiness of the participants that is brought into focus by אֱמֶת in the compound expression. The genuineness, permanence and reliability is not so much an attribute of חֶסֶד as of the parties who are involved in the חֶסֶד, whether it be God to human or human to human—the

---

1.	Morris (1981: 60) notes several variants of 'love' used in different translations.

relationship between them is an unwavering, enduring, reliable commitment to each other in which חֶסֶד is the appropriate action.

5. *Overview*

This chapter has shown that the compound expression חֶסֶד וֶאֱמֶת resembles חֶסֶד more closely than אֱמֶת.

1. The frequency of occurrence (Table 10.1) indicates that the distributions of חֶסֶד וֶאֱמֶת and חֶסֶד have a greater resemblance than the distributions of אֱמֶת and חֶסֶד וֶאֱמֶת.
2. Consideration of the collocates of the three items (Tables 10.2 and 10.3) shows that חֶסֶד וֶאֱמֶת is found in close association with more collocates of חֶסֶד than of אֱמֶת.
3. Examination of passages in which חֶסֶד וֶאֱמֶת occurs in parallel with other items indicates that this compound expression may be regarded as a simple semantic item, and suggests that the semantic area of חֶסֶד וֶאֱמֶת is closer to that of חֶסֶד than to that of אֱמֶת.
4. The expression חֶסֶד וֶאֱמֶת appears in many passages whose context exhibits features like those proposed by Wright as characteristic settings for the use of hendiadys. Consequently חֶסֶד וֶאֱמֶת must frequently be considered as an example of hendiadys, confirming the conclusion that it is on many occasions a single semantic item. This, however, raises problems as the translator attempts to convey the richness and complexity encompassed by the expression חֶסֶד וֶאֱמֶת in its various contexts.

Chapter 11

CONCLUSION

1. *Linguistic Aspects*

A. *Lexical Fields*

Principles of structural linguistics, which have been previously applied
to lexical fields consisting of biblical words found either in the Hebrew
Old Testament or in the Greek New Testament, have not been used to
examine the word חֶסֶד. The present study has shown that it is possible
to investigate חֶסֶד in a lexical field. It has produced some valuable
results, confirming insights gained in previous studies, and providing
insights into the nature and meaning of חֶסֶד that have escaped the attention of previous investigators. The methodologies of earlier investigations have not been superseded; rather, the present methodology should
be used alongside the earlier ones in such a way that they supplement
one another.

Earlier studies have not used computer facilities to store and retrieve
information; indeed, such facilities did not exist when many of these
studies were made. The vast amount of information collected in the
examination of the field in the present study could not have been
handled adequately without using a computer. For studies of such
lexical fields, access to a computer is most advisable and extremely
beneficial: its speedy and accurate rearrangement of data places a
selected item in a variety of environments, making it much easier to
observe the item from different aspects.

B. *Structure*

The structure of a language is exhibited in the relationships existing
between the units of the language, here taken to be words. Methods
employed in a structural approach to the analysis of language have
been applied to the investigation of the relationships between words,

examining both the situational contexts and also the linguistic environments in which the words occur.

The situational context includes the types of parties and entities involved in each occurrence of a member of the lexical field. The use of חֶסֶד and the derivatives of אהב with non-personal entities provides a feature that differentiates between them, while the use of חֶסֶד and the derivatives of רחם with persons shows that they resemble one another.

Examining the linguistic environment reveals syntagmatic and paradigmatic relationships between members of the field. Word strings in which the elements occur were considered from three different aspects. On the syntagmatic axis are word-pairs that frequently occur together in fairly close proximity. The collocations of elements with other words reveal both resemblances and contrasts between elements, leading to preliminary definitions of the formal meaning of certain elements. Also on the syntagmatic axis are strings of words containing verbs as well as members of the field. These reveal that חֶסֶד and חֵן contrast in their usage with the verbs עשׂה and מצא. Investigation of paradigmatic relationships centres on words substituted for elements in certain strings. This aspect led to the discovery of a contrast between חֶסֶד and טוב.

These relationships between words help to throw light on the meanings of related words, but meanings can be compared more effectively by determining sense-relations, including synonomy, antonomy, hyponomy and compatibility, between the words. These relations can in turn be deduced by investigating sentences containing the words, with a view to finding relations of implication between the sentences. It had been hoped that such sense-relations would provide a major contribution to the present investigation, but there is in the corpus very little material that is suitable for determining relations of implication between sentences.

C. *Synchrony*

This study has been confined to a synchronic investigation of a field in the corpus as it existed at a fixed point in time. Such a study is an essential prerequisite to any diachronic investigation of the same field, but the magnitude of the task undertaken precluded any extension to other points of time. The present study is structured in such a manner that it is not possible to consider the development that has undoubtedly occurred in the concept during the compilation of the various documents which form the Hebrew Bible. The methods adopted can be adapted to remedy this deficiency, by first partitioning the text into various sections according to the time of their composition. A collocation profile of חֶסֶד for each section of the text will then reveal whether the composition of the field changes from one section to another. Similarly, a diachronic study of the distribution of חֶסֶד in the various sections of the text may indicate significant changes, from section to section, in the nature of the agent and patient with which חֶסֶד is used.

Insights into the nature and meaning of חֶסֶד have been gained either by considering the complete picture or by examining individual passages. A synchronic study exposes the researcher to a tendency to level out the results by importing into each occurrence of the word insights that have been discerned in its other occurrences. It is clear that חֶסֶד refers to a rich and varied concept; in order to resist the levelling out tendency, it must be remembered that insights gained from individual passages do not necessarily apply to each and every occurrence of the word.

A preliminary excursion has been made in a slightly different direction, applying these principles to compare the lexical field of חֶסֶד in DSS with that in *BHS* (Clark 1992: 50-53). חֶסֶד occurs 50 times in the Qumran documents considered and approximately 250 times in *BHS*. The distributions of חֶסֶד in the two sources afford examples of similarities—for example, its much more frequent use with God as agent than with a human agent—and of contrasts—for example, DSS uses plural forms of חֶסֶד more frequently than *BHS*. The actual number of collocations with חֶסֶד in DSS is usually much greater than in *BHS*; and several words not considered as collocates in *BHS* have been noticed occurring frequently with חֶסֶד in DSS. Other distinctive features are: the expression חֶסֶד וֶאֱמֶת has been found only once in DSS (21 times in *BHS*); and עשׂה takes חֶסֶד as object only once in DSS (40 times in *BHS*).

2. *Insights Confirmed*

Insights obtained in previous studies of חֶסֶד have been confirmed in the present study. A few of those considered to be more significant are noted briefly.

A. חֶסֶד—*Güte*

Although Stoebe (1971: 600, 601; cf. 610) adopts this 'translation' as the heading for his article, he points out that this is only an imperfect rendering of the word חֶסֶד, and that the breadth of its meaning in its secular usage cannot be expressed exactly by a single German word. That 'goodness' is an approximation to the meaning of חֶסֶד has been confirmed while examining passages that contain the verb עשׂה and the noun טוב, for each of these occurrences conforms to the constraints devised by Sakenfeld for חֶסֶד. According to Sakenfeld's criteria, טוב is a substitute for חֶסֶד in these passages, so טוב and חֶסֶד may be regarded as synonyms.

B. חֶסֶד *and* חֵן

Lofthouse (1933) found several features that distinguish חֶסֶד from חֵן. Some of these are confirmed in the present study, including:

1. חנן refers to an action, which cannot be enforced or claimed, that passes from a superior to an inferior;
2. חֵן is used only rarely of God, but chiefly of people between whom there is no specific tie or bond;
3. when חֵן is used in making a request, it is a rather elaborate way of saying 'please'.

C. *God as Patient*

It has been suggested that חֶסֶד is rarely—if ever—directed by a human to God. In these rare cases it is necessary to weaken the concept so that חֶסֶד becomes something like 'loyalty' or 'devotion'. However, when the patient is defined as 'the one for whose benefit' the action is performed, it has been shown that in these doubtful cases it is not God but other humans who are the beneficiaries. Thus the study has confirmed that, while חֶסֶד is used with both God and humans as agent, the patient is always human but never divine.

3. *Fresh Insights*

Former researchers did not concentrate on the relationships of חֶסֶד with other words. Insights gained by investigating such relationships are summarized briefly here.

A. *Essential Components*

אֱמֶת and אֱמוּנָה have both been found as essential components of חֶסֶד.

Glueck perceived a very close link between חֶסֶד and אֱמֶת. He expresses this in many ways, but never in a succinct statement like the one above. He frequently uses the word 'loyalty', but it is difficult to decide whether it is a rendering for חֶסֶד or for אֱמֶת. When both agent and patient are human he says (1967: 40, on Gen. 20.13) that חֶסֶד is 'not merely love...but...at the same time loyalty', for, although חֶסֶד is used alone here, it is still possible to visualize אֱמֶת next to it. Again, when God is agent (p. 72, on Gen. 24.27) the appearance of חֶסֶד together with אֱמֶת or אֱמוּנָה emphasizes 'the quality of loyalty inherent in the concept' חֶסֶד. On several occasions Glueck suggests that either חֶסֶד or אֱמֶת may be rendered by 'loyalty'. Divine חֶסֶד is glossed as 'loyalty' (p. 95, on Ps. 23.6; Ps. 13.6; cf. p. 102, H), and so is human חֶסֶד (p. 50, on 2 Sam. 16.17); but divine חֶסֶד וֶאֱמֶת is 'love and loyalty' (p. 54, on 2 Sam. 2.6), and in their religious usage (p. 57, on Hos. 4.1) human אֱמֶת and חֶסֶד are glossed as 'loyalty' and 'love' respectively. Glueck also claims that loyalty is inherent in חֶסֶד (pp. 50, 72) and belongs to חֶסֶד (p. 102, F); חֶסֶד embraces אֱמֶת (p. 54), includes אֱמֶת (p. 55, C1), and comprises אֱמֶת (p. 57). In addition, he says that 'loyalty and love' are two of the 'component parts of the general concept' of human חֶסֶד (p. 55, D).

Hills (1957: 9) also recognizes the close relationship between between חֶסֶד and אֱמֶת; the frequent use of אֱמֶת with חֶסֶד emphasizes the *trustworthiness* that 'is necessary where the חֶסֶד act is the fulfilment of a promise in the future' and the *constancy* 'demanded in cases where חֶסֶד must be prolonged over an extended period to meet a continuing need'.

While Glueck and Hills draw attention to the relationship between the terms חֶסֶד and אֱמֶת, the present study shows that both אֱמֶת and אֱמוּנָה are essential components of חֶסֶד when God is agent as well as when the agent is human.

B. *Commitment*

חֶסֶד and טוב can be regarded as synonyms according to the parameters that Sakenfeld set for situations in which חֶסֶד is the expected response. However, a closer examination of passages in which טוב is substituted for חֶסֶד in syntagms containing the verb עשה reveals a commitment between the parties involved when חֶסֶד, but not when טוב, is used. This provides a distinguishing feature that Sakenfeld's methodology did not require. Sakenfeld has more recently suggested 'faithfulness' and 'loyalty' as acceptable translations of חֶסֶד, and she maintains that the latter is particularly apposite for almost all instances of human חֶסֶד.

She also defines human חֶסֶד (1985: 131) as 'a freely undertaken carrying through of an existing commitment to another who is in a situation of need'. Hills, however, had earlier[1] spoken of human חֶסֶד as an enduring responsibility for another in which there is 'implied an unconditional, lifelong commitment to him and his need'.

The methodology adopted in the present study has shown that a deep, enduring, personal commitment to each other is an essential feature of situations in which one human party extends חֶסֶד to another. This is a mutual, bilateral commitment, unlike the unilateral commitment proposed by both Hills and Sakenfeld.

C. חֶסֶד וֶאֱמֶת

If אֱמֶת is an essential component of חֶסֶד, why is the composite expression חֶסֶד וֶאֱמֶת used so frequently? This expression is often described as an example of hendiadys, and an examination of the nature of this figure of speech provides an answer to the above question. Whenever חֶסֶד וֶאֱמֶת occurs with God as agent it is always in a setting of complexity, dignity, elevation, grandeur, remoteness from ordinary experience, solemnity or sublimity. These characteristics are also present in its occurrences with a human agent in some of the narrative passages and also in some of the poetical passages.

4. *The Content of* חֶסֶד

A. *Benefits Flowing from* חֶסֶד

An indication of the richness and variety of the content of חֶסֶד can be obtained by listing some of the benefits that are seen to result from the expression of חֶסֶד. Many of these benefits have been mentioned but not emphasized in the discussion of different passages. Speaking of human חֶסֶד, which he discerns as rendering basic assistance and meeting crucial needs, Hills (1957: 3-5) says that the 'benefits granted by חֶסֶד... are unlimited in their variety and extent' and include deliverance from death, proper burial of the dead, perpetuating a man's name in his descendants, protection from harm, guidance on a journey, material support, fellowship and consolation, and restoration of the sanctuary.

Table 11.1 sets out a selection of the benefits that have been found

---

1. In a private communication, dated 24 July, 1961.

to flow from חֶסֶד. Each of these benefits was listed fairly frequently in a column of PERDAT headed OUTCOME, but together they account for slightly less than two-thirds of the occurrences of חֶסֶד. Brief notes on some of the cases of human חֶסֶד emphasize the breadth and variety of its content.

BENEFIT	AGENT	
	God	Human
Assistance	10	2
Blessing	4	4
Davidic Dynasty	8	–
Deliverance	28	2
Forgiveness	12	1
Preservation	10	4
Worship	69	1

Table 11.1. *Benefits Flowing from* חֶסֶד

1. 'Assistance' is rendered to Abraham by Sarah (Gen. 20.13), who claims to be his sister, and to Jacob by Joseph (Gen. 47.29), who promises to bury him with his fathers.

2. 'Blessing' in each case refers to a special provision by Yahweh, not by humans; it is invoked by David on the men of Jabesh-gilead for the חֶסֶד they demonstrated in their burial of Saul (2 Sam. 2.5), by Naomi on Boaz (Ruth 2.20), and by Boaz on Ruth (Ruth 3.10).

3. 'Deliverance' for Rahab and her parents is the manifestation of the חֶסֶד requested by Rahab and promised by the spies in Jericho (Josh. 2.12, 14); at Joshua's command, this one family is spared at the destruction of Jericho (Josh. 6.17, 22-25). The spies, and Joshua, act as Yahweh's representatives; here, as in other cases, it is Yahweh who delivers.

4. 'Preservation' of life is the content of the חֶסֶד offered to the man of Bethel (Judg. 1.24) and requested by Ben-hadad (1 Kgs 20.31), and it results from the חֶסֶד shown by the Kenites to the people of Israel (1 Sam. 15.6).

5. 'Worship' is almost always evoked by חֶסֶד יהוה rather than by human חֶסֶד; this may also be true in Ps. 101.1, but the context suggests that the psalmist is moved to praise Yahweh as he contemplates the upright conduct of his fellow human beings.

Three out of every four occurrences of חֶסֶד are with God as agent. It is therefore not surprising that the benefits are attributed to חֶסֶד יהוה

more frequently than to human חֶסֶד. The figures show that it is over-whelmingly divine חֶסֶד that leads to deliverance, forgiveness and worship. The establishment of the Davidic dynasty is never attributed to the חֶסֶד of human beings; it is always Yahweh's חֶסֶד that is at work.

B. *Comparison of* חֶסֶד *with Other Elements*

Derivatives of חנן, with basic meaning 'favour', 'graciousness', are used to indicate that one person is well-disposed towards another. The following contrasts are among those which help to distinguish them from חֶסֶד:

1. relative status of participants is important with the חנן deriva-tives but not with חֶסֶד;
2. commitment between participants is important with חֶסֶד but not with the חנן derivatives;
3. practical expression of the attitude is important with חֶסֶד but not with the חנן derivatives.

Derivatives of רחם, with basic meaning 'compassion', 'mercy', include רַחֲמִים, which often resembles חֶסֶד very closely. Some distinguishing features are:

1. commitment between participants is important with חֶסֶד but not with רַחֲמִים;
2. רַחֲמִים is sometimes a factor that contributes to Yahweh's expression of חֶסֶד.

Derivatives of אהב, with basic meaning 'love', contrast in many ways with חֶסֶד. These contrasts include:

1. אהב derivatives, but not חֶסֶד, are frequently directed to inanimate entities by both Yahweh and humans;
2. אהב derivatives, but not חֶסֶד, are frequently directed by humans towards Yahweh;
3. Yahweh's אַהֲבָה for Israel is his basic reason for making them his 'chosen people'. Hence it is fundamental to the relation-ship in which they express their mutual love for each other and in which Yahweh also extends his חֶסֶד towards Israel.

Derivatives of שנא, with basic meaning 'hate', are antonyms of the אהב derivatives; they are in marked contrast with חֶסֶד and rarely occur in close association with it.

Derivatives of אמן, with basic meaning 'faithful', 'reliable', are used very frequently in situations that involve a non-personal entity; indeed, the contribution of these derivatives is almost double the average contribution of all the roots to this area. The verb takes an inanimate object on several occasions when the subject is either God or a human; many times אֶמֶת and אֱמוּנָה are used attributively with inanimate entities, and once a verbal form is found as an attribute of חֶסֶד. Although they contrast in this way with חֶסֶד, nevertheless both אֶמֶת and אֱמוּנָה are also found to be essential components of חֶסֶד.

5. *Formal Definition of* חֶסֶד

The formal definition proposed for חֶסֶד in Subsection 3Bc of Chapter 4 is based on its collocations with other lexical items. This is now augmented by taking into account its distribution, comparing it with the distributions of other elements. The figures in brackets indicate the approximate percentage of occurrences in situations involving God to Human, Human to Human, and Human to God respectively.

1. The distribution of חֶסֶד resembles that of
   a. רַחֲמִים very strongly   (80–20–0);
   b. אֶמֶת and אֱמוּנָה not so strongly   (40–30–10).
2. The distribution of חֶסֶד contrasts with that of
   a. אהב and אַהֲבָה strongly   (20–70–10);
   b. שׂנא very strongly   (10–80–10).
3. The tendency of חֶסֶד to collocate with
   a. אֶמֶת is very strong;
   b. רַחֲמִים and אֱמוּנָה is not so strong;
   c. אהב is weak.
4. For items with which it collocates frequently, the collocation profile of חֶסֶד
   a. resembles that of אֶמֶת;
   b. contrasts with those of רַחֲמִים and אַהֲבָה.
5. For items with which it collocates rarely, the collocation profile of חֶסֶד
   a. resembles those of אֶמֶת, רַחֲמִים and אֱמוּנָה;
   b. contrasts with that of אהב.

6. The resemblance of collocation patterns with that of חֶסֶד is
   a. greatest for רַחֲמִים;
   b. strong for אֱמֶת;
   c. not quite so strong for אֱמוּנָה;
   d. weaker for אהב.

There is a general agreement between the situational tendencies and the collocational trends, in that רַחֲמִים, אֱמֶת and אֱמוּנָה tend to resemble חֶסֶד, while אהב and אַהֲבָה tend to contrast with חֶסֶד.

6. *Individuals and* חֶסֶד

חֶסֶד is extended to—or by—the same person on several occasions. However, the material was arranged for investigation in a way that has prevented consideration of different occurrences of חֶסֶד with the same person. A brief summary of the circumstances in which the word חֶסֶד is used with Abraham, Joseph and David gives further indication of the richness and variety of the concept.

A. *Abraham*
Abraham is the recipient of חֶסֶד in six passages.

Abraham and Sarah had a pre-arranged understanding that when they ventured into foreign countries she would allow it to be known that she was Abraham's sister—referred to as her חֶסֶד to him in Gen. 20.13. This, Abraham reasoned, would reduce the likelihood that he would be murdered for the sake of his attractive wife.

Abimelech claims to have treated Abraham well (called חֶסֶד in Gen. 21.23) during his sojourn in Gerar, and he asks Abraham to deal favourably in the future with him and his posterity.

Abraham's steward, sent to find a wife for Isaac, three times refers to Yahweh's חֶסֶד extended to his master: twice he requests it (Gen. 24.12; Gen. 24.14) and once he gives thanks for it (חֶסֶד וֶאֱמֶת, v. 27). Then he requests it from Laban and Bethuel (again חֶסֶד וֶאֱמֶת, v. 49). The result is that Rebecca leaves her home and becomes Isaac's wife.

B. *Joseph*
Joseph is twice said to be the recipient of חֶסֶד—once from Yahweh in Gen. 39.21; this results in the jailer viewing him favourably and entrusting the care of the prisoners to him. Consequently Joseph is

well placed to help the butler, from whom he requests חֶסֶד (Gen.. 40.14). This leads eventually to Joseph's appointment to take charge of the granaries in Egypt during the years of plenty and of famine. While Joseph is still second in the land of Egypt, Jacob requests חֶסֶד וֶאֱמֶת from him in connection with his burial (Gen. 47.29).

Only on these three occasions is חֶסֶד associated with Joseph. חֶסֶד never plays a part in the relationship between Joseph and his brothers. Joseph's commitment to them is obvious—to the writer of the account and to the readers, but not to the brothers. He provides food for them, he desires to see Benjamin and Jacob again, he arranges for them to settle in Goshen; these are all indicative of Joseph's commitment to his family. Yet the brothers' relationship with him commenced as hatred and later was tinged with fear and distrust (Gen. 50.15-21). חֶסֶד, it seems, is a most appropriate term to apply to the actions proposed by Joseph in vv. 19-21; but the brothers' distrust rules out any commitment to Joseph on their part and thus precludes the use of the word חֶסֶד here. In many ways, Joseph's dealings with his brothers parallels Yahweh's expression of חֶסֶד to wayward Israel.

C. *David*

David is featured frequently with חֶסֶד, both as agent and as patient. In his relationships with other men, David requests חֶסֶד from Jonathan (1 Sam. 20.8) who promises to inform him how Saul reacts to his absence from the king's table. In return, Jonathan requests David to extend חֶסֶד to him and his descendants (vv. 14-15). Subsequently, David keeps his promise, seeking out Mephibosheth (2 Sam. 9.1-7), and he persists in treating him favourably over the years (2 Sam. 19.24-30; 21.7). He also attempts to show his goodwill to Hanun (2 Sam.10. 2; 1 Chron.19.2) but is rebuffed.

David prays that Yahweh will extend חֶסֶד וֶאֱמֶת to the men of Jabesh-gilead who buried Saul's body and thus prevented its further defilement at the hands of the Philistines (2 Sam. 2.6). There are many references to the חֶסֶד of Yahweh to which the historian attributes the establishment of the Davidic dynasty (e.g. 2 Sam. 7.15; 1 Kgs 3.6; 8.23, etc.). The Chronicler also refers to this persisting commitment of Yahweh to David and his descendants, and the psalmist likewise alludes to it on several occasions.

7. *Summary*

חֶסֶד is peculiarly and distinctively a Hebrew word, the content of which can be determined by investigating it in the culture of the Hebrew people as it is discerned in the Hebrew Bible.

חֶסֶד cannot be adequately translated in many languages, including English.

חֶסֶד is not merely an attitude or an emotion; it is an emotion that leads to an activity beneficial to the recipient. The relative status of the participants is never a feature of the חֶסֶד act, which may be described as a beneficent action performed, in the context of a deep and enduring commitment between two persons or parties, by one who is able to render assistance to the needy party who in the circumstances is unable to help him- or herself.

The use of the word in the Hebrew Bible indicates that חֶסֶד is characteristic of God rather than human beings; it is rooted in the divine nature, and it is expressed because of who he is, not because of what humanity is or needs or desires or deserves. Yahweh's tenacious commitment to Israel even in the face of their blatant and persistent rebellion demonstrates that חֶסֶד is an enduring quality of God. This commitment leads him to punish his wayward people and to regulate their punishment in such a way that they desire to return to him. Although it is not at the time apparent to Israel, חֶסֶד יהוה is still available and Yahweh awaits the opportunity to manifest it again when his people repent and return to him.

Yahweh expects his people to emulate this quality that he so frequently demonstrates, even though people's expression of it can be only a pale reflection of Yahweh's. As Morris (1981: 81) has well said of חֶסֶד, 'In men it is the ideal; in God it is the actual'. חֶסֶד is a supreme human virtue, standing as the pinnacle of moral values.

1. שׂנא is remote from חֶסֶד;
2. חֶסֶד is closely related to חנן; it includes 'grace' and 'mercy', but it is much more than grace and mercy;
3. חֶסֶד is close to רַחֲמִים; it includes 'compassion', but it is not merely compassion;

4. חֶסֶד is close to אֱמוּנָה; it includes 'faithfulness', 'reliability', 'confidence', but it is not merely faithfulness, reliability, confidence;

5. חֶסֶד is not very close to אהב; while it includes 'love', its connotations are much broader than those of love.

These illustrations are of human rather than divine חֶסֶד. It has been frequently noted that, even though his unfaithful rebellious people are unaware of it, God continues to direct חֶסֶד towards them. His ultimate aim, and his great desire, is that his people will repent and return to him, renewing the relationship that had its origin in the covenant he made with Abraham.

BIBLIOGRAPHY

1. The following works deal specifically with the word חֶסֶד: Bowen 1938; Clark 1976; Clark 1989; Clark 1992; Dickey 1976; Gitay 1979; Glueck 1927; Glueck 1961; Glueck 1967; Hills 1957; Johnson 1955; Kuyper 1964; Lofthouse 1933; Margot 1974; Peacock 1980; Sakenfield 1978; Sakenfield 1985; Stoebe 1951; Stoebe 1952; Stoebe 1971; Whitley 1981; Zobel 1986.

2. An asterisk * prefixed to a date in this bibliography indicates that reference is being made to the article as it appears in the collection specified. The date is the year in which the article was first published (or the address was given); the page number(s) refer to the page(s) in the collection. Thus, words quoted from Firth (1957a: 181) will be found on page 181 in Palmer's reprint of the article which was originally published in 1957.

Ackroyd, P.R. and C.F. Evans (eds.)
 1970 *The Cambridge History of the Bible*, I (Cambridge: Cambridge University Press).

Aitchison, J.
 1972 *General Linguistics* (London: English Universities Press).

Albrektson, B.
 1963 *Studies in the Text and Theology of the Book of Lamentations* (Studia Theologica Lundensia, 21; Lund: Gleerup).

Allen, L. C.
 1983 *Psalms 101–150* (WBC, 21; Waco, TX: Word Books).

Andersen, F.I.
 1986 'Yahweh, the Kind and Sensitive God', in O'Brien *et al.* 1986: 41-88.

Andersen, F.I. and D.N. Freedman
 1980 *Hosea* (AB, 24; New York: Doubleday).

Avishur, Y.
 1971 'Pairs of Synonymous Words in the Construct State (and in Appositional Hendiadys) in Biblical Hebrew', *Sem* 2: 17-81.

Balentine, S.E.
 1980 'A Description of the Semantic Field of Hebrew Words for "Hide"', *VT* 30: 137-53.

Barr, J.
 1961 *The Semantics of Biblical Language* (Oxford: Oxford University Press).
 1968 *Comparative Philology and the Text of the Old Testament* (Oxford: Clarendon Press).

1968a   'The Image of God in the Book of Genesis—A Study of
          Terminology', *BJRL* 51: 11-26.
1972   'Semantics and Biblical Theology—A Contribution to the Discussion',
          Congress Volume, Uppsala 1971 (VTSup, 22; ed. J.A. Emerton *et al.*;
          Leiden: Brill): 11-19.
1976   'Biblical Theology', *IDBSup*, 104-11.

Bazell, C.E., J.C. Catford, M.A.K. Halliday and R.H. Robins
1966   *In Memory of J.R. Firth* (London: Longmans Green).

Bierwisch, M.
1970   'Semantics', in Lyons (ed.) 1970: 166-84.
1972   'Generative Grammar and European Linguistics', *CTL* 9.1: 313-42.

Birkeland, H.
1955   'Some Linguistic Remarks on the Dead Sea Scrolls', *Interpretationes
          ad Vetus Testamentum pertinentes Sigmundo Mowinckel* (ed.
          N.A. Dahl *et al.*; Oslo: Forlaget Land og Kirke): 24-35.
1956   'Some Reflexions on Semitic and Structural Linguistics', *For Roman
          Jakobson* (compiled by Morris Halle *et al.*; The Hague: Mouton): 44-
          51.

Bloomfield, L.
*1926   'A Set of Postulates for the Science of Language', *Language* 2: 153-
          64 (reprinted in Joos 1967: 26-31).
1935   *Language* (revised British edn; London: Allen & Unwin [New York,
          1933]).
1939   'Linguistic Aspects of Science', *International Encyclopedia of Unified
          Science*, I.4 (ed. O. Neurath *et al.*; Chicago: University of Chicago
          Press).

Botterweck, G. J. and H. Ringgren (eds.)
1973–   *Theologisches Wörterbuch zum Alten Testament* (Stuttgart:
          Kohlhammer).
1974–   *Theological Dictionary of the Old Testament* (ET of Botterweck and
          Ringgren 1973–; Grand Rapids: Eerdmans).
1986   *TDOT*, V.

Bowen, B.M.
1938   'A Study of CHESED' (PhD dissertation, Yale University).

Briggs, C.A.
1907   *A Critical and Exegetical Commentary on The Book of Psalms*, II
          (ICC; Edinburgh: T. & T. Clark).

Bright, J.
1965   *Jeremiah* (AB, 21; New York: Doubleday).
1972   *A History of Israel* (OTL; London: SCM Press, rev. edn).

Brongers, H.A.
1965   'Merismus, Synekdoche und Hendiadys in der Bibel–Hebäischen
          Sprache', *OTS* 14: 100-14.

Bruce, F.F.
1963   *The Books and the Parchments* (London: Pickering & Inglis).

Burres, K.L.
1970   *Structural Semantics in the Study of the Pauline Understanding of
          Revelation* (PhD dissertation, Northwestern University).

Childs, B.S.
    1974   *Exodus* (OTL; London: SCM Press).
Chomsky, A.N.
    1957   *Syntactic Structures* (The Hague: Mouton).
    1965   *Aspects of the Theory of Syntax* (Cambridge, MA: M.I.T. Press).
Clark, G.R.
    1976   'The Concept יהוה חסד in the Old Testament' (MA thesis, University of
              Melbourne).
    1989   'The Word חֶסֶד in the Hebrew Bible' (PhD dissertation, University of
              Melbourne).
    1992   'חֶסֶד—A Study of a Lexical Field', *Abr Nahrain* 30: 34-54.
Cole, R.W. (ed.)
    1977   *Current Issues in Linguistic Theory* (Bloomington: Indiana University
              Press).
Coseriu, E.
    1969   *Einführung in die Strukturelle Linguistik* (Tübingen: Narr).
    1973   *Probleme der Strukturellen Semantik* (Tübingen Beiträge zur
              Linguistik, 40; Tübingen).
Coseriu, E. and H. Geckeler
    1974   'Linguistics and Semantics', *CTL* 12.1: 103-71.
    1981   *Trends in Structural Semantics* (Tübingen: Narr).
Crystal, D.
    1965   *Linguistics, Language and Religion* (Faith and Fact Books, 13;
              London: Burns & Oates).
    1980   *A First Dictionary of Linguistics and Phonetics* (London: Andre
              Deutsch).
Dahood, M.
    1965   *Psalms*, I (AB, 16; New York: Doubleday).
    1968   *Psalms*, II (AB, 17; New York: Doubleday).
    1970   *Psalms*, III (AB, 17A; New York: Doubleday).
Davidson, A.B.
    1962   *An Introductory Hebrew Grammar* (rev. J. Mauchline; Edinburgh:
              T. & T. Clark).
Dentan, R.C.
    1963   'The Literary Affinities of Exodus 34:6-7', *VT* 13: 34-51.
Dickey, F.L.
    1976   *The Development of the Hebrew Idea of* ḥesed *in the Biblical
              Literature* (DMin dissertation, School of Theology at Claremont).
Donald, T.
    1963   'The Semantic Field of "Folly" in Proverbs, Job, Psalms, and
              Ecclesiastes', *VT* 13: 285-92.
    1964   'The Semantic Field of Rich and Poor in the Wisdom Literature of
              Hebrew and Accadian', *OrAnt* 3: 27-41.
Driver, S.R.
    1913   *Notes on the Hebrew Text...of the Books of Samuel...*(Oxford:
              Clarendon Press, 2nd edn).
Dumortier, J.-B.
    1972   'Un rituel d'intronisation: le Ps 89:2-38', *VT* 22: 175-96.

Durham, J.I.
1987   *Exodus* (WBC, 3; Waco, TX: Word Books).
Eichrodt, W.
1961   *Theology of the Old Testament*, I (OTL; London: SCM Press).
1967   *Theology of the Old Testament*, II (OTL; London: SCM Press).
1970   *Ezekiel* (OTL; London: SCM Press).
Eikmeyer, H.-J. and H. Rieser (eds.)
1981   *Words, Worlds, and Contexts* (New York: de Gruyter).
Elliger, K. and W. Rudolph (eds.)
1984   *Biblia Hebraica Stuttgartensia* (editio minor; Stuttgart: Deutsche
            Bibelgesellschaft.
Engler, R.
1975   'European Structuralism: Saussure', *CTL* 13.2: 829-86.
Erickson, R.J.
1980   'Biblical Semantics, Semantic Structure, and Biblical Lexicology: A
            Study of Methods, with Special Reference to the Pauline Lexical Field
            of "Cognition"' (PhD dissertation, Fuller Theological Seminary).
Even-Shoshan, A. (ed.)
1977–80   *A New Concordance of the Bible*, I-III (Jerusalem; Kiryath Sepher).
1983   *A New Concordance of the Old Testament* (one volume edn, with
            English introduction by J.H. Sailhamer; Jerusalem: Kiryath Sepher).
Firth, J.R.
*1951   'Modes of Meaning', in *Essays and Studies* (The English Association,
            1951; repr. in Firth 1957b: 190-215).
1951a   'General Linguistics and Descriptive Grammar', *TPS* 1951: 69-87.
*1953   'Linguistic Analysis as a Study of Meaning', in Palmer 1968: 12-26.
*1955   'Structural Linguistics', in *TPS* 1955: 83-103 (repr. in Palmer 1968:
            35-52).
*1956a   'Philology in the Philological Society', *TPS* 1956: 1-25 (repr. in
            Palmer 1968: 53-73).
*1956b   'Linguistics and Translation' (paper read at Birkbeck College,
            London, June 1956; published in Palmer 1968: 84-95).
*1956c   'Descriptive Linguistics and the Study of English' (paper read in
            Berlin, May 1956; published in Palmer 1968: 96-113).
*1956d   'A New Approach to Grammar' (paper read at Bedford College,
            London, 1956; published in Palmer 1968: 114-25).
*1957a   'A Synopsis of Linguistic Theory, 1930–55', in *Studies in Linguistic
            Analysis* (Special Volume of the Philological Society, Oxford; Oxford:
            The Philological Society): 1-31 (repr. in Palmer 1968: 168-205).
1957b   *Papers in Linguistics, 1934–1951* (London: Oxford University Press).
Fodor, J.A. and J.J. Katz (eds.)
1964   *The Structure of Language: Readings in the Philosophy of Language*
            (Eaglewood Cliffs, NJ: Prentice-Hall).
Fowler, R.
1974   *Understanding Language* (London: Routledge & Kegan Paul).
Fox, M.V.
1973   'Jeremiah 2:2 and the "Desert Ideal"', *CBQ* 35: 441-50.

Freedman, D.N.
*1972 'Prolegomenon to G.B. Gray, *The Forms of Hebrew Poetry*', in Freedman 1980: 23-50.
1980 *Pottery, Poetry, and Prophecy* (Winona Lake, IN: Eisenbrauns).
Fries, C.C.
1954 'Meaning and Linguistic Analysis', *Language* 30: 57-68.
1963 'The "Bloomfield" School', in Mohrmann *et al.*, 1963: 196-224.
Geckeler, H.
1971 *Zur Wortfelddiskussion* (Munich: Wilhelm Fink).
1971a *Strukturelle Semantik und Wortfeldtheorie* (Munich: Wilhelm Fink).
1973 *Strukturelle Semantik des Französischen*, Tübingen: Max Niemeyer).
1981 'Structural Semantics', in Eikmeyer and Rieser 1981: 381-413.
Gesenius, H.F.W.
1966 See Kautzsch 1966.
Gibson, A.
1981 *Biblical Semantic Logic* (Oxford: Basil Blackwell).
Gitay, Y.
1979 Review of Sakenfeld 1978, *JBL* 98: 583-84.
Glueck, N.
1927 *Das Wort ḥesed im alttestamentlichen Sprachgebrauch als menschliche und göttliche gemeinschaftsgemässe Verhaltungsweise* (BZAW, 47; Berlin: Töpelmann.
1961 2nd edn of Glueck 1927.
1967 *Hesed in the Bible* (ET of Glueck 1927 by A. Gottschalk; Cincinnati: Hebrew Union College).
Gordon, R.P.
1986 *1 and 2 Samuel* (Exeter: Paternoster Press).
Gottlieb, I.B.
1970 'Scientific Method and Biblical Study', *Tradition* 11: 44-54.
Greenberg, M.
1983 *Ezekiel 1–20* (AB, 22; New York: Doubleday).
Greimas, A J. *et al.*
1970 *Sign, Language, Culture* (Janua Linguarum, Series Maior, 1; The Hague: Mouton).
Hagner, D.A. and M.J. Harris (eds.)
1980 *Pauline Studies* (Exeter: Paternoster Press).
Halliday, M.A.K., A. McIntosh and P. Stevens
1964 *The Linguistic Sciences and Language Teaching* (London: Longmans).
Harris, Z.S.
1951 *Methods in Structural Linguistics* (Chicago: University of Chicago Press).
Harrison, R.K.
1970 *Introduction to the Old Testament* (London: Tyndale Press).
Haugen, E.
1951 'Directions in Modern Linguistics', *Language* 27: 211-22.
Helm, P.
1982 Review of Gibson 1980, *Philosophy* 57: 421-22.

Hertzberg, H.W.
1964   *I and II Samuel* (OTL; London: SCM Press).
Hillers, D.R.
1964   'A Note on Some Treaty Terminology in the Old Testament', *BASOR*
            176: 46-47.
1972   *Lamentations* (AB, 7A; New York: Doubleday).
Hills, S.O.
1957   'The ḥesed of Man in the Old Testament' (unpublished paper delivered
            at the November meeting of the Biblical Colloquium in Pittsburg).
Hockett, C.F.
1968   *The State of the Art* (Janua Linguarum, Series Minor, 73; The Hague:
            Mouton).
Honeyman, A.M.
1952   'Merismus in Biblical Hebrew', *JBL* 71: 11-18.
Hooke, S.H.
1962   Review of Barr 1961, *JTS* 13: 128-30.
Householder, F.W.
1971   *Linguistic Speculations* (Cambridge: Cambridge University Press).
Hymes, D.
1964   'Directions in (Ethno-) Linguistic Theory', *American Anthropologist*
            66: 6-56 (Special Publication: Transcendental Studies in Cognition).
Hymes, D. and J. Fought
1975   'American Structuralism', *CTL* 13.2: 903-1176.
Ikegami, Y.
1967   'Structural Semantics: A Survey and Problems', *Linguistics* 33: 49-67.
Jenni, E. and C. Westermann (eds.)
1971   *Theologisches Handwörterbuch zum Alten Testament*, I (Munich: Chr.
            Kaiser Verlag).
Johnson, A.R.
1955   'חֶסֶד and חָסִיד', *Interpretationes ad Vetus Testamentum pertinentes
            Sigmundo Mowinckel* (ed. N.A. Dahl *et al.*; Oslo: Forlaglt Land og
            Kirke).
Joos, M.
1967   *Readings in Linguistics*, I (Chicago: University of Chicago Press, 4th
            edn [originally published 1957]).
Kaddari, M.Z.
1973   'A Semantic Approach to Biblical Parallelism', *JJS* 24: 167-75.
Katz, J.J. and J.A. Fodor
1963   'The Structure of a Semantic Theory', *Language* 39: 170-210
            (reprinted in Fodor and Katz 1964: 479-518).
Kautzsch, E. (ed.)
1966   *Gesenius' Hebrew Grammar* (2nd English edn trans. A.E. Cowley;
            London: Oxford University Press).
Kedar, B.
1981   *Biblische Semantik: Eine Einführung* (Stuttgart: Kohlhammer).
Kempson, R.M.
1977   *Semantic Theory* (Cambridge: Cambridge University Press).

Kittel, G. (ed.)
    1933–   *Theologisches Wörterbuch zum Neuen Testament* (Stuttgart: Kohlhammer).

Kittel, R. (ed.)
    1962   *Biblia Hebraica* (Stuttgart: Württembergische Bibelanstalt).

Koehler, L. and W. Baumgartner (eds.)
    1958   *Lexicon in Veteris Testamenti Libros* (Leiden: Brill).

Koerner, E.F.K.
    1975   'European Structuralism: Early Beginnings', *CTL* 13.2: 717-827.

Kuyper, L.J.
    1964   'Grace and Truth', *Int* 18: 3-19.

Lambdin, T.O.
    1973   *Introduction to Biblical Hebrew* (London: Darton, Longman & Todd).

Lampe, G.W.H. (ed.)
    1969   *The Cambridge History of the Bible*, II (Cambridge: Cambridge University Press).

Lehrer, A.
    1974   *Semantic Fields and Lexical Structure* (Amsterdam: North-Holland Publishing).

Lepschy, G.C.
    1970   *Survey of Structural Linguistics* (London: Faber & Faber).
    1975   'European Structuralism: Post-Saussurean Schools', *CTL* 13.2: 887-902.

Lesser, A.H.
    1982   Review of Gibson 1980, *JSS* 27: 80-81.

Lindars, B.
    1981   Review of Riesener 1979, *JTS* 32: 192-94.

Lisowsky, G.
    1958   *Concordance to the Hebrew Old Testament* (Stuttgart: Württembergische Bibelanstalt).

Loesch, K.T.
    1982   'Hendiadys', *PMLA* 97: 99.

Lofthouse, W.F.
    1933   'חֵן and חֶסֶד in the Old Testament', *ZAW* 10: 29-35.

Lyons, J.
    1963   *Structural Semantics* (Oxford: Basil Blackwell).
    1966   'Firth's Theory of "Meaning"', in Bazell *et al.*, 1966: 288-302.
    1968   *Introduction to Theoretical Linguistics* (London: Cambridge University Press).
    1970   'Generative Syntax', in Lyons (ed.) 1970: 115-39.
    1974   'Linguistics', *Encyclopaedia Britannica: Macropaedia*, X (Chicago: Helen Hemingway Benton): 992-1013.
    1977   *Semantics* (London: Cambridge University Press).
    1977a   *Chomsky* (Hassocks, Surrey: Harvester Press, 2nd edn [originally published London, 1970]).

Lyons, J. (ed.)
    1970   *New Horizons in Linguistics* (Harmondsworth: Penguin Books).

Margot, J.-C.
    1974   'And his Love is Eternal (Psalm 136)', *BT* 25: 212-17.
Marshall, I. H. (ed.)
    1977   *New Testament Interpretation* (Exeter: Paternoster Press).
Matsuda, I.
    1976   'The Structure of Mental Activities in Biblical Hebrew', *Annual of the Japanese Biblical Institute* 2: 79-99.
McCarter, P.K.
    1980   *I Samuel* (AB, 8; New York: Doubleday).
    1984   *II Samuel* (AB, 9; New York: Doubleday).
McKane, W.
    1970   *Proverbs* (OTL; London: SCM Press).
    1986   *A Critical and Exegetical Commentary on Jeremiah*, I (ICC; Edinburgh: T. & T. Clark).
Mitchell, T.F.
    1975   *Principles of Firthian Linguistics* (London: Longmans).
Mohrmann, C., A. Sommerfelt and J. Whatmough (eds.)
    1963   *Trends in European and American Linguistics 1930–1960* (Utrecht: Spectrum).
Moran, W.L.
    1963   'The Ancient Near Eastern Background of the Love of God in Deuteronomy', *CBQ* 25: 77-87.
Morris, L.L.
    1981   *Testaments of Love* (Grand Rapids, MI: Eerdmans).
Moule, C.F.D.
    1962   Review of Barr 1961, *Theology* 65: 26-27.
Nida, E.A.
    1964   *Toward a Science of Translating* (Leiden: Brill).
    1972   'Implications of Contemporary Linguistics for Biblical Scholarship', *JBL* 48: 73-89.
    1972a   'Linguistic Theories and Bible Translating', *BT* 23: 301-308.
    1975   *Componential Analysis of Meaning* (Leiden: Brill).
    1975a   *Exploring Semantic Structures* (Munich: Wilhelm Fink).
Nida, E.A., J.P. Louw and R.B. Smith.
    1977   'Semantic Domains and Componential Analysis of Meaning', in Cole (ed.) 1977: 139-67.
North, C.R.
    1964   *The Second Isaiah* (Oxford: Clarendon Press).
O'Brien, P.T. and D.G. Petersen (eds.)
    1986   *God who is Rich in Mercy* (Sydney: Anzea Publishers).
Oehman, S.
    1953   'Theories of the "Linguistic Field"', *Word* 9: 123-34.
Palmer, F.R.
    1976   *Semantics: A New Outline* (London: Cambridge University Press).
Palmer, F.R. (ed.)
    1968   *Selected Papers of J.R. Firth, 1952–59* (London: Longmans Green).
Pardee, D.
    1980   Review of Sakenfeld 1978, *JNES* 39: 244.

1981   Review of Riesener 1979, *CBQ* 43: 630-32.

Peacock, H.F.

1980   'Translating "Mercy", "Steadfast Love", in the Book of Genesis', *BT* 31: 201-207.

Quemada, B.

1972   'Lexicology and Lexicography', *CTL* 9.1: 395-475.

Rabin, C.

1970   'Hebrew', *CTL* 6: 304-46.

Riesener, I.

1979   *Der Stamm* עבד *im Alten Testament: Eine Wortuntersuchung unter Berücksichtigung neuerer sprachwissenschaftlicher Methoden* (BZAW, 149; Berlin: de Gruyter).

Roberts, B. J.

1969   'The Old Testament: Manuscripts, Text and Versions', in Lampe 1969: 1-26.

Robins, R.H.

1957   'Aspects of Prosodic Analysis', *Proceedings of the University of Durham Philosophical Society*, I (Series B, no. 1): 1-12.

1971   *General Linguistics: An Introductory Survey* (London: Longman Group, 2nd edn [originally published 1964]).

1979   *A Short History of Linguistics* (London: Longman Group, 2nd edn [originally published 1967]).

Rothwell, W.

1962   'Medieval French and Modern Semantics', *Modern Language Review* 57: 25-30.

Sakenfeld, K.D.

1978   *The Meaning of Hesed in the Hebrew Bible: A New Enquiry* (HSM, 17; Missoula, MT: Scholars Press).

1985   *Faithfulness in Action: Loyalty in Biblical Perspective* (Philadelphia: Fortress Press).

Sampson, G.

1980   *Schools of Linguistics* (London: Hutchinson).

Saussure, F. de

1960   *Course in General Linguistics* (ed. C. Bally and A. Sechehaye; trans. [from the French] W. Baskin; London: Peter Owen).

Sawyer, J.F.A.

1967   'Root Meanings in Hebrew', *JSS* 12: 37-50.

1967a   'Context of Situation and *Sitz im Leben*', *Proceedings of the University of Newcastle upon Tyne Philosophical Society* (no. I.11; ed. J.A. Richardson): 137-47.

1968   'An Analysis of the Context and Meaning of the Psalm-Headings', *Transactions of the Glasgow University Oriental Society* 22: 26-38.

1972   *Semantics in Biblical Research* (SBT, 2nd ser., 24; London: SCM Press).

1974   'The Meaning of בְּצֶלֶם אֱלֹהִים ('In the Image of God') in Genesis I–XI', *JTS* 25: 418-25.

1981   Review of Riesener 1979, *JBL* 100: 468-69.

Sebeok, T.A. (ed.)
   1963–76   *Current Trends in Linguistics* (The Hague: Mouton), vols. 1-14.
Seiler, H.J.
   1967   'Toward an Exploration of the Lexical Field', *To Honor Roman Jakobson*, III (Janua Linguarum, Series Maior, 33; The Hague: Mouton): 1783-98.
Shults, F.L.
   1974   שלם *and* תמם *in Biblical Hebrew: An Analysis of the Semantic Field of Wholeness* (PhD dissertation, University of Texas at Austin).
Silva, M.
   1972   Semantic Change and Semitic Influence in the Greek Bible (PhD dissertation, University of Manchester).
   1980   'The Pauline Style as Lexical Choice', in D.A. Hagner *et al.* 1980: 184-207.
   1983   *Biblical Words and their Meaning: An Introduction to Lexical Semantics* (Grand Rapids: Zondervan).
Simpson, J.M.Y.
   1979   *A First Course in Linguistics* (Edinburgh: Edinburgh University Press).
Sinclair, J.McH.
   1966   'Beginning the Study of Lexis', in Bazell *et al.* 1966: 410-30.
Snaith, N.H.
   1944   *The Distinctive Ideas of the Old Testament* (London: Epworth Press).
Sørensen, H.S.
   1967   'Meaning', *To Honor Roman Jakobson*, III (Janua Linguarum, Series Maior, 33; The Hague: Mouton): 1876-89. Also published as 'Meaning and Reference' in Greimas *et al.* 1970: 67-80.
   1970   'A Semiotic Solution to the Logical Problem of Existential Statements', in Greimas *et al.* 1970: 81-88.
Speiser, E.A.
   1964   *Genesis* (AB, 1; New York: Doubleday).
Spence, N.C.W.
   1961   'Linguistic Fields, Conceptual Systems and the *Weltbild*', *TPS* 1961: 87-106.
Stoebe, H.J.
   1951   'Gottes hingebende Güte und Treue חֶסֶד וֶאֱמֶת, Bedeutung und Geschichte des Begriffes חֶסֶד' (ThD dissertation, University of Münster).
   1952   'Die Bedeutung des Wortes *Häsäd* im Alten Testament', *VT* 2: 244-54.
   1971   'חֶסֶד—Güte', in Jenni *et al.* 1971: I, 600-21.
Swellengrebel, J.L.
   1962   Review of Barr 1961, *International Review of Missions* 51: 206-10.
Talmon, S.
   1970   'The Old Testament Text', in P.R. Ackroyd *et al.* 1970: 159-99.
Tangberg, K.A.
   1973   'Linguistics and Theology: An Attempt to Analyze and Evaluate James Barr's Argumentation in *The Semantics of Biblical Language* and *Biblical Words for Time*', *BT* 24: 301-10.

Thistleton, A.C.
1977 'Semantics in New Testament Interpretation', in Marshall 1977: 75-104.

Thompson, J.A.
1963 The Vocabulary of Covenant in the Old Testament (PhD dissertation, Cambridge University).
1974 'The Significance of the Verb *Love* in the David–Jonathan Narratives in 1 Samuel', *VT* 24: 334-38.
1980 *Jeremiah* (NICOT; Grand Rapids, MI: Eerdmans).

Thorne, J.P.
1965 Review of *Constituent Structure: A Study of Contemporary Models of Syntactic Description*, by P. Postal, *Journal of Linguistics* 1: 73-76.

Trier, J.
1931 *Der deutsche Wortschatz im Sinnbezirk des Verstandes* (Heidelberg).
1934 'Das sprachliche Feld. Ein Auseinandersetzung', *Neue Jahrbücher für Wissenschaft und Jugenbildung* 10: 428-49.
1973 *Aufsätze und Vorträge zur Wortfeldtheorie* (ed. A. van der Lee and O. Reichmann; Janua Linguarum, Series Minor, 174; The Hague: Mouton).

Ullendorff, E.
1970 'Comparative Semitics', *CTL* 6: 261-73.
1981 Review of Wells 1980, *JSS* 26: 356-57.

Ullmann, S.
1957 *The Principles of Semantics* (Glasgow: Jackson, 2nd edn [first published 1951]).
1962 *Semantics: An Introduction to the Science of Meaning* (Oxford: Basil Blackwell).
1972 'Semantics', *CTL* 9.1: 343-94.

Vassilyev, L.M.
1974 'The Theory of Semantic Fields: A Survey', *Linguistics* 137: 79-93.

Wartburg, W. von
1969 *Problems and Methods in Linguistics* (trans. J.M.H. Reid, from the 2nd French edn [1963]; Oxford: Basil Blackwell [originally published as *Einfuhrung in Problematik und Methodik der Sprachwissenschaft* (Tübingen, 1943)]).

Wells, P.R.
1980 *James Barr and the Bible: Critique of a New Liberalism* (Phillipsburg, NJ: Presbyterian and Reformed Publishing Company).

Wernberg-Møller, P.C.H.
1973 Review of Sawyer 1972, *JTS* 24: 215-17.

Westhuizen, J.P. van der
1978 'Hendiadys in Biblical Hymns of Praise', *Sem* 6: 50-57.

Weinfeld, M.
1970 'The Covenant of Grant in the Old Testament and in the Ancient Near East', *JAOS* 90: 184-203.

Weiser, A.
1962 *The Psalms* (OTL; London: SCM Press).

Whitley, C.F.
    1981   'The Semantic Range of חֶסֶד', *Bib* 62: 519-26.
Wright, G.T.
    1981   'Hendiadys and *Hamlet*', *PMLA* 96: 168-93.
Zobel, H.-J.
    1986   'חֶסֶד', in G.J. Botterweck *et al.* 1986: 44-64.

INDEXES

INDEX OF REFERENCES

INDEX OF AUTHORS